EDITH BLAKE'S WAR

Krista Vane-Tempest is the daughter of a teacher and was raised in country New South Wales. She studied law, English, history and politics at the Australian National University then worked as a lawyer before starting to write. In her spare time, she is a volunteer guide at the Australian War Memorial. She lives in Canberra with her husband and three children.

'Beautifully written and an engaging read, *Edith Blake's War* opens a window on unsung areas of Australian nurses' service at war. Krista Vane-Tempest's meticulous research enhances understanding but never intrudes, as Sister Blake's own voice brings her wartime experiences vibrantly to life. An ultimately moving book born of connection to family across generations.'

JANET BUTLER

'Edith Blake's story powerfully evokes the horrors and dangers of nursing during the Great War while capturing the poignant and special bond Australian nurses forged with Anzac soldiers. Krista Vane-Tempest deftly weaves the larger context of the war throughout Edie's remarkable letters home and gives her the long overdue recognition her courage warrants.'

PETER REES

'More than a biography, Krista Vane-Tempest has penned a tribute to the contribution and sacrifice of Australian women during the First World War. In doing so, she has rediscovered the evocative story of Edith Blake, nurse to the Anzacs and British troops and whose life was tragically lost in that terrible conflict.'

KARL JAMES

EDITH BLAKE'S WAR

The only Australian nurse
killed in action during
the First World War

KRISTA VANE-TEMPEST

NEWSOUTH

A NewSouth book

Published by
NewSouth Publishing
University of New South Wales Press Ltd
University of New South Wales
Sydney NSW 2052
AUSTRALIA
newsouthpublishing.com

© Krista Vane-Tempest 2021
First published 2021

10 9 8 7 6 5 4 3 2 1

This book is copyright. Apart from any fair dealing for the purpose of private study, research, criticism or review, as permitted under the *Copyright Act*, no part of this book may be reproduced by any process without written permission. Inquiries should be addressed to the publisher.

A catalogue record for this book is available from the National Library of Australia

ISBN: 9781742237398 (paperback)
         9781742249964 (ebook)
         9781742249933 (ePDF)

Design Josephine Pajor-Markus
Cover design Nada Backovic
Cover images (*top*) Studio portrait of Sister Edith Blake, Queen Alexandra's Imperial Military Nursing Service Reserve, AWM P11193.004; (*bottom right*) *Glenart Castle*, AWM PS1195; (*bottom left*) Sister Edith Blake at 17th British General Hospital, AWM P11193.006.
Printer Griffin Press, part of Ovato

All reasonable efforts were taken to obtain permission to use copyright material reproduced in this book, but in some cases copyright could not be traced. The author welcomes information in this regard.

CONTENTS

LIST OF ABBREVIATIONS   vii
PROLOGUE   viii
PREFACE   x

1. GETTING STARTED   1
2. EDIE AT THE COAST   6
3. AUSTRALIA GOES TO WAR   16
4. WHY THE BRITISH?   24
5. LEAVING AUSTRALIA   29
6. INTO THE BLUE   36
7. THE LANDINGS   46
8. ON DUTY ONCE MORE   52
9. PYRAMIDS BY MOONLIGHT   58
10. IN THE LAND OF UNCERTAINTY   66
11. CULTURE SHOCK   70
12. ARRIVAL IN ALEXANDRIA   75
13. FLIES, FAECES AND FOOD   83
14. NOT ONE WHOLE MAN   92
15. THE FORTUNES OF WAR   103
16. NOTHING DOING ON THE PENINSULA   112
17. SUCH A CHRISTMAS WE HAVE HAD   118
18. DON'T THINK THAT I'VE LOST MY HEART   127
19. WAITING FOR THE NEXT MOVE   133
20. IT IS AN EDUCATION   138
21. SUNBURN, SAND – AND SLACK   145

22	THE NICEST SHIP I HAVE BEEN ON	155
23	PASSING THROUGH ALL DANGERS	165
24	THE WAR AT SEA	172
25	ENGLAND AT LAST	177
26	BACK TO THE OLD PLACE	186
27	'A PLEASANT VOYAGE'	191
28	SOMEWHERE ON THE ATLANTIC OCEAN	199
29	I'M NOT GOING TO NURSE ANY GERMANS	210
30	OUR FEELINGS ARE VERY MIXED HERE	214
31	THESE MEN HAVE TO WORK	222
32	THE FOOD QUESTION IS A SERIOUS ONE NOW	230
33	MURDER IN MY HEART	235
34	'BABY KILLERS'	242
35	IT IS DELIGHTFUL WALKING HERE	248
36	FAMILY FOOTSTEPS	253
37	FOR WEAL OR WOE	257
38	HMHS *GLENART CASTLE*	268
39	A VERY BOISTEROUS CRADLE	273
40	TAKING LEAVE	282
41	WHAT THE FISHERMEN SAW	288
42	THE SINKING	292
43	THE NEWS THEY HAD DREADED	302
44	AFTER THE WAR	310

EPILOGUE	316
ACKNOWLEDGMENTS	318
BIBLIOGRAPHY	320
NOTES	331

LIST OF ABBREVIATIONS

AAH	Australian Auxiliary Hospital
AAMC	Australian Army Medical Corps
AANS	Australian Army Nursing Service
ACCS	Australian Casualty Clearing Station
AGH	Australian General Hospital
AIF	Australian Imperial Force
ATNA	Australasian Trained Nurses' Association
BGH	British General Hospital
CCS	casualty clearing stations
HMAS	His Majesty's Australian Ship
HMAT	His Majesty's Australian Transport
HMHS	His Majesty's Hospital Ship
HMS	His Majesty's Ship
OC	Officer Commanding
MO	Medical officer
POW	prisoner of war
QAIMNS	Queen Alexandra's Imperial Military Nursing Service
QAIMNSR	Queen Alexandra's Imperial Military Nursing Service Reserve
RAMC	Royal Army Medical Corps
RFC	Royal Flying Corps
RMS	Royal Mail Ship
RNAS	Royal Naval Air Service
SMS	Seiner Majestät Schiff (His Majesty's Ship)
SS	Steam Ship
USS	United States Ship
VAD	Voluntary Aid Detachment

PROLOGUE

In the early hours of 26 February 1918, His Majesty's Hospital Ship (HMHS) *Glenart Castle* steamed into the Bristol Channel, heading for France to pick up wounded men from the killing fields of the Western Front. On board was a thirty-two-year-old Australian nurse, Edith Blake.

As HMHS *Glenart Castle* cut through choppy waters whipped up by a cold wind, crews on passing fishing boats observed her lights blazing from bow to stern, her white hull clearly displaying the broad green band and red crosses that identified her as a hospital ship.

Unbeknown to the ship's company, a German U-boat lurked in the waters below. The submarine, UC-56, stalked *Glenart Castle* in silence for over an hour, her torpedoes at the ready.

Shortly before 4 am the crew of the *Glenart Castle* was changing shift when an almighty explosion ripped the ship's hull open like a tin can and smashed her starboard decks. Men in the starboard engine room were killed immediately; others were thrown across the decks or tossed from their bunks as the ship lurched violently. HMHS *Glenart Castle* shuddered to a halt and was cast into darkness.

Although Germany had promised to respect the safe passage of hospital ships in those waters, UC-56 had taken deadly aim and fired.

Survivors told a Naval Court of Enquiry what happened next.[1] Men ran to their lifeboat stations and began to lower the boats in response to six piercing shrieks from the steam whistle. Water gushed into the ragged hole and the ship listed starboard. In the darkness below, people groped for the doors and stairways that

Prologue

would deliver them to the boat decks. Then the call 'EVERY MAN FOR HIMSELF!' went up.

Waves dashed lifeboats against the broken hull. As the ship rolled further starboard, men worked desperately to launch the portside boats. Some of these made it to the heaving surface and were set free. Others dangled from the davits (cranes that swing out to launch lifeboats) as the ship groaned and her bow strained towards the dark sky, tipping the boats' screaming occupants into the sea. When the ship plunged down sternwards, some boats were swamped by the wall of wash. People still clinging to the ship jumped for their lives and were sucked under.

It took just seven or eight minutes for the *Glenart Castle* to sink. Of more than 180 crew and medical personnel on board, only twenty-nine men survived.[2] In the subsequent official enquiry, no-one could say what had happened to the eight nurses whose mission was to save lives.

So it was that Edith Blake's war came to an end in the black waters of the Bristol Channel. To the best of our knowledge she was the only Australian nurse killed in action in the First World War.

PREFACE

I grew up knowing only that my grandmother's eldest sister, Edith, was a nurse who died serving in the First World War when her hospital ship was sunk by a German submarine.

I didn't know that it had been a British ship, or where it had sunk. I didn't know that during the war she had nursed near the hellholes of Gallipoli and the Western Front. I didn't know that because she had served with the British military nursing service, her name would not appear on the Australian War Memorial's Roll of Honour, the nation's wall of remembrance.

When I asked Dad, he said that the family never really discussed it, although his grandfather Charles, Edith's father, had taken a set against the Irish because he believed the Republicans had provided safe harbour to the U-boat that sank his daughter's ship. Dad was just two when the old man died and his only recollection of his grandmother, my great-grandmother Kate, was as 'a lady in black' who did not like to be disturbed by noisy little boys.

After the war, people sought different ways to cope. Many did not want to talk about it, for Australia had suffered mightily. No man, woman or child was untouched; everyone had lost a loved one or knew someone who had. No-one's pain was special. The sight of men on crutches or with pinned sleeves or bandaged eyes was common. The smell of decay lingered on the breath of those who had been gassed. Many thought it unseemly to acknowledge the invisible wounds of the mind and heart.

By the time I was born, my grandmother Alice was a widow aged seventy living on her own in a weatherboard home in the Sydney suburb of Sans Souci. The house backed on to Kogarah Bay,

Preface

a shallow scoop out of the northern shore where the Georges River empties into Botany Bay. My father was raised with his brothers in that house. Their Auntie Grace, Alice's other sister, had lived next door; their grandparents two doors down. When the king tides came the boys would dive from the verandah into 3 or 4 feet of water – provided their mother wasn't looking. Alice couldn't swim. She was scared of the sea and was never reconciled to the sight of her boys larking around in the bay.

By the 1980s my grandmother had moved into a retirement village, living independently. She had been barely 5 feet tall at the peak of her own nursing career, and nine decades of gravity had deprived her of several inches. As she entered her nineties, she moved into a room in the village's high-dependency complex so her last material possessions, a modest reflection of a long life, were shared out among the family. I was nineteen or twenty, and I quickly claimed my great-aunt Edith's 1915 diary.

I thought the diary was the only surviving relic of Edith's war years; Dad wasn't aware of anything else. However, in 2011 my stepmother Pat was tapping away at her computer researching family history when my father shuffled off to the bedroom and retrieved a plastic shopping bag he had stuffed at the bottom of a wardrobe. The bag contained an assortment of my late grandmother's old personal papers, which my uncle had passed on to my father a few years earlier.

'Might be something useful in there', said Dad as he handed Pat the bag, then retired to his chair to continue his crossword. He had never looked inside it. 'In there' were family photos and letters, including 138 letters that Edith had written home throughout her war service. We hadn't known they existed. Her youngest sister had been their loving, silent, sole custodian for decades.

The letters were separated into three thick bundles tied with string: one each for 1915, 1916 and 1917–18. Many ran to four or five sheets, secured by a rusty pin. The paper had browned and mottled with age, the edges were somewhat ragged, but in faded ink flowing over hundreds of pages and about 100 000 words, Edith Blake had chronicled her war service. She wrote home almost every week to 'Dear Mum, Dad, Grace and Queen'.

Queen? 'Oh yes', said Dad, sounding slightly surprised, as if I should have known. 'Mum was always Queenie; no-one called her Alice.'

Edith's letters, in which she chatted to her family about who and what she had seen, revealed her to be educated, intelligent, conservative, practical, earnest and courageous, with a dry sense of humour. And a loving daughter and sister: she invariably signed off, 'Much love from Edie'.

Nearly a century after it was silenced, I could hear Edie's voice. This is her story.

1
GETTING STARTED

The year she turned twenty-three, Edith Blake was considering her options. It was Mr and Mrs Blake's view that each of their three daughters would contribute to her upkeep until she was married, when she would become her husband's responsibility.

Charles Blake was a hard worker, keen to build up his business and improve his family's circumstances. From humble beginnings as a carrier – carrying goods, or even people, in his horse-drawn cart – for years now had traded from premises in Abercrombie Street, Chippendale, as a vendor and agent for Farmers and Dairymen's Milk Co Ltd. Charles had an entrepreneurial streak and his decision some five years earlier to expand and diversify his business Blake & Co by opening refreshment rooms in Enmore Road near their Marrickville home was a success, although he had flirted with bankruptcy in the past. His girls need not work in dirty or dangerous jobs to survive, but nor could the Blakes easily afford to keep a stable full of unmarried offspring.

Edith, affectionately known as Edie, was the eldest, born in Darlington, an inner-Sydney suburb wedged between the University of Sydney and the Devonshire Street Cemetery, from which, within years, old bones would be dug up to make way for Central Railway Station. When his pregnant wife's time came, Charles put Catherine up into his cart and they rattled the short distance to a cottage hospital in Shepherd Street where their first daughter duly entered the world on 22 September 1885. Although Edith grew up to serve as a nurse in the biggest war the world had yet known, that was a long way in the future, and unimaginable on the day she was born.

In fact, the Australia she was born into was completely different, a collection of colonies that had yet to federate into a single nation.

In eighteen months the Blakes would be blessed with another daughter, Grace, and, ten years afterwards, with Alice, known as Queenie. The family were photographed together in 1900 in what looks like their Sunday best. It may have been the annual Farmers and Dairymen's Milk Co picnic. Charles is sporting an embroidered smoking hat. On the back of the photo, someone has written 'Picnic at Long Nose Point'.

By 1908, there was no sign of suitors in the offing for Edie or Grace. Both girls enjoyed reading and were more inclined to in-depth conversation than small talk; Edie later lamented that she did not have a 'glib tongue'.[1]

Of the two, twenty-year-old Grace's future was better assured. She liked to sew. Both the older girls knew how to draft patterns and copy the fashions they saw in Mark Foy's, update old dresses or take them apart and make them into something new. For the past two years, Grace had been employed by the Department of Public Instruction as a dressmaking teacher.

Their youngest sister was just twelve years old and still attending Enmore Superior School, a 2-mile walk from home. Queenie would go on to attend Bracondale College, a finishing school for young ladies established in nearby Petersham by the Misses Haviland. At Bracondale, girls were taught 'English in all branches … French, Latin, Drawing, Painting, Sewing, Music, Physical Drill'[2] and the skills necessary to keep a clean, economical and healthy house, including rudimentary home nursing and 'how to make good tea'.[3]

Edie's choices were limited. While she could make simple garments, she had no inclination to make it her profession as Grace had. In many ways she was like her father: intelligent and willing to take a calculated risk; sometimes impatient, liking to keep herself busy and declaring that hard work never disagreed with her. Teaching or governessing were possibilities, but she had a mind to

Getting started

try something else. By now, largely driven by the pioneering nurse Florence Nightingale and her methods, nursing was a profession: an acceptable choice for middle-class girls – or the unmarried eldest daughter of the Blake family.

In the spring of 1908, Edith Blake caught a tram to Little Bay, where the Coast Hospital (later renamed Prince Henry Hospital) was situated. There were always many more applicants for trainee nursing positions there than could be accepted, but after she had applied three times her determination was rewarded. Edie had at last secured an interview with the matron.

A series of beaches punctuates the rugged coastline between Sydney Harbour and Botany Bay. At the southern end of this strip is the protected cove of Little Bay. When a smallpox epidemic afflicted Sydney in 1881, it was the isolation of Little Bay, coupled with its protected beach and the fresh sea breezes thought to blow away the miasma of disease, that saw the site selected for a sanitary camp.

The smallpox victims were brought in by boat and carried up to bell tents huddled on a hill above the sand dunes, surrounded by scrub. The temporary camp was formally commissioned some months later as the Coast Hospital, but faced an uncertain future until in 1884 it was recognised as a hospital for infectious diseases.[4] Separate wards were built for sufferers of diseases including smallpox, typhoid, male venereal diseases and leprosy. Miss Jean McMaster was appointed the first matron in 1891, soon after she had completed her three-year nurse's certificate at the Prince Alfred Hospital. In turn, she instituted a three-year certificate course for student nurses at the Coast. The training at both hospitals was based on the Nightingale method: at its core were hygiene, cleanliness, diet, fresh air, sunshine and discipline (and nun-like white veils).

The road Edie walked down is still there, lined with the same soldierly column of Norfolk pines. By the time she arrived at the hospital, it looked more like a village, too well ordered and integrated to be lonely. It boasted airy weatherboard wards with galvanised iron roofs, large windows and wide verandahs, scattered across the grassy slopes above the beach. Although there was a pier, patients were generally brought in by horse-drawn ambulance or, more recently, the electric tram that directly served the hospital. The neat white buildings were tethered by a network of narrow roads bordered with neat white fences, across an area so vast that the matron did her rounds in a horse and cart driven by a 'bob-a-day' man.[5] Bob-a-day men (elderly pensioners or otherwise unemployable men who were charged with a variety of odd jobs, for which the Coast Hospital provided them quarters and paid double the sixpence per day paid by other state hospitals) dressed in old corduroys and government-issue blue linen shirts wielded hoes, taming the coastal heath into vegetable gardens, chook runs and pastureland.[6] To the south lay the lazarets (accommodation for leprosy patients), staff cottages, laundry and stables, and a pond on which people went punting. Beyond the hospital the Pacific Ocean glittered and swelled rhythmically.

Miss Alice Watson had replaced Miss McMaster in 1905. Her thick red hair was swept back in two wings from a centre parting. In her broad Scottish brogue she asked questions to satisfy herself that the applicant was intelligent, stable, mature, and physically strong enough for the work.[7] Tall girls were preferred; Edie wasn't tall, but evidently exceeded the 5-foot limit.[8]

The matron had a straightforward manner that inspired respect. In the future when serving in a distant war, Edie wrote warmly about Miss Watson and was always delighted when she received letters from her. On this day Miss Watson's enquiries were no doubt searching yet typically tactful. Perhaps she surprised Edie by asking her to take off her shoes and present her feet for inspection. One could not expect to be a nurse with fallen arches, and Miss Watson kept a lorgnette pinned to her bosom for just such purposes. Edie's arches apparently passed muster.[9]

Night and day shifts were each twelve hours.[10] Miss Blake must attend lectures, pass examinations and learn cookery tailored to

Getting started

invalids. On top of board and lodging, as a probationer she would receive £10 per annum for three months (£2 10 shillings, pro rata) and £20 per annum for the next nine months. Her salary would increase by £5 increments every six months until she graduated. A new nurse needed the wherewithal – very likely her family's assistance – to afford the textbooks and her first uniforms, for the starting pay was a pittance. Edie would essentially be working for her keep.

2
EDIE AT THE COAST

Edie commenced her training at the Coast Hospital in November 1908. She was given swatches of material to get her uniform made up. Some nurses had theirs made at David Jones in the city. Edie probably asked her sister Grace to make hers.

Although the government and the Australasian Trained Nurses' Association (ATNA) officially recognised a three-year training certificate, Miss Watson had that year increased the Coast Hospital's to four years, which had the advantage of being recognised in Britain.

The Coast staff lived and worked closely together. They called themselves 'Coasters'. The strong sense of community was in part forged by the hospital's relative isolation, but the glue binding them was the leadership provided by Miss Watson and the medical superintendent, Dr Reginald Millard, who enjoyed an excellent relationship. Miss Watson even taught the Millard children to play the piano.[1] Both were well liked and respected. Each was exacting but fair and shared the expectation that staff should work diligently and care for their patients as people, not mere 'cases'. The nurses trusted Matron. They knew that she would hear them out and support them when dealing with the health system hierarchy. Edie would learn that not all matrons stood up for their nurses like this.

Miss Watson practised what she preached. She took special care of the Coast's leper community. Although provided with physical comforts that exceeded those of many Australians, including croquet and tennis lawns, the use of a rowboat on the lake and a bathing house on the beach, they were nonetheless cut off from their lives, families and employment. Not only did the kindly matron organise regular entertainment for them and co-opt nurses with a talent to sing, recite or play piano, but she insisted that her senior sisters join her for a weekly afternoon tea on the beach with them. Matron Watson visited the lazarets almost every day for a cup of tea and conversation, shaking hands and offering precious human contact in her knowledge that confinement under the *Leprosy Act* was due in no small part to an ancient stigma rather than real risk of contagion.[2]

Edie was one of the first eleven nurses to complete the new four-year Coast certificate. The women who would become her closest friends started training the year after her: Clarice Dickson and Dorothy Cawood in April, and, in December, Mildred Crocker Brown. In keeping with professional courtesy, they never called each other by their first names. Despite living and working together, staff often did not even know each other's first names. To Edie, her best friends were 'Dick', 'Cay' and 'Crock' or 'Crocker Brown' – drawing on Mildred's middle name to distinguish her from all the other Browns.

Clarice Dickson was four years older than Edie. She had been born near St George in the vast Queensland plains 300 miles west of Brisbane, but after her father's death her mother returned to the Kurrajong area of her youth, in the lower Blue Mountains in New South Wales, and remarried. These events brought Dickson to Sydney, where she earned her mental nursing certificate at Callan Park Hospital for the Insane at Rozelle, before commencing training in general nursing.

Dorothy Cawood was from Parramatta. Almost a year older than Edie, she was the youngest of seven children and had followed her sister Minnie into nursing. Her mother was England-born and her father a carpenter and member of the Parramatta Volunteer Rifles. She and Dickson became particular friends: they were both sensible and mature and marked out for leadership.

Mildred Crocker Brown was a few years younger than the others, born in 1889 in Auburn in Western Sydney. A bright student at Methodist Ladies' College in Burwood, Crocker Brown was distinguished by being, as Edie reminded her family on several occasions, the 'tall one', although, at an impressive 5 feet 11 inches, it was unlikely that they would forget her. The height came from her father, William, who had come from Nantucket Island 'for a look-see' at Australia, then married Amy Crocker and stayed.[3]

Miss Watson ran a tight ship. She used a large 'chessboard' in her office to plot the rosters of her nurses and female staff, and at eleven o'clock every night the senior nurse of every ward had to provide a report on new admissions and patients' conditions. It was Miss Watson's habit to slide a white umbrella along cupboard tops to check for dust and she insisted her nurses look immaculate no matter the task or the season.[4] Hair had to be tucked neatly under a white cap; uniform had to be topped with a white apron and its detachable white collar and cuffs must be starched and clean – or the wearer must sponge or change them.

Edie's days often began before dawn. On day shift there was time for a quick cup of tea before each nurse lined up to fill a bucket with hot water from the large kitchen cauldron then lug it to the ward where they had to sponge five patients, make five beds, put out the dirty linen and bedpans, then cut and butter bread for the patients' breakfast, before they could have their own breakfast at 7 am.

Although the bob-a-day men helped scour the floors, nurses did everything else in the wards. First-year probationers swept verandahs and scrubbed what must have seemed like every surface: lockers, dressers, even the huge tables in the wards – duties which the nurses called 'slushies'. Probationers, or 'pros', had to learn how to change bedpans; sponge patients; dress burns, sores and wounds; make and apply poultices; and give enemas.[5] In the evenings, furnaces in the ward boiler rooms had to be stoked and the blackened glass of the kerosene lanterns cleaned and the wicks trimmed, ready for the nurses on night duty.[6] Nine years later, in 1917, when Edie was nursing in Surrey, England, she revisited this time in a letter of encouragement to Queenie, who was commencing her training:

While reading your letter my own pro days came back. Oh Dear! How hard it was to stick to the job! How I wanted to throw down my broom or scrubbing brush & run over to Matron & tell her I couldn't stop & when I went to bed at night, with my tired feet rubbed with methylated spirits, how I wished that the morning would never come. But when I entered my second year I felt a different being altogether. Though I had sometimes to do a day here & there 'Proing' & I didn't mind it. The second year is the happiest year of training, you will find it so as you go on. You won't mind getting up in the morning, to see how a very bad case was progressing, & you begin to realise, that perhaps the little bit you do for that patient, you may be helping to get him better. In the 3rd & 4th year, the responsibility is felt more, then you begin to worry & if you are not careful, become irritable & then sometimes the pro may feel that irritability of that nurse.

Dear me Queen! I seem to be giving you a sermon or a lecture! I don't mean to, these thoughts keep coming into my brain. I wouldn't be a 'Pro' again at the Coast for all the money in China. But would do my second again any day. (24 August 1917)

On top of these duties Edie attended classes, filling exercise books over her four years of training with notes on subjects such as Anatomy and Physiology, General Nursing, Medical and Surgical Nursing, Hygiene, Infectious Diseases and Materia Medica, on which she had to pass annual examinations. From England, Edie told Queenie,

> I have here all my nursing books, & wouldn't be without them, when training I studied from them, & now I use them for reference ... get a well bound exercise book ... with the pages numbered. Copy your lectures into the book & have the 2nd 3rd & 4th year lectures in one book, before you begin leave a few pages for index. If you do this you will find the book excellent

for reference. I have most of my lectures in one book, but it was badly bound & the leaves are coming out. I must recopy it one day. I'm not looking forward to the job. (24 August 1917)

The Coast was a public hospital and many patients were the city's poorest and most vulnerable. Nurses found themselves sponging grimy skin, shaving lice-infested heads, directing blowlamps on to the bunks to kill bed bugs, and washing dirty garments. Heaven forbid that Matron caught any of them wrinkling their noses in disgust; even the filthiest rags must be treated with respect as they might be the only clothes a patient had. Miss Watson impressed upon her girls that 'no matter how objectionable a patient was, he was some mother's son and must be treated with kindness and dignity'.[7]

'Pros' also had to learn to deal with the most offensive sights and smells. Farm girls grew up with the cycle of life, sickness and death; but girls from towns or the city, like Edie, had more to learn. Nursing methods were not for the faint-hearted: the women were practical and became inured to the various symptoms of a sick or injured human body.

For example, the distinctive sweet smell of rot on the breath pervaded the diphtheria ward: some said it was a smell never forgotten.[8] A bacterial infection spread by coughing and sneezing, diphtheria is barely known now, but was common in those days. Diphtheria patients were often children. Thick creamy patches formed on the tonsils, which spread rapidly and thickened like leather, potentially causing suffocation or releasing toxins that could bring on heart failure. Clarice Dickson's first ambulance duty saw her tossing around in the wagon as they galloped along Sydney's rough roads, hooves flashing and bell clanging, rushing a young diphtheria victim to hospital for an emergency tracheotomy.[9] Although there was no diphtheria vaccination available at the time, an anti-toxin that could save lives if given soon enough became available in Edie's third year. After the anti-toxin was administered, nurses gently swabbed the infected throat with sodium chloride solution for several days[10] until the diseased patches softened enough to be cleaned away from the tonsils with a soft cloth stretched over a finger.[11]

With its specialisation in infectious diseases, the Coast insisted upon the highest standards of hygiene. The nurses learned the latest methods for isolation and antisepsis to prevent cross-infection and re-infection. There were separate wards for different infectious diseases, and a 'locked ward' for men with venereal diseases. Coast nurses also learned the mantra 'Flies, faeces, food equals typhoid'.[12] Outbreaks were common in cities where people lived close by their waste. The sisters wore rubber gloves when touching typhoid patients or anything belonging to them, and crockery had to be boiled after use.[13]

When Edie took her turn in the infectious wards she had to live, eat and sleep there. Nurses in those wards often worked seven days a week and longer than the standard shifts. They had to scrub their hands – and everything else – vigilantly and wear a mask and cap, and were not allowed to leave these wards until they had bathed and changed their clothes. Despite all precautions, a small number of sisters were infected. Edie herself caught a dose of diphtheria: merely touching an infected droplet with a cut finger could be enough. The few staff who died were buried nearby in the Coast Hospital Cemetery.

Coast nurses became experts at recognising symptoms of different conditions and in the treatment of each. They could differentiate the rashes caused by diseases such as measles, rubella and scarlet fever, to the extent that it was stipulated in later years that a patient with a rash could not be admitted until examined by a senior nurse.[14] Nurses were well placed to observe changes in their patients, and some doctors, including Dr Millard, were comfortable asking their opinion of a patient's condition. However, the nurses knew their place and that they must never offer an unsolicited opinion. Miss Watson insisted that nurses 'never diagnose and never, never suggest treatment'.[15]

Patients suffering typhoid or diphtheria usually required five to six weeks' bed-rest to recover, but it could take months, and it was the nurses who ensured that they were comfortable, hydrated and fed, who massaged their muscles and flexed their limbs so that they could get back on their feet in due course. These were the days, long before the discovery of sulfonamides (the first effective antibacterial drugs, introduced in 1935) and penicillin (not discovered until 1928, and not widely available until after the Second World War), when the key to recovery was bed-rest to allow the body to heal. Conscientious nursing could be the difference between life and death.

Nurses learned to treat a persistent high temperature with frequent cool sponges, or in extreme cases to wrap the patient in a wet sheet to make a 'wet pack'. Glycerine and borax or a weak carbolic solution were used to swab dry lips and mouths. Though drugs such as aspirin, bromides, narcotics and sedatives were available, it was standard practice to try to soothe headaches with cold (or sometimes warm) compresses and massage. Pressure points on the bedridden were massaged with methylated spirits and dusted with zinc powder, and, from day one at the Coast, probationers learned the importance of pulling bedsheets tight to eliminate the creases that could cause bedsores. Nurses monitored and reported anything unusual, but the head nurse decided what to bring to the doctor's attention. Soiled linen was soaked in carbolic solution then boiled, while infected waste was boiled then buried.

Making and keeping a diet chart and understanding cookery for invalids were integral to the Coast training. Food was simple and wholesome and demonstrated the British belief in the restorative power of a good cup of tea. Meals were served according to a strict schedule. Oatmeal or semolina for breakfast, with bread and butter and a cup of tea. Dinner at midday was generally roast beef or mutton with vegetables and gravy. Biscuits and tea at 2 pm were followed at 5 pm by sago and milk or bread and butter with tea, then cocoa at 7 pm.[16] Certain conditions required specialised diets. A typhoid patient initially received liquids in small doses, then jellies and purees. The Coast kitchen fare was, for some invalids, the most nutritious they would ever eat. The doctors were known to keep undernourished children in hospital longer than was strictly necessary in order to feed them a little more good food, before they returned to the dirty lanes and tiny cottages in Sydney's cramped and dishevelled heart. Edie could barely imagine what it was to live like that, although her mother, Kate, had had a rough start to life.

Catherine (Kate) Canham had been born in 1859 in Parramatta Street (modern Broadway) amid the breweries and public houses of Chippendale and Ultimo, when Sydney was a frontier city of fewer than 100 000 souls, cut off from Europe by 14 000 miles via ship – some three months' travel. Kate's parents had both come to the young colony for a better future. Her father, John, and his brother had been childhood orphans raised in a Cambridge workhouse. At the age of twenty-three, blacksmith John struck out alone on a £5 passage to Sydney. There he met Margaret Deely, one of the thousands of impoverished young girls who flooded into the colony on assisted passages to escape the cold, damp shadow of Ireland's Great Potato Famine.[17] John and Margaret married at St Mary's Cathedral and set about producing five children.

Edie's mother, Kate, was their second child. She was raised in Waterloo, a new suburb rising out of the swamps on the city fringe. Here ramshackle workers' cottages crowded like crooked teeth between the slaughterhouses, tanneries, boiling-down works and wool-washes. Here her father, John, came home in the evenings, his face and arms sweaty and black with soot from his smithy. Here Margaret died, twelve years after arriving in the colony. Kate was just six years old. Little wonder that she told her own daughters that they had it easy, saying, 'You were born with silver spoons in your mouths'.

As her training progressed, Edie would have undertaken more duties. Stocking the drug cupboard. Administering drugs like morphia.[18] Assisting in the infectious wards and undertaking ambulance duty as a second-year trainee. Changing dressings in the surgical wards in her third year: skills that Edie and her colleagues did not know would soon become so vital. They learned the methods of antisepsis and asepsis introduced by Joseph Lister, a professor of surgery at the University of Glasgow. Lister's ideas – of sterilising instruments and washing hands before surgery, cleaning a wound with bacteria-killing chemicals such as weak carbolic acid he called 'antiseptics' then dressing it to prevent new bacteria from entering – had been revolutionary when he first presented them in the 1860s. Before this, many a patient died of infection introduced by a physician's own hands. Matron Watson herself instructed her nurses in bandaging and the different kinds of rolls and folds needed to bind a leg, arm or scalp wound.[19] By her fourth year, Edie was taking charge of wards, assisting in the operating theatre, and running 'special' cases where patients received one-on-one care.[20]

There were worse places to be than the Coast Hospital. Fresh air and sunshine abounded. Convalescents of all ages lay in daybeds on the verandahs or went to the beach under the nurses' supervision. Sea breezes brought relief from the sticky heat of summer, though in winter Little Bay was buffeted by strong south-easterlies and nurses wrapped their capes tight and ducked their heads against the sea spray as they tramped between the buildings. One was blown off a verandah by a southerly buster and broke her ankle.[21]

Edie stayed on after she completed her training in 1912. Her friends Dickson, Cawood and Crocker Brown stayed too. There was a sense of camaraderie among the sisters. Between shifts they studied together, picnicked on the beach and had tea and cakes at La Perouse. They hiked up the northern headland, which had views towards the city, clambered over the rocks on the southern shore, and paddled in Little Bay. Some activities were shared with the doctors, but never swimming. A rock pool had been constructed at Matron McMaster's insistence, who feared that her charges might be swept out to sea or taken by a shark. The only sharks that concerned Miss Watson were of the human variety and, a stickler for propriety, she insisted that there be no mixed bathing in the bay, even though it was now commonplace (in strictly regulated neck-to-knee swimming costumes) on Sydney's beaches.

Edie visited her family on her days off or enjoyed Sydney's many attractions with her sisters and colleagues. The nurses could go out to dinner or a dance. They risked being grounded if they missed the hospital's 10 pm curfew, although there was a monthly midnight late pass.[22] For their annual holidays, trips to the Blue Mountains or sea cruises were popular among the nurses. Edie had been to the Blue Mountains, but she had not been out of Australia since a childhood family visit to England. The *Australasian Nurses' Journal* was full of items to catch a girl's eye. Nurses contributed articles about their exciting experiences travelling or working overseas. Among the advertisements for disinfectants, baby formulas, soaps and 'Anthony Horderns' Famous Low Prices for Fashionable Footwear' were ads such as this July 1914 offer of an eight-week tour of the New Hebrides:

> Where are You Going to For Your Holiday, Nurse?
>
> This is a Daily question and yet, not one easily answered off-hand. Nurses are not millionaires – they must always study ways and means …
>
> Next tour sails 1st September.

By then, Australia would be at war.

3

AUSTRALIA GOES TO WAR

In the Australian winter of 1914 life at the Coast proceeded according to routine.

Domestic news was dominated by the likelihood of a federal election being called, labour disputes, and the dry weather affecting large swathes of the country, prompting the New South Wales government to convene a conference of its departments to consider drought relief and mitigation measures.

Newspapers reported on international matters of interest. The question of Home Rule (self-government) for Ireland. Suffragettes setting off bombs, lighting fires and damaging artworks in Britain and France. Salacious divorces. Daredevil aerobatic feats. Douglas Mawson's return from the Antarctic and Ernest Shackleton's preparations to go. Border tensions between the United States and Mexico.

European politics also featured heavily in the Australian newspapers. The Balkans were at war in 1912 and 1913, and the treaty system that seemed to be dividing Europe into two was cause for increasing concern. The 28 June 1914 assassination in Serbia of the presumptive heir to the Austro-Hungarian throne was reported on 30 June and for a few days afterwards.

By late July, another Balkan war seemed inevitable. Most Australian press and political opinion considered deplorable the prospect that this conflict could escalate into war across Europe, but accepted that, as a matter of honour and duty to its allies, Britain too might have to declare. Australia was now in the middle of an election campaign, but both the government and soon-to-be-elected opposition pledged Australia's support. Prime Minister Joseph Cook said, 'If it is to be war – if the Armageddon is to come – you and I shall be in it … If the old country is at war, so are we'.[1]

At the turn of the century, the British Empire held power over more than 400 million people – nearly a quarter of the world's population – with territories so far-flung it was dubbed 'the Empire on which the sun never sets'. England had been at the forefront of the industrial revolution and London was the world's trade and financial hub. The defence of the British Isles had long rested on control of the seas through an immensely strong navy and a political policy of supporting equilibrium among the countries on the continent. Any imbalance of power, like the rise of an aggressive, expansionist country, could threaten Great Britain's security. The assassination of Archduke Franz Ferdinand and the aggression and triggering of treaty clauses that followed meant that it would be almost impossible for Britain to remain neutral.

Australia, as a newly minted nation still under the banner of 'British Dominion', continued to closely identify itself with the old country. Little more than a century after the First Fleet had landed, most white Australians saw themselves as British. When a reception was held at Sydney's Town Hall for the outgoing governor-general Lord Denman in April 1914, he presciently proclaimed to loud cheers and applause,

> Australia, the most British of all the Dominions, is achieving a great reputation throughout the Empire for what she has done and is doing in the matter of defence, and I trust your reputation will not only be maintained but enhanced … I will be able to assure the King – if his Majesty needs it – that he has no more loyal subjects in any part of the world than the people of Australia.[2]

Britain declared war on Germany on 4 August 1914. Such was Australia's devotion to the old colonial power that the Australian government considered Britain's declaration enough for Australia to be at war too and did not feel the need to declare war on its own behalf. Around the country, Australians were ready to answer the call. Men began knocking on the doors of Victoria Barracks in Sydney and Melbourne and other enlistment points across the nation in the wake of the news, eager to join up. Few voices were raised against the war, especially in the initial dash to get involved before it was over.

Due to the terms of the *Defence Act*, Australia could not send its standing forces overseas, and instead had to put together a new military force. It was decided to create the Australian Imperial Force (AIF) out of volunteers, and to send it to fight as a part of the British Expeditionary Force. Within a month of the declaration of war Australia had raised its initial commitment of 20 000 men: a division of infantry (18 000 men) and a brigade of light horse (2000 men, plus horses). Around one-fifth of the AIF had been born in the United Kingdom and many more were the offspring of parents born there.[3] While some Aboriginal men – ineligible to serve because they were not 'of substantial European background' as required by enlistment standards – successfully joined the AIF, for the most part it was a force composed of young white men.

The Australian government also committed a medical force to go with the AIF. A small number of Coast staff enlisted immediately, including two male medical attendants who left to join the army. Dr Reginald Millard, who had worked at the Coast Hospital since 1908, was also a member of the standing force, the Australian Army Medical Corps (AAMC). He was also quick to volunteer for the AIF, doing so just a few weeks after the outbreak of war in Europe. Aged forty-six at the time, and far beyond the maximum age limit for soldiers (thirty-eight years in August 1914, which was increased to forty-five years in June 1915), the experienced doctor would serve with the AAMC on Gallipoli, in France and in England for the duration of the war.

The initial medical commitment to the war was 1000 medics to staff one field ambulance (100 beds), one light horse field ambulance (sixty beds), one clearing hospital (200 beds), two stationary hospitals (200 beds each) and two general hospitals (530 beds each).[4] After appealing to medical practitioners, the authorities were swamped with offers. Initially, as many doctors were turned away as could be accepted. While Millard had been successful, other Coast doctors had to wait. Dr Thomas Furber was accepted for service in January 1915; Dr Thomas Frizell was accepted in March.

War fever gripped the nation. The nurses got into the spirit as the men around them enlisted. They knew their own professional skills would be useful: hundreds wanted to serve but did not know how or where to apply. The 15 August 1914 edition of the *Australasian Nurses' Journal* said, 'Since the war broke out, many enquiries have been received from nurses anxious to join the Army Nursing Service, in case nurses may be required'. It advised them to send their applications to a Miss Gould.[5]

Ellen 'Nellie' Gould had been the first lady superintendent in the new NSW Army Nursing Reserve and continued this role during her time in South Africa in the Boer War. When, in 1902, the Australian Army Nursing Service (AANS) was formed, Gould was an obvious choice to become its senior nursing administrator. Now, in a new war, she was again ready to serve in building the AANS for service abroad. When war broke out, the AANS sent notices asking its Reserve sisters if they were prepared for home or overseas service because, although as reservists they could be called up,[6] overseas service for nurses required volunteering just as with the soldiers. Fully qualified ATNA members could also apply, but first opportunity went to the Reserves. The army sought mature, fully trained nurses. They had to be aged between twenty-one and forty,[7] single or widowed, of British parentage or a naturalised British subject, with at least three years' training in 'a duly recognised civil General Hospital'.[8]

Coasters were among those eager to serve. Edie's friends Clarice Dickson and Dorothy Cawood applied and Edie too was quick off the mark. Australia had officially been at war a week when she obtained a reference from Matron Watson to support her application to the AANS. It stated simply, 'Sister E Blake has been on the nursing staff at The Coast Hospital since 16.11.1908 and holds the certificate of training issued by the institution. Her work and conduct are good'.[9] For Edie, apart from the skills she had to offer, there was the added attraction of getting to England and visiting her father's family, whom she had not seen since she was seven years old.

Edie's father, Charles Blake, carried Suffolk in every syllable he uttered, but when he arrived in Sydney at the dawn of the 1880s, this was hardly unusual. He hailed from Dallinghoo, a village near Ipswich. His father, Andrew, Edie's grandfather, owned and operated a combined smithy, carpentry and wheelwright's premises that made and repaired agricultural vehicles, machinery and implements, but, as the second of six sons, there was no way for Charles to make a living there, even if he had wanted it. Instead, he had landed half a world away in the colony of New South Wales.

Charles' mother, Frances, had died in 1864 following a miscarriage, a year after his seven-year-old sister Sarah died from diphtheria. His father did his best to raise their four young sons alone, assisted only by a housekeeper who was competent but powerless to tame them. The boys ran wild, and were later described as 'thoroughly out of hand', although they did attend the village school.[10] At Christmas 1867 the students gave the teacher a signed bible ahead of her impending nuptials. Inscribed 'Presented to Miss Edbrooke by the children of the Dallinghoo School as a token of affection', it was signed by every child, including Charles, Henry and James Blake. In January 1868, Miss Matilda Edbrooke married their father. Four more children, Alice, Matilda (Tilda), Andrew William (Will) and Frank, would later join the family.

After the marriage, the boys were sent to board at Kesgrave Hall in Ipswich. Andrew could afford the fees with the proceeds of sale of his brother's farm near Chicago, after his brother was killed fighting in the American Civil War.[11] At Kesgrave Hall, twenty boarders 'slept on hard boards and their main amusements were football and walking to Kesgrave Church on Sundays'.[12]

On completing his education, Charles, was apprenticed to Ransomes agricultural machinery makers at Ipswich, but it didn't suit him. He was independent, restless and bored. Eager for an opportunity to carve out a different life for himself, in 1873 Charles Blake went to sea. Family lore suggested he ran away, and perhaps he was prepared to do so; however, he was apparently convinced by the local rector, the well-connected Reverend Walford, that if he wanted to go to sea he should do so gainfully employed by upright people, while receiving proper instruction and qualifications to set up his future. Walford helped secure the fourteen-year-old an apprenticeship with Brocklebank's merchant shipping company of Liverpool.[13]

Charles sailed on Brocklebank clippers to the far east – Hong Kong, Singapore and Calcutta – developing a lifelong love of the sea. Each voyage took many months, the longest nearly a year, as ships sailed south of the Cape of Good Hope to catch the favourable winds that slung them across the Indian Ocean and back. Although the Suez Canal had opened in 1869, it was a route practical only for steamships. At the end of four years, Charles received a reference confirming that he had completed his apprenticeship, having 'conducted himself with sobriety and attention to his duties'.[14]

Australia's sun and opportunities must have called like a siren's song in comparison to Victorian Britain, and Charles jumped ship in Sydney. 'Jumping ship' could be licit, whereby a sailor was permitted to disembark at a port of his choice when his term of service was complete, or illicit, which could see an absconder sought by the law. Family lore again stepped in, suggesting that when his ship docked in Sydney, the captain scarpered and Charles jumped too. However, he may be the crew member 'Chas Blake' from Suffolk who arrived on the steamship *Northumberland* on 28 October 1879, in which case he may have carried a letter of introduction from the Reverend Walford that he could present to the Anglican Church in Sydney to receive assistance.[15] Either way, here he was, a fit young man barely more than twenty, at a boom time in a bustling city with a population of more than 200 000 that would double again in the next decade.

Confident, with a short dark beard and hair slicked back in a natty quiff, his solid Blake build made even more muscular by years of labour on the merchant ships, Charles acquired a horse and cart and set up business as a carrier. Keen as he had been to leave England, he was proud of his homeland and never lost contact with the family he had left behind.

Edie found the youthful exploits of the father she adored inspiring. She was eager to please him and desperate not to miss out. However, there was a long list of nurses eager to serve and few applicants were chosen. When the first convoy of troopships steamed out of Albany on 1 November 1914, it carried a contingent of just twenty-five Australian Army nurses. Edie was not among them.

Less than a month later, arrangements were underway for a second convoy. On a steamy day under threatening skies in late November 1914, crowds gathered on a Sydney wharf beneath the *Kyarra* as the ship made preparations to join that second convoy.[16] The passenger liner had been requisitioned earlier in the month for conversion into a hospital ship and she was painted white, with a broad green band and large red crosses on her sides. A red cross flag flapped high on the masthead and the Australian flag swung proudly from the stern. Cramming the decks were scores of khaki-clad men, and nurses in long grey dresses topped with short red capes. The Queenslanders wore white muslin caps, while the forty

New South Wales sisters wore grey bonnets.[17] Edie was surely there, searching among these for familiar faces, as Clarice Dickson and Dorothy Cawood were on board, along with Dr Wallis Mervyn Alfred (Mervyn) Fletcher, who had recently spent two years as a junior medical officer at the Coast Hospital.

The smiling voyagers flung coloured streamers over the throng below. The air shivered with an approaching storm and great thunderclaps elicited shocked 'oohs' from the crowd as the ship's engines roared into life. Edie must have watched with mingled longing and envy as the ship slowly pulled away. Again, she was not on board. She was not among the chosen few.

Those on the *Kyarra* did not know where they were headed, but they probably assumed she was bound for France.[18] Her next stop was Melbourne, where authorities were mortified to discover that beneath hospital equipment and supplies she was carrying hundreds of tons of coal, wool, tallow and hides – all contraband, for the Hague Convention protected a hospital ship provided she was not carrying 'stores of war'. Naval authorities had declared that the *Kyarra* was carrying no such material, and even the petrol had been drained from the tanks of the motor ambulances on board. Now the offending material was hurriedly unloaded, which at least made room for extra ambulances, equipment and Red Cross comfort packages.[19]

Before long, Edie got her chance to serve. But when she did sign up, it was with the British.

4

WHY THE BRITISH?

In her letters home during her service, Edie didn't say why she enlisted, still less why she enlisted with the Imperial nursing service. In fact, she never applied to the British. The Australians allocated her to them.

Like the AANS, the British Queen Alexandra's Imperial Military Nursing Service (QAIMNS) had been formed in 1902. There were some 2500 members of QAIMNS Regulars and Reserves in 1914; by the war's end there would be about 10 000.[1] Grace Wilson, principal matron of the AANS in 1914, later explained that 'the great difference was the existence (in the British Service) of a permanent nucleus, the QAIMNS, thoroughly trained in military administration, and with a knowledge of the routine returns required by the Army Departments; whose status, and place, in the military organisation was well established and known within the medical service'.[2]

Although the AANS nurses had the status of officers, they did not wear badges to indicate their rank (or receive officers' rates of pay).[3] The lack of clear lines of command concerning the AANS in the early days of the war gave rise to tensions as the first contingents of AANS arrived in Egypt. In a world governed by rank, who gave orders to whom? To whom did orderlies answer? Were nurses' arrangements (such as promotion and leave) and their work (such as rosters) to be directed by the matron – or by the medical unit's commanding officer, who held rank in the army?

The hierarchy question gave rise to a bitter clash at No. 1 Australian General Hospital (1AGH) in Cairo between respected

Why the British?

matron Miss Jane Bell and the Officer Commanding (OC), Colonel William Ramsay Smith. Both claimed to be responsible for all matters concerning the nurses and were each of a personality that would not give an inch. Ultimately, both were recalled to Australia in mid-1915, '[bringing] to the Australian medical service in Egypt a reputation for indiscipline and incapacity that was not soon lived down'.[4]

To some Australian nurses seeking overseas service, joining the QAIMNS Reserve (QAIMNSR) was a means to an end. Several who were in England when the war started joined the QAIMNSR there. Others followed a route advocated by the *Australasian Nurses' Journal*, which suggested in the September 1914 edition that, while 150 nurses had their names on the AANS waiting list, others had paid their own way to England, 'doubtless thinking that if they are on the spot they may have a better chance of being sent on duty at the earliest possible moment',[5] although in March 1915 the Journal warned that some nurses making the journey to England had been disappointed.[6]

As it was, Edie's chance had arrived. In early 1915 the British War Office offered to accept some of the Australian nurses who had volunteered for overseas service but had found no place in the small AANS. For a time, nurses trying to enrol for service were 'somewhat high-handedly' appointed to either the AIF or the QAIMNSR with little choice between the two.[7] Junior Sister Edith Blake was one of the AANS applicants allotted to the QAIMNSR, together with two other Coasters: Sisters Eena Copeman, from Edie's year, and Elsie Graham, who had graduated two years ahead. All three understood that they were, at least for now, serving with the British – which was more than one Australian who enlisted with the QAIMNSR who claimed not to understand, until she was steaming across the Indian Ocean, that when she had applied to join the Australians she 'might be detailed for service with the British Nursing Service'.[8] Another complained, 'We reckoned this quite unfair of the Defence

Department. We had not asked to go with the British. I offered for service with Australian Hospitals, and was only told a few days before we left that I was to serve with the British, and that was the end of it'.[9]

Within a month of being told to present themselves for examination, the three Coasters were heading off to war.

The quota of nearly 130 Australian QAIMNS Reserves was despatched overseas on His Majesty's Australian Transport (HMAT) *Malwa* on 6 April 1915, HMAT *Orontes* on 14 April 1915 and HMAT *Mooltan* on 15 May 1915.[10] Edie, Copeman and Graham were among the first to depart. Things moved so expeditiously that their working and administrative arrangements were not fully settled before they left, as Edie wrote home from the *Malwa*:

> Got Dad's letter in Adelaide, and also a little budget from different nurses. We shall get no more mail till we reach London which will be about the 14th of May. I don't know whether I told you about the questions I put to Miss Solling? Well I asked her what would be our duty when we arrived in England & also why we were called to England. She thinks that we will probably be in charge of wards put aside for the wounded as there are very few trained nurses in England. Lord Kitchener it seems is not satisfied with the treatment the wounded are getting. If that is the reason we will probably be made Sisters, but that will only be another £10 added to the £40. Which is not much is it?
> (11 April 1915)

Despite being the senior sister on the *Malwa*, Miss Wilhelmina (Minna) Sölling was no wiser than Edie as to why they were being sent to the British and what would happen to them. She had been matron of Crown Street Women's Hospital in Sydney, but, like Edie and nearly everyone else, accepted a reduction in rank, and pay, when she joined up. The AANS received £60 per annum, the

Why the British?

QAIMNSR just £40 (plus allowances), which was about one-third of an AIF private's base pay of 6 shillings a day (about £110 per annum, equivalent to the average daily wage). The Australians were on a better wicket all round: the AIF private's pay was a little over three times the British Tommy's, which caused angst in Egypt, where Australians splashed their cash on donkey rides, souvenirs, warm beer, and women.

As a junior sister at the Coast Hospital, Edie's salary had been £80, twice her QAIMNSR pay. Apart from commenting that it was 'not much' Edie did not complain, because she understood that it would be topped up to equal her Coast pay. The Department of Public Health agreed that 'the difference between Sister Blake's military and official pay should be paid by the Government as in the cases of the others who joined the Expeditionary Forces'.[11] Because she had been 'allocated' to the Imperial forces, she would be treated like the AANS. This decision was signed off only after Edie was in the middle of the Indian Ocean. The arrangement did not run smoothly. Five months later she wrote:

> Grace says that Dad is receiving from the Coast £2.1.6 per month. This works out at £24.18.0 per annum. I received at the Coast £80 per annum & I'm only getting here £40. Well £40 & £24 will only bring the amount up to £64, won't it? The Coast must be making a mistake. I do not want to be a grab all, but I think the Coast should pay the amount they said they would. I think they are mistaking my pay, for the Australian nurses who get £60. While the RAMC [Royal Army Medical Corps] is only getting £40. (1 September 1915)

The Coast was in error and the confusion about Edie's top-up pay (whether it was payable, how much and who would be responsible to pay it) continued, but, before the year was out, she gave up worrying about it.[12] (It was not until late 1921 that newspapers across Australia carried an article stating that the 'Commonwealth Government recently approved the payment of war gratuity to those nurses who were selected and sent abroad by the Defence Department in 1915 for service with Queen Alexandra's Imperial Military Nursing Service', inviting eligible nurses to apply, stating their period of service.[13]) Besides, the QAIMNSR had one significant advantage over the AANS: certainty. Nurses who volunteered for the AANS signed up, like the soldiers, for the unknown duration of the war. In contrast, QAIMNS Reserves signed twelve-month contracts. If they didn't like it, they could come home after a year, potentially at their own expense.

The Australian Army subsequently insisted, for purposes of 'safeguarding the interests of Australian nurses and the autonomy of their service', that if the Imperial government wanted the services of more Australian nurses, they must serve as members of the AANS.[14]

Serving with the British was a decision that Edith Blake would question more than once as she nursed overseas, and it was one that would have major repercussions. She couldn't know this in the Sydney autumn of 1915, but it didn't matter. She was on her way.

5
LEAVING AUSTRALIA

Edie had prepared herself for war. At the back of a black 1915 Collins Paragon Diary she wrote the addresses for her uncles Harry and Will in London, and aunt Alice in Bristol. The family would send their letters to Edie care of Harry, for no-one knew what her address in England would be.

On Easter Saturday 1915 she went to say goodbye to her family, who were now living in Sans Souci. Her father, Charles, had come on in the world. Blake & Co had flourished, and Charles had run the refreshment rooms in Enmore Road until 1915, when Edie wrote, 'So glad Dad has sold out, & for such a good figure too. The speculation of the shop, if not a comfortable one, proved a profitable one. I can just imagine the tea & coffee service in amongst the afternoon tea things. Also the clock on the dining room mantlepiece'. (20 August 1915).

Edie had been working at the Coast when Charles rented out their Marrickville home and built a weatherboard bungalow on a substantial Sans Souci parcel. She knew how much her father enjoyed tinkering around their new home, directing his restless energy to new projects. He planned to construct a sea wall to protect his land from inundation by the king tides. And perhaps a pier for his motor launch. When overseas she eagerly sought and followed news of additions and improvements:

> A verandah along the kitchen is a great improvement I should imagine. If you had an awning up on the verandah Mum

wouldn't have so many flies in the kitchen. (1 September 1915)

Queenie gave me an illustration of the new fence, how pretty it will be. Is it of wood with a foundation of brick? & the paths too, Dear Me! I shall have to be prepared to see great changes when I come home, or rather shall I know the house when I do come? I suppose Dad will be thinking of the boat soon as it must be getting warmer now. Tell Dad he mustn't do as Paddy did, who wanted to lengthen his days by stealing a few hours from the night. (24 September 1915)

I should like to see the place now it is fixed up. I suppose Dad will paint the house soon. (24 October 1915)

What work it must have been building the sea wall. I'm sorry the roses haven't bloomed too well, perhaps the soil isn't good enough for them. (23 November 1915)

What have you called the boat? I would love to see the garden. 'Myelash' [malesh] (Arabic for 'never mind'). (6 February 1916)

At the Coast Hospital there were farewells for Edie and Sisters Copeman and Graham. More Coasters would soon follow them to the war. Similar toasts were taking place across Sydney, wishing colleagues 'farewell and a happy reunion at the close of the war'.[1] Amid 'promises of letter writing' from both sides (Diary, 3 April 1915), each received the gift of a hot water bag from the Red Cross Society and their train tickets to Melbourne, where they were to meet the ship. Miss Watson wished her girls well. Matron gave Edie a new, more positive yet typically economical, reference that last day:

Leaving Australia

April 4th 1915

Sister Blake has been a member of the nursing staff at the Coast Hospital since November 1908. She leaves today for Europe as a staff nurse in the RAMC [Royal Army Medical Corps]. She has proved herself an excellent nurse & food manager. I can confidently recommend her for any position of trust.

A Watson, Matron[2]

A second reference from the Office of the Director General of Public Health in Sydney, dated 6 April 1915, had to catch up with Edie overseas. It added that during Sister Edith Blake's time at the Coast Hospital 'she has had excellent experience in medical, surgical and infectious nursing, and ward management; she was in charge of the operating theatre for five months. Her work and conduct are good'.[3]

The three Coasters were among those joining the QAIMNSR who caught an 8 pm train from Sydney's Central Station. Edie's new trunk contained her Coast uniforms and a few dresses besides.

'[There were] many on the platform to see us off', she wrote in her diary. 'Travelled 1st class.' They had dinner in the dining car:

> For the first time tasted clear soup, to my mind it isn't appetising, a few pieces of carrots & peas floated in it. It seemed so strange to watch the passing scenery while eating ... Of course couldn't sleep in the train it rocked as if we were at sea but didn't get as far as losing my tea. Some of the nurses did. (6 April 1915)

They arrived in Albury at 7 am and changed trains, a necessity because the former colonies had built railway lines with different track widths. Rattling along in a Victorian train Edie could now see the 'fearfully dry' countryside (Diary, 4 April 1915), on which she commented again when her ship called into Adelaide and Perth. Having lived her life east of the Great Dividing Range, she had been insulated from the worst of Australia's harsh climate. Thin brown sheep, hollowed-out cattle, patchy brown grasses and parched rocky paddocks bore testament to the drought that held the southern half of the continent in its grip and encouraged more than a few men to enlist as rural work dried up. (In Adelaide it actually rained, which Edie bemoaned while acknowledging that the locals 'were glad ... as they have felt the drought more ... than anywhere' (11 April 1915).)

It was almost 1 pm when they arrived in Melbourne:

[T]here was no one to meet us, we were hanging about the dingy station for about an hour before it was decided to look after ourselves. Today we have to go to [Victoria] barracks to get further instructions. It seems to me everything is badly managed, we do not know if we will get all we have spent refunded. It will practically cost £1.0.0 before we get on the boat. (6 April 1915)

The Sydneysider inevitably compared Melbourne to her home city. She was impressed but stubbornly parochial:

Yesterday we went to the botanical gardens, it is really a very beautiful spot. Don't think they are better than the Sydney gardens, but they are much bigger ... The Melbourne streets are good, very wide and all straight but they all seem to me to be all alike. The trams are cable & they stop wherever you hail them & all fares are 3', they are not nearly as up to date as ours & I don't understand where they are going, names of places seem to be all over them. Tell Queen she is to save up her shilling a week & come to Melbourne to meet me when I come back. (6 April 1915)

They met Miss Sölling the next morning, caught a tram to the port and boarded Royal Mail Ship (RMS) *Malwa*, a P&O liner requisitioned as a troopship. Most of her passengers were bound for the front to serve as soldiers or medics. Officers, including RAMC doctors, travelled First Class. Other ranks, including the nurses, were relegated to Second Class. Civilian passengers included officers' wives and Dr Hubert Orr, a dentist on a visit to London.[4]

> We left Melbourne 3pm Tuesday & ran into a storm but we seemed to run quickly out of it. Didn't feel at all sick, went to dinner 7pm (swell hours). The dinner was 7 courses: 1st course soup, second fish, 3rd beef, 4th chicken, 5th sweet, 6th icecream, 7th fruit. The first 4 I went through & thoroughly enjoyed it. Then I had enough. So went on deck & promenaded till 9pm. It was too cold to remain up so came down.
>
> Went to bunk & lost my dinner much to my disgust for I thought I was holding tightly.
>
> Slept all night, but did not feel like breakfast so went without. About 10am a gentleman spoke to me. The gentleman was no other than Dr Orr of Lismore, the husband of the Matron of that hospital. We have chatted & promenaded the deck nearly all day. Am feeling very well, had luncheon, feel just as well as if I were on land. It will be dinner soon. At 2.30pm Dr Yeates came and chatted to me for about an hour, then I introduced him to Graham & Copeman. He came over from the first class, he says it is too swanky for him. French is spoken by the waiters. Everyone has to dress for dinner. Most of the women smoke. Dr says that most of the other Doctors would feel more comfortable in the second class. (7 April 1915)

Dr Orr had spied the nurse looking peaked after her rough night at sea:

> [He p]roved very companionable. Brought beef tea to me, very nice having no breakfast. Promenaded deck 19 times which equals a mile ... The acquaintance with Dr Orr causes comment. Fortune told & cards good luck, but trouble on board foretold (hope not true). Introduced [a new QAIMNSR sister] to Dr Orr. Tells him how disappointed she is to find that he is a married man, as she weaved a romance between he & I. (Diary, 7 April 1915)

The *Malwa* docked in Port Adelaide for a day. The nurses took a train into the city, finding it clean and pretty: 'It happened to be Belgian Flag day. The King of the Belgians Birthday, everybody bought a flag & the proceeds went to the Belgium fund. The city was decorated, it was such a pity it rained' (11 April 1915).

Britain had entered the war when Germany invaded Belgium, whose neutrality Britain had guaranteed. Germany's reprisals for Belgian resistance – a campaign of atrocities dubbed the 'Rape of Belgium' – were well publicised and exaggerated, as if the truth was not sufficiently abominable. Australians enthusiastically campaigned for 'poor little Belgium'. The *Australasian Nurses' Journal* advertised numerous fundraisers and in March asked nurses to pay a weekly subscription to 'The ATNA [Australasian Trained Nurses Association] Belgian Relief Fund' to 'feed a few of these starving people ... who have lost everything'.[5] It reinforced the view that this was a 'right' war to fight.

From Adelaide the *Malwa* headed for Fremantle, and Edie suffered again:

> Much to my disgust have been sick most of the time since [leaving Adelaide]. Today feel much better. We are in sight of

land. It is such a comfort to see land again. This ill named bight has acted up to its traditions. It was a moderate sea so I've been told. But it seemed to me to be rough. (11 April 1915)

On Monday 12 April 1915, the *Malwa* docked at Fremantle for several hours and Edie visited Perth with a small group of nurses, including a former Coast nurse she had first met on the railway platform in Albury, of whom she wrote, 'Nurse Swannell is very companionable, she was trained several years before me' (15 April 1915).

Swannell would become one of her closest friends. Five years older than Edie, Evelyn Ellen Swannell was intelligent, level-headed and mature, one of eight children of a pioneer family[6]; her father, Thomas, had been a government surveyor in the Richmond–Windsor district near the Hawkesbury River, where Evelyn was born. She was the first of her family to serve in the war. Her brother Frederick, a veterinary surgeon, would enlist and serve, but for now was safe.

After completing her routine inspection of the city's botanical gardens and public buildings, Edie sniffed: 'Perth has narrow streets but rather nice buildings. Sydney seems very much ahead of any other states' capitals. Adelaide & Perth [are] really nothing to look at. The streets look poor, the station platforms are like our sidings in the country' (15 April 1915).

At 4 pm, the ship set off for Ceylon. Passengers leaned on the railing and watched as Western Australia's flat coastline receded in the late afternoon sun.

Edie wrote in her diary, 'Bid a long farewell to Australia. Wonder if' – she scratched this out – '*when* we will return'.

6

INTO THE BLUE

On their first morning in the Indian Ocean, RMS *Malwa*'s passengers undertook a safety drill. Edie found it rather exciting. 'We had to don life belts in order to know how to use them in case of an accident. The crew had fire drill, also boat drill' (15 April 1915).

The next order of business was to organise games and entertainment, for the ship was full of fit young people – and it would take them nine long days to reach Colombo:

> [W]e had a meeting to form a committee for the arrangements of sports. Since then all sorts of games have been played in tournaments. I have been in them all except card playing, that game is going on now. All the gentlemen paid in 5/- each & the ladies 2/6 each. After a deduction of tipping the deck steward the money is to go to the Belgium fund instead of prizes for sports. Dr Orr is treasurer.

> I have enjoyed the games very much. Today & yesterday I played in ladies singles ['Did not win a game' (Diary, 14 April 1915)], tomorrow we play in doubles with the gentlemen. Doubt if that will be better because the men play much better than the women. The men play cricket on deck & don't they enjoy it. I wish I were a man they seem to enjoy everything so thoroughly.

> Yesterday morning Dr Orr set all the men going skipping ropes, then with trapeze climbing & all sorts of antics, which I found very amusing.

> Last night we had a concert, some of the passengers play well, also sing. We had a dance afterwards, the deck steward put down boracic acid to make the floor slippery. But the ship rolled a bit & the floor was a bit hard. I had one dance with a doctor from the 1st saloon. The other side do not favour us much with their presence, I mean the doctors. (15 April 1915)
>
> Today had a very nice game of deck quoits. I'm not too bad a hand at [it], but still am not good … Some time today there is to be a potato race for ladies, egg & spoon race for gentlemen, whistling competition for both sexes, cock fighting whatever that may be, also high jumping for men. (17 April 1915)

After three days at sea, Edie was still coming to terms with the adventure: 'It is so hard to realize, we are in a different ocean. Hope we shall be able to see the Cocos Islands when we pass. I should like to see the Emden very much' (15 April 1915).

Newspapers had extensively reported His Majesty's Australian Ship (HMAS) *Sydney*'s triumph over Seiner Majestät Schiff (SMS) *Emden*, a German light cruiser that had been raiding shipping in the Indian Ocean with great success. In November 1914 the *Sydney Morning Herald* carried a report from a British eyewitness in France that 'the destruction of the *Emden* caused immense satisfaction in all the ranks. At one place, where the trenches were close, the news was passed on, with comments to the enemy. As the result the Germans fired heavily on our trenches for some time'.[1]

Edie did not get her wish to see the beached wreck. The *Malwa* ploughed on uninterrupted in the lonely expanse of ocean:

> Yesterday we sighted a boat on the horizon nose first. Everyone was excited, & made all sorts of conjections [sic]. It is the only object we have seen since we left Fremantle besides the ship we are on. As she came close she looked very like our own boat.

Some said it was the Mooltan, while others declared it was the Mongolia. A whistle blew, our flag, a Union Jack with a red background, went up, & soon afterwards a flag appeared at the stern of the other boat. They say there are plenty of flying fish, but never manage to see any. We have been teasing Copeman about hallucinations of sight, for she is the only one who sees them. (15 April 1915)

The heat and humidity increased as they approached the equator. Although for Edie seasickness was a thing of the past, Evelyn Swannell suffered dreadfully. They were in a cabin without a window to offer the benefit of a horizon or a breeze and it was 'like a hot house' (17 April 1915).

Miss Sölling was loath to alter accommodation arrangements, so they spent as much time as possible in the public rooms or promenading the deck for fresh air and exercise, crossing off the days until the blessed relief of dry land. Amid the games and concerts, the doctors put the men through physical drills and presented lectures to the nurses on first aid, dressings, fractures and arresting haemorrhage. Edie wrote letters, sewed, read *Les Miserables* and attended Sunday church service in the First Class saloon.

There were other distractions. Although she had enjoyed the innocent thrill of 'causing comment' with her acquaintance of the safely married Dr Orr, Edie scorned the onboard flirtations around her:

Imagine a number of people cooped up together, with very little to do ... The men are rather nice taking them collectively. I have had very little to do with them but I see them, & the women too. The women casting sheep's eyes at them, but the opposite sex seem adamant. Most of them are going to war, going home most of them to form the King Edwards Horse. 22 of the women are nurses. Only a few are on pleasure bent. I'm afraid some of the nurses are not having the good time they expected, & look a bit down. We have a nurse who is sitting quite close to me now with a gentleman, every now and again I hear a most absurd voice affected to the highest degree, they keep chipping in to me, asking the gentleman's name, they tell me I'm too interested [in my letter] to be writing to my people. (15 April 1915)

Romances between nurses, RAMC and soldiers were common enough, although officially frowned upon. At home or war, marriage almost invariably marked the end of a nurse's career.[2] Fraternisation between the sexes on the *Malwa* was restrained compared with activities on other ships. Aboard the *Orsova* in August 1915, canoodling between couples in darkened corners all over the ship earned the nurses a lecture from a senior officer and suppression of the ship's newspaper.[3]

Apart from betraying impatience with simpering flirts, Edie's comments exposed parochialism and jealousies among the nurses. After what followed in Ceylon she confided, 'There is no feeling of unity amongst the nurses. We Coasters seem to agree & get on together better than the others & we keep to ourselves which seems better & is less trouble' (23 April 1915).

The *Malwa* docked in Colombo early in the morning on 21 April 1915 and remained in port until 6 pm the following day. Edie, Eena Copeman and Elsie Graham booked a trip to Kandy through Cooks: 'With tips the trip cost £2.5. It was so delightful that I don't think that was too much, besides being several degrees cooler' (23 April 1915).

The Coasters travelled separately. Edie was miffed that they had not been asked to join Miss Sölling's party, but smugly confident that their professional arrangements were superior:

Miss Solling & two PA [Prince Alfred] nurses went to Kandy too. The day before we landed at Colombo Miss Solling asked us what we were going to do. She did not think that we would care to pay £3 to Kandy. It was plainly seen we were not wanted. No one seemed to know what the cost would be, so we decided to go to Cooks & see. Three gentlemen took Miss Solling & the two nurses, but did not book through Cooks. Consequently we had everything arranged for us. They were behind us in everything …

The train journey lasts 4 hours which took us into the heart of the island & into the mountains. The scenery was gorgeous … We passed tea plantations, banana & coconut groves. Cinnamon trees, also nutmeg & cocoa bean trees. The country has very rich vegetation, & is so green, so different to parched Australia. We reached Kandy 1.40 pm.

A carriage was waiting for us to take us to the hotel, a very large clean place, & well appointed. After lunch, we were told the carriage was waiting for us to take us to Lady Hortons drive. I can't describe the beauty of this drive. At a point the guide took us to a look out overlooking Kandy lake. Here we had to give our first tip, & gave too much, as we found out afterward. We drove through native villages, which are very squalid & smelly. We were shown the sacred elephants which I don't think are any more sacred than I am. The elephants went through all sorts of tricks. One was 90 years old, with enormous tusks. They were bathing. Coming back we went through the Temple of the Tooth. This is a very old peculiar building … (The tooth it seems is a tooth belonging to Buddha).

We gave the guide a Rupee between us which he said was not enough, he haggled & haggled with us [so] that to get rid of him we gave him another. But it seems to me whatever you give them, it is not enough. After dinner at the hotel we had a rickshaw ride, I enjoyed this immensely. We went round the lake. At first I did not like to get into a vehicle drawn by a human being. But got over that … While in the rickshaw the sun was setting, & the sky was reflected in the water, so imagine how beautiful it all was. That night I slept in a bed, it was so comfortable after the bunk. Graham & Copeman had a two bedded room but I had to have a room to myself, at first I felt a bit nervous for everywhere you went there seem[ed] to be a native servant in front or at the back of you.

The next morning we drove to the Paradeniya gardens, which are considered the best in the world. The roads would do Dad's car good they are in excellent condition, the huge trees on either side made them very shady. The gardens are really beautiful … We took the train back to Colombo from Paradeniya, got into Colombo just half an hour before we were to be back to the boat. So we had afternoon tea at the Great Oriental Hotel, the biggest in Colombo.

A bangle took my fancy at Kandy. It is supposed to be moonstones & silver, whether it is or not I don't know but it is a curio & I thought of Queen's birthday but I don't think I shall post it till I get to England. I gave 4 ½ rupees for it. They wanted at first 8 but I beat them down to the 4 ½. But in all probability it isn't worth a rupee. (23 April 1915)

Edie had visited Ceylon during the family trip to England when she was seven years old and was delighted to find her memory was not wanting:

As far as I can remember the natives wear more than they did 20 years ago. Many of them will have a European coat & loin cloth & a straw hat. There were some who wore circular combs in their hair. The hair was long & fastened in a knot. For the life

of me I could not tell the men from the women. Their babies are
beautiful. Copeman went into raptures over them, & wanted me
to adopt. They would be alright to adopt if they didn't grow up.
They were fat, shiny & pretty.

My memories of Colombo did not deceive me, the buffalo carts I
remember well, they are just the same, also the markets which we
had to pass to go to the station. The only thing I did not see were
the men in canoes. In Colombo the boys ran after the people
saying they had no father or mother & were hungry, but I did
not see this. From the train we threw 10 cents & 5 cent pieces
to the piccaninnies who picked them up backwards with their
eyelids. Their bodies were wonderfully supple, wished mine was.
(23 April 1915)

As the *Malwa* made west across the Arabian Sea, the cabin Edie
and Evelyn Swannell shared deep below decks became almost
unbearable. The Coasters and the nurses from Adelaide were the
only nurses travelling in cabins without portholes.

When we tackled [Miss Sölling] about [it], she said we would
have to take our chances – Graham, Copeman or I, do not care,
but Nurse Swannell has been very sick until Colombo, she thinks
she would be better in a cabin with a porthole.

Last night slept on deck, it was beautiful but at 5.30am we were
turned out, so as to allow the Lascars [Indian sailors] to scrub
the deck. Went then into the music room, but at 6am [were]
turned out again, so after we both got up on deck to watch the
men drill, this is rather interesting. Don't think I shall sleep in
the cabin again. We do not know what to do with ourselves, it
is so hot in the cabin when you wake up, the pillow & bed [are]

saturated with perspiration. We have a beautiful breeze ahead of us. We have had several heavy showers, they say they are the monsoonal rains. (23 April 1915)

A few days later they rounded the Horn of Africa and turned in to the Gulf of Aden. The gulf was the gateway to the Red Sea, which in turn led to the Suez Canal, and the military camps full of Australians training in Egypt. Now the war seemed much closer, as they passed a troopship with a band on board playing 'Tipperary'. The following morning they reached Aden itself, a Yemeni port established by the British as a protectorate to support their steamer traffic to and from India. It had an uneasy relationship with surrounding tribes and the Ottomans:

> A dirty, dusty, dry, desolate place. Would not like to live there. It is fortified, & has a thousand troops (territorials) feel sorry for them, for there is nothing to see or do. On the Harbour there was a Warship. No one was allowed to take a camera on shore or they would be confiscated. We went ashore & took a car to the tanks. These tanks supply the town. We were told [they] were made by King Solomon. They are hewn out of rock & hold millions of gallons of water. There were 5 tanks in all. The Arabs went around the town selling the water in sheep skins. Did not get any, for the water in the tanks looked dirty, & the dirty Arabs were swimming in them. (29 April 1915)

They only stayed an hour on shore, but before the *Malwa* left port Miss Sölling received startling instructions. The nurses were to leave the ship at Suez:

> We all felt as if a thunderbolt had descended upon us. Everyone is disappointed. I felt it too, for now I do not know when I

shall get your letters. Six weeks seem long enough time, but goodness knows when we will get them now. I have written to Uncle Harry, telling him what has happened. I do not think I shall want any money. I have nine pounds on me, & if we go to Cairo or Dardanelles, or any other place, we will be kept & paid, & don't think I shall be spending any money. Getting off at Suez sounds as if we will be going to Egypt, as there is a railway connecting the Suez with Cairo. Perhaps we will have to relieve the people there. (29 April 1915)

The *Malwa* hugged the Yemeni coast then turned north into the Red Sea, passing more and more ships as she went. Sea traffic here was now subject to the will of the British, who had seized the Suez Canal after the Ottomans entered the war and closed it to all but Allied and neutral shipping. Ottoman forces had raided the canal only two or three months before the *Malwa* passed through, trying to gain control of the quickest naval route between Europe and both India and the Pacific. The British maintained a staunch defence of the canal for many months:

> We had a great send off from the boat. The night before we got into Suez we had a dance & concert. One gentleman got up & spoke on behalf of the nurses, we should be suffering from swelled heads. On leaving the boat the cheers from the passengers would have deafened you. Everybody shook hands with us more or less. (5 May 1915)

The nurses were medically examined then taken ashore by tender. Edie scribbled a postscript to her letter:

> Just arrived at Suez. The instructions are that we are to proceed to Heliopolis a hospital in Cairo. I'm not off the boat & don't know when we will get to Cairo. Oh dear, when shall I get your

letters? Hope war news is true we heard, we all were very excited. For war news is very scarce. We hear that the Australians have captured 8,000 Turks.[4] Most of the nurses are anxious as they have brothers at Dardanelles.

Love to all. Hope all of you are well.

Love from Edie (29 April 1915)

The nurses next boarded a train for Cairo.

7

THE LANDINGS

Although the first contingent of Australian and New Zealand troops left Albany bound for England, camps on the wintry Salisbury Plain were not ready for them and it was decided they would complete their training in Egypt, where they could help defend the Suez Canal.

The Ottoman Empire had entered the war on the side of Germany on 29 October 1914, when it used its newly acquired warships, the *Goeben* and the *Breslau* (renamed *Yavûs Sultân Selîm* and *Midilli* respectively) to conduct raids on Russian ports on the Black Sea. Over the following days, Russia, France and Great Britain declared war on the Ottomans. The outbreak of hostilities in this quarter was not unexpected, with increased German influence in Turkey. A German commander even closed the Dardanelles without direct orders from the Ottoman government. A narrow strait in Turkey's north-west known from antiquity as the Hellespont, the Dardanelles had long played an important role in history. The armies of Xerxes and Alexander the Great had crossed it and Lord Byron had swum it. Both shores were lined with forts, and now the waters were also seeded with mines.

While the defensive measures in the Dardanelles were formidable, it seemed to some to offer a back door to the war. As the fighting in France ground to a trench war deadlock and Tsar Nicholas appealed for assistance, the British War Council, at the behest of the first lord of the Admiralty, Winston Churchill, suggested a speedy naval attack to capture Constantinople. It was hoped that re-opening the strait would allow transport of munitions, grain and oil through

The landings

the Sea of Marmara and the Bosphorus and into the Black Sea, the only warm water sea route to Russia, and could potentially allow military forces to attack Germany from a different direction. There were a number of different viewpoints of what should happen after the Dardanelles was opened, but all relied on the straits being forced first.

Britain and France commenced their attempt on the Dardanelles with a naval bombardment of its forts in February 1915. On 18 March, a British and French naval fleet tried to force its way through the straits, but failed dismally in the face of determined fire from the Ottoman forts and a well-mined waterway. Three Allied battleships were sunk, at least three more were seriously damaged, and as many as 700 British and French seamen were killed or wounded in the endeavour.

Rather than the attempt to force a way through being called off, a land invasion was hurriedly planned despite the original determination that this should be a naval campaign alone.[1] The antipodeans training in Egypt were ideally placed to take part in this new campaign, landing on the western side of the Gallipoli peninsula in the hopes of forcing their way overland and attacking the Dardanelles forts from behind. The Australians would have their first taste of action in the rugged pink hills above what would become known as Anzac Cove.[2]

The first Australian boots hit the sand shortly before 4.30 am on 25 April 1915. They belonged to Australians of the 3rd Brigade – Queenslanders of the 9th Battalion, South Australians of the 10th Battalion and Western Australians of the 11th Battalion.[3] While the initial shouts and rifle shots ripped through the pre-dawn calm at Anzac Cove, Edith Blake and her fellow Coasters were thousands of miles away, asleep on the *Malwa*.

The Anzac area was relatively lightly defended when the landings commenced, but the Ottomans were able to rush reinforcements to the rugged ridges above Anzac Cove in short order. As more and more Australians were landed at the cove throughout the day, the Ottomans rallied and increased their defensive rifle and machine-gun fire on the attackers. Somewhere among these was Miss Sölling's youngest brother. As his sister and her colleagues on the *Malwa* breakfasted and attended divine service on a quiet Sunday in the thick air of the Arabian Sea, twenty-one-year-old Lieutenant Eric Sölling was shot dead.[4] Reports would reach Miss Sölling soon after she arrived in Cairo, but there was confusion. Even as the authorities notified the family that Eric had been killed in action, Miss Sölling telegraphed them with the well-meaning but incorrect news that he had a leg wound. This sparked a flurry of anguished cables and must have only increased Miss Sölling's pain once she knew the truth.[5]

While the *Malwa* was navigating the Gulf of Aden, then the 1400-mile length of the Red Sea, the Australians and New Zealanders scrabbled to gain a foothold at Anzac Cove. The French came ashore at Kum Kale, on the Asiatic side of the Dardanelles. On the European shore, the British met fierce opposition at Cape Helles. Here, in disastrous landings at 'V' Beach, hundreds were slaughtered as they disembarked from ships' boats and the beached landing ship the *River Clyde*. Australian QAIMNSR nurse Agnes (Beryl) Corfield wrote that a man told her 'the Wednesday of the Retreat of Mons (supposed to be the worst day of the war) was like heaven to the terrible Sunday of Gallipoli'.[6] Off the coast of Cape Helles, the sea literally ran red with the blood of British soldiers.

None of the Allied forces reached their first day's objectives. Not then, not ever during the blighted eight-month campaign. The Ottomans were not only better prepared and equipped with German weaponry and officers' support (under German field marshal Limon von Sanders) than the British War Council had anticipated, but they fought passionately for their country. At Anzac Cove, led and inspired by their own Colonel Mustafa Kemal (who would make his reputation here, later becoming the first president of the Turkish republic), the Ottomans rallied quickly and halted the advance.

The landings

Isolated parties of Anzacs penetrated further inland that first day than they ever would again, later having to withdraw a little to establish a firm defensive perimeter.[7] The commander-in-chief of the Mediterranean Expeditionary Force, General Sir Ian Hamilton, accepted the view of naval commanders that immediate evacuation was impossible and told his infantry, 'You have got through the difficult business, now you have only to dig, dig, dig until you are safe'.[8]

The diggers dug in. It took days to reorganise the muddled Australian and New Zealand battalions and establish a strong perimeter on the heights above Anzac Cove. The ridges above the cove became scarred with trench lines that barely moved for the duration of the campaign. Allied soldiers were never safe. Almost every inch of the land they held was vulnerable to the Ottoman guns, and snipers posed a constant threat.

Under medical arrangements the wounded were first brought down to dressing stations on the beach. Those who could do so made their own way – walking, limping or crawling hundreds of yards. Some were helped on sure-footed little donkeys, while 'cot cases' were stretchered down the treacherous gullies. Wounded men were to be evacuated by barge to waiting hospital ships.

Yet, immediately after the landings, wounded men lay on the beach in the sun, parched and at the mercy of flies, for many hours, or even days, before being evacuated. On 25 April just one hospital ship, the *Gascon*, waited off Anzac Cove, together with transports and troopships. On the ships, casualties languished in dirty field dressings and bloodied uniforms, or blankets if their tunics had been cut off, while medical staff struggled to hydrate them or clean their wounds due to a lack of clean water.[9] Poor lines of communication meant that the transport ship SS *Hindoo*, delayed by storms and carrying essential medical staff and equipment, lay off Cape Helles for three days without unloading her vital cargo. Consequently, hospital ships were left critically understaffed and underequipped.

One wounded officer brought to Egypt on an ordinary transport in a trip lasting three days and nights recounted that there were just three doctors and twenty-six orderlies to attend 1346 patients.[10] The captured German liner *Lutzow* was pressed into service as a temporary hospital ship. Her patients were identified by old luggage labels and placed under the care of one veterinary officer and one orderly (with 130 horses) who worked to exhaustion in what a surgeon later described as 'the dirtiest, nastiest boat I have been on'.[11]

The medical arrangements for the campaign were based on an estimate that the 75 000-strong British force would incur around 3000 casualties, but in the fortnight after the landings, nearly 16 000 wounded (more than one-fifth of the landing force) were evacuated to Alexandria.[12] Almost half remained there. The rest went on to Malta, England, and almost 5000 to Cairo – mostly into the Australian hospitals.[13]

Hotels, schools and similar properties in Egypt were commandeered to make way for hospitals to support the Allied war effort. Completed in 1910, the Heliopolis Palace Hotel was billed as the most luxurious hotel in Africa and the Middle East. Featuring a blend of Moorish, Persian, Islamic and neoclassical styles, it was the jewel of Heliopolis, the new city raised from the desert a few miles north-east of central Cairo for the leisure and indulgence of the elite. The hotel was now repurposed as 1AGH.

1AGH accommodated about 1000 patients, but, as the casualties from Gallipoli poured into Cairo in late April, it expanded dramatically[14]. Auxiliary hospitals were established in nearby schools, clubs, a factory and even Cairo's Luna Park, a former amusement park where beds were set up on the adapted ice skating rink and 'anywhere a space could be found … in the Pavilion patients came from the joy wheel, laughter house, skeleton house, scenic railway, & bandstand to be dressed. They used "the Mysterious Cavern" as a dressing room'.[15] The ticket booth was lined with mosquito netting and became an operating theatre.[16]

The landings

No. 2 Australian General Hospital (2AGH) was established in the Mena House Hotel near the Australian Army camp at Giza, but in early May 1915 transferred to Ghezireh Palace, a palace near the centre of Cairo that had been converted into a hotel twenty years earlier. Between them, Ghezireh and Mena House (retained as an auxiliary hospital) accommodated 1000 patients.[17]

The *Malwa* carried twenty-one Australian nurses who were to serve with the QAIMNSR.[18] The train was waiting when they arrived at Suez at noon on Sunday 2 May 1915. Looking out the window as they rolled west they saw desolate country: mile upon mile of sand and bare rocky rises. As they approached Cairo, there were more signs of habitation: palm trees, rock walls, and shepherds tending herds of skinny goats. Everything bore a patina of dust.

It took them half a day to travel fewer than 90 miles to Cairo, where an ambulance waited to take them to Heliopolis.

8
ON DUTY ONCE MORE

The column of ambulances rattled down Cairo's dark streets. The Coasters huddled against the night's chill as walls and alleyways flashed by in the flickering headlights. At last, the convoy turned down a long palm-fringed driveway and crawled to a halt before the erstwhile Heliopolis Palace Hotel, an enormous building styled with arches and domes and bold striped columns.

Inside, marble staircases curved up to balconies held aloft by soaring columns. Brightly coloured friezes decorated the walls. Where ladies and gentlemen had once mingled in silks, robes and suits, khaki-clad medical officers circulated among rows of patients on low beds. The nurses' rooms were on the second floor, furnished with little more than similar hard, narrow beds.[1] They must have been too tired to care.

The next morning, 3 May 1915, Edie went to work.

Dear Mum & Everybody,

Well, am on duty once more ... we arrived [at the 'Palace Hospital' at] midnight. The building is really the finest building I have ever seen. Have been lost twice in it already. We breakfasted at 8.30am & on duty 10am in the [Luna Park] skating rink. There are about 800 patients & 4 nurses you couldn't imagine what it was like & how the nurses welcomed us.

All patients were wounded at the Dardanelles. The very bad patients are at Alexandria, & those in the rink have slight

wounds, but all need dressing. I'm on night duty tonight, in a
place connected with the rink, I'm the only woman here & I
have no orderly, but one patient gets up if I want him. There
are 73 patients. One patient is very ill I'm afraid he is likely
to be delirious & there are several others who need continual
attention. (May 1915)[2]

The men in Edie's care were relatively lightly wounded, but the sheer number was almost overwhelming. Her task was vital, for they were not yet out of the woods. Two suffered severe haemorrhage, and the 'likely to be delirious' patient was running a temperature of 104 degrees as his body fought an infected bullet wound in his shoulder (Diary, 3 and 5 May 1915). Even with early, thorough cleaning and disinfection, and regular follow-up, infection could strike where recovery had seemed possible. One Australian wounded on the first day of the landings at Anzac Cove had written home bullishly from Alexandria that he was slightly wounded and though not yet healed was fit enough to go back. He died three weeks later.[3]

The highest standards of hygiene were critical. Best practice dictated that nurses' hands must be washed and soaked in a weak carbolic solution before and after touching patients, and instruments and equipment sterilised. Wounds which had had treatment on the battlefield, in casualty clearing stations (CCS) and in transit, still needed to be cleaned. They were irrigated with saline solution, debrided, fragments of bone and debris picked out with probes, then dressed with an antiseptic solution such as iodine or carbolic acid. Local anaesthetic eased the pain of cleaning serious wounds. Some soldiers came in missing chunks of flesh the size of a fist, or worse, which required nurses to work in pairs to place waterproof sheets and bowls underneath to catch blood and water before packing the hole with antiseptic-soaked gauze. Shrapnel generally made a much larger, messier wound than a bullet; but if a bullet hit bone, it was likely to shatter it. Fresh from her civilian hospital, Edie was seeing for the first time the carnage wrought when metal tore into flesh and bone.

A bad wound could take an hour to clean, dress, bandage and, if necessary, splint. Some needed to be dressed several times a day. Yet best practice was not always possible. Sister Ellen King, one of Edie's contemporaries at Luna Park, described the primitive conditions:

> [T]here were absolutely no conveniences. The sterile? water was brought us by a native servant from the cookhouse ... [one] day when we had almost finished one jug of sterile? water we found a large onion in the bottom. There was an absence of even antiseptics ... Kerosene tins were converted into arm & foot baths, dressing trays, sterilizers, and many other useful things. There were no sterilized dressings, gauze was placed in 1% solution of picric acid overnight and in the morning diluted with sterile water.[4]

Despite the difficulties, King conceded, 'Under this treatment many of the wounds did very well indeed'.[5] Edie wrote 'I shall never forget entering [Luna Park] for the first time. It was then I realised what war meant, but still 75% of these men went back to the Dardanelles' (25 June 1915).

The newly arrived Australian nurses had little more than their civilian uniforms with them. One Australian Army nurse, who departed Australia in June 1915, remarked to her mother, 'Go easy and not burst yourself giving to Patriotic funds. It is a humbug from start to finish, look at us how much it cost in Australia, then since coming to London have had to buy Primus stoves, Mackintoshes, gumboots, Mess kit ...'[6] Edie didn't even get the chance to shop; she and her comrades had to borrow mess kit:

> We are not properly equipped and it is very awkward. Every nurse has her own cutlery & enamel ware. At meals we seem to

be depriving somebody of a fork spoon or cup ... This morning
our luggage, or part of it for part is still at Suez, was taken to
front entrance & we haven't seen it since. Found this foolscap so
using it to write & when my pen runs out will have to stop. It is
cold here, so different when on the boat. Seen very little of Cairo
yet. (5 May 1915)

At first, Edie felt off-kilter. She missed her family and had to get used to new routines. She had not been the closest of friends with Eena Copeman and Elsie Graham in Sydney, but, in this strange place, the Coasters were allies. Besides, they expected to move on soon: 'Don't think it will do to address my letters yet to Egypt. For the nurses on the Kyarra will be here in a fortnight's time, & we may go on to London when they arrive or they may keep us here till the Dardanelles campaign is over ... Don't think I would care to stay here' (5 May 1915).

The appearance of an old colleague momentarily raised her spirits. 'We go to the Palace for meals & while I was there standing in the spacious hall waiting instructions & feeling a bit homesick, I heard a footstep behind me.' It was Dr Furber: the 'first familiar face', other than her colleagues, she had seen (5 May 1915).

Thomas Furber had departed Australia in a flurry: within one month of enlisting in January 1915, he had left the Coast Hospital, married former Coaster Irene Corbett, and steamed out of Sydney as a captain in the AAMC.[7] He was in Cairo when the Gallipoli campaign commenced. Edie wrote,

> There is no base hospital near the Dardanelles. Dr Furber tells me that they have been operating day & night. Had about 7 hours sleep in three days. Train loads upon train loads of patients come in. The nurses simply admit the patients, if they can dress the wounds they do, no other work can be done ... We talked for about ½ hour, he knew I was here & came to

find me. He is one of the principal doctors at the Palace, & says he will do his best to have Copeman Graham & I to work under him, he has 80 patients in the Palace Hospital. If he can manage it, we will be fortunate. (5 May 1915)

For a week Edie had about 100 patients in her care; then they received a surge of men, likely from Cape Helles following a second failed attempt to capture the village of Krithia and the nearby heights of Achi Baba.

> When I came on duty, motor car after motor car arrived with patients, till they brought in 350. The day orderlies stayed up till 1am, several patients got up and helped, & how we all worked, for all had a bath, & put to bed, & the wounds dressed. Many of the wounds had not been dressed for days while some had not been dressed since they were wounded on the field. They were so tired. Nearly all were British tommies. The Captain (medical officer) came into the ward, & called attention. He gave a speech asking the Australians to give the Britishers a hearty welcome, it is the first time I have ever heard cheering & clapping at midnight in a hospital ward. On Thursday night 20 more came in, but their wounds were more severe, & the patients were very sick.
>
> On Tuesday a cablegram was read out to the patients from the King, congratulating them on their bravery in the Peninsula of Gallipoli near the Dardanelles. (16 May 1915)

Suddenly Edie's 'ward' had more than 500 patients, 'mostly shoulder wounds, fingers shattered, [but] all could help themselves to bed' (Diary, 12 May 1915).

Soon after she arrived in Cairo, Edie heard the sound of male voices raised in song. The sisters ran outside and saw columns of khaki-clad Australians with emu feathers wafting proudly in the bands of their slouch hats and dust kicked up by their boots: '[It was] the light horse soldiers on foot on their way to the front … Almost all the boys waved us goodbye. The boys were very cheerful singing at the tops of their voices "Are we downhearted? No!" Tipperary' (Diary, 8 May 1915).

Elsie Graham's brother Donald was among them. He had enlisted with the first wave in August and had been training at the light horse camp at Maadi on Cairo's outskirts. Now the nineteen-year-old upholsterer was on his way to catch a train to Alexandria, where, the next day, his regiment would board a ship bound for Gallipoli.[8]

Like Donald Graham, most of these men had proved themselves able to handle a horse on enlistment. Nevertheless, in camp they were made into true light horsemen, capable of fighting on horseback and on foot, and responsible for properly managing their mounts to meet the daily demands of a harsh desert campaign. The horses would be vital for transporting men and provisions, with little time for rest and limited water and feed.[9] For now though the men were leaving their horses behind, as they had no use for them at the Dardanelles.

As she watched the light horsemen march out in waves, Edie smiled brightly but felt miserable:

> [I] stood at the gate waving to them, & they yelling goodbye to me, some stepping out of the ranks to shake hands. 10,000 men are expected next week, some telling me that they are going straight to the Dardanelles … It makes one's heart ache to see these men going, wondering how many will ever return. (16 May 1915)

9

PYRAMIDS BY MOONLIGHT

By mid-May Luna Park Auxilliary Hospital held 1620 patients, tended by a staff of six officers, fifteen nurses and forty other ranks.[1] The nurses from the *Malwa* were quartered in what Edie called 'Prince Ibrahim's Palace', a mansion built for a prince of the khedive, at Heliopolis.[2] They continued to work in the Australian hospitals, unsure of where and when the British authorities would move them.

> The *Kyarra* arrives today with the reinforcement of nurses, but am still wondering how the RAMC nurses will fare. No more patients have come into Heliopolis for the last few days, but the work has become heavier. Egypt is not a fit place to nurse in Summer. It is fearfully hot. So have been wondering if a base will be formed nearer the Dardanelles. The *Kyarra* nurses will make a great difference to us, for we are working under heavy pressure. Two of the Coast nurses, Graham & Swannell, have been sick, & one of the Adelaide nurses has gone under. As for me I never felt better. I know I'm looking fresher than in Sydney, have not had a headache, or the slightest feeling of inconvenience since I've been here. The trip across the ocean did me good I suppose, but manual work never upsets me. (23 May 1915)

Knowing she might receive orders to leave at any time, Edie saw as much of her friends and Cairo as possible. Sometimes she cadged a lift, but often tramped 4 miles across the desert in sturdy stockings and ankle-length dress.

Pyramids by moonlight

Had a glimpse of the Nile yesterday for the first time. Went to Ghezireh Palace to see Dick & Cay. They are very comfortable at this hospital. The Palace is a beautiful place, it belonged to the late Sultan's Grandfather … Strange to say, one of the soldiers was playing on the piano the 'Barcarole' he played well, & it sounded well … The spaciousness of the place lends beauty to the music, & it resounds in the immense hall. (15 May 1915)

The pyramids attracted newcomers like bees to a honeypot. Soldiers of the AIF were camped at Mena at the base of the pyramids and the men climbed them often, removing their boots for the slippery ascent and carrying candles at night. Archie Barwick, a private in the Australian 1st Battalion, wrote that the Chephren pyramid was most dangerous, and it was put out of bounds after three men were killed one day attempting to climb it.[3] The troops were eventually forbidden from climbing the Sphinx or any pyramid other than Cheops, 'and that only from North-East corner'.[4] Edie was enthralled:

> This afternoon our Matron got a car for us & we went to the Pyramids. I think the Sphinx & the Pyramids are a most wonderful sight … Though the Sphinx is huge, I thought it was bigger. We were then taken to a temple of the Sphinx. We walked on alabaster, while the walls are of granite blocks. How the Egyptians got those granite rocks there is the mystery of the world. The largest crane in the world & the most powerful could not lift half the weight of these blocks. The Sphinx & Pyramids were built thousands of years before the Israelites were in Egypt, before Moses & Aaron.
>
> I had a camel ride. A weird experience it is riding one. The animal sits down, the Arabs lift you on to the saddle, the animal rises first on his fore feet & you feel like you are rising miles in the air, & over the camel's tail, & then when he rises on his hind

legs one feels as if you are going over his head. I have heard some say that the motion of a camel was that of the sea, & made you sea-sick, but I felt that my inside would be jerked out, & when the animal ran I felt as if I would fall off …

Will send you a photo sitting on a camel in the shade of the Sphynx by the next mail …

Love to you all from Edie (15 May 1915)

The photo was enclosed with her next letter: 'Do you recognise me under the chin?' (23 May 1915)

Eager to capture everything, she bought a small camera to record her adventures.

Have been out a good deal. Last Monday went to the Museum in Cairo. I never cared for museums at any time, but of course one must not miss this place, as the mummies of the old Egyptian Pharaohs are seen here. For Egypt must have been the most wonderful place. The mysteries are beyond one's comprehension. I told you in my last letter about the Pyramids. Well the mummies we saw at the Museum were taken from these pyramids. The preservation is wonderful … The body is dark looking & very shrunken, some hair is seen but it is golden looking, though I think the hair changes after death. Even the muscles of the body are seen. I did not like looking at them, they are horrible & uncanny …

On Thursday went to the mosque, the Arabic & Moslem place of worship. This is another beautiful & wonderful structure but is only 100 years old. It was built after the invasion of Napoleon. And the architecture is the same as that of the Mosque at Constantinople (wonder if I shall ever see it). We entered the

Pyramids by moonlight

courtyard shod in queer looking slippers, ever so much too big tied round the ankles & have pointed turned up toes. How I wished I could take a snap. The courtyard is all marble, there is a fountain in the centre made of marble, the moslems wash hands face & feet five times a day ... The Moslems always kneel facing the east, for Mecca (the Moslem holy city) is East of Egypt ... The guide took us round the outside of the mosque. I did not think we were so high up, for here the whole panoramic view of Cairo is seen, also the Nile & the Pyramids beyond.

Hope I don't make you weary with these descriptions of places, for it is hard to make others see with your eyes. Wish you could see it too. For I shall never forget this place as long as I live. (23 May 1915)

Edie was always keen to hear news of Coasters. 'Two of the Coast Drs will arrive soon with the 10,000 men, so when they do, there will be 7 Coast nurses of my time & 5 Coast doctors. So we shall not be in want of familiar faces' (23 May 1915).

Four Coast nurses were due on the *Kyarra*, and over two dozen more Coast-trained nurses would land in Egypt in the next few months. Coast doctors Millard, Furber and Fletcher were already in Egypt, with Thomas Frizell and John James soon to arrive. Dr Mervyn Fletcher became a regular feature in Edie's letters.

Do you remember me speaking of Dr Fletcher at the Coast? He wrote to me last week asking me to go to dinner at the Grand Continental Hotel. Unfortunately on night duty so couldn't go, so he asked to have afternoon tea there instead, but I [received] the letter some 2 hours after the appointed time so we have arranged to see the pyramids by moonlight, he says that pyramids by moonlight is much better than rockhopping at the Coast. I'm looking forward to this, a number of nurses are going to take a car there & they will drop me at Mena House. Hope he will suggest a moonlight flitter down the Nile in a felucca (an Arab boat). Don't think there is a romance attached to it. Far from it where Mervyn Fletcher is concerned. (23 May 1915)

Edie's assurance that there was no romance attached failed to convince her sisters: she later referred in an aside to 'Dr Fletcher (the one Gracie thinks I've lost my heart to)' (23 January 1916). Yet it appears the doctor was merely a companionable colleague for seeing the sights around Cairo and with whom she could share a joke:

I had dinner in town one night with Dr Fletcher from Sydney. He took me round the poorer streets of Cairo. As we passed along, saw a cow standing at a door. A man was milking her after a while he took the milk into the house. The cow & milkman went to the next house, the same performance happened again. I wonder if the Board of Health will ever bring that arrangement of selling milk into force! (23 July 1915)

In late May, Edie wrote,

Two red cars took us to see the Pyramids by moonlight. And as Mena Hospital is at [the] foot of [the] pyramids, thought I would go & see Dr Fletcher. Dr took me over the Hospital, we also saw the Sphinx smile. Coming home, found out that the Manager's wife of Shephe[a]rd's Hotel (the biggest Hotel in Cairo) has invited all the nurses to call and have cool drinks, which we did. (29 May 1915)

Shepheard's was a favourite haunt of military officers, along with the city's wealthier classes. Heavy drapes absorbed the echoes of chattering voices and clattering boots. Pashas in long white robes and red fezzes padded over the marble floors on slippered feet. Edie's group must have headed for the relaxed cane settings and palms on the famous terrace where, seduced by the glamour and high spirits, Edie drank pretty glasses of punch:

> The drink was in large wine glass[es] ... The stuff was sherry coloured containing oranges, bananas & apples, I'm afraid that there were too many oranges in it, which made it bitter. On arriving home, hardly recalled going to bed. Woke up with a large head, which ached, & feeling terribly thirsty. The temperature of the heat of day was 106° [Fahrenheit] in the shade. The thirst was awful & so was the headache, also the vomiting, could hardly do my dressings, had to ask to go off duty. When I found to my horror that I was suffering from a recovery, we had had champagne cups the night before, & as I was not used to wine & any strong drink it had upset me. (29 May 1915)

In the throes of the ensuing illness she scolded herself: 'Did not know what it was I was drinking. Should have had more moral courage' (Diary, 31 May 1915). But she later saw the funny side: 'Today I feel as right as a bank. Of course, the Doctors, Matron, & everybody concerned think it fit & proper to tease me. I shall not forget the incident or what it cost, I do not know how people can drink after suffering from a recovery' (29 May 1915).

Edie was more cautious when invited to a moonlight flit down the Nile organised by the doctors. They glided downstream from the Nile Bridge, on a river busy with feluccas crammed with leisure-seekers, merchant traffic, and fishermen on the shore. As the sky turned red then purple then black, Edie's party sipped cold drinks and ate a sumptuous dinner of iced soup, fish, ham, cakes and fruit. Edie noted,

> I was the only one who was a teetotaller, but of course no one took much, the men took shandies, the ladies wine &

lemonade ... I don't wonder people rave about the moonlight on the Nile ...

We did not get back to Cairo till 12.45am. In the tram going back to Heliopolis, the car stopped. We wondered why, so waited for some considerable time. When one of the Drs got out to see what was the matter he found the driver & conductor fast asleep. We arrived at the Palace 2am. (4 June 1915)

Wartime Egypt offered more freedom than the watchful eyes of Sydney society – although the military expected strict standards of behaviour. A nurse could be escorted in public by a man, but she could not risk being caught in a compromising position with one: for that she could be sent home, like the nurse who was found sitting in a tent alone with a soldier after 10 pm. Her claim that she did so to help him overcome his tendency to drink too much was not accepted.[5] They knew they sailed close to the wind at times. Australian QAIMNSR nurse Beryl Corfield told her friend Lizzie with a wink, 'Now we have [a] pledge here, it is "I vow & declare that I will not divulge anything that I see or hear in Egypt during the present war"'.[6] One afternoon Edie and Evelyn Swannell went looking for Groppi's, a renowned Swiss patisserie popular with European blue-bloods, politicians and now service personnel:

Don't think I told you what Sister Swannell & I did on our last 1/2 day off, I wouldn't dream of doing it in Sydney. We wanted to find Groppi's, a place noted for ices & afternoon tea. We asked many soldiers for the place is full of them, & none of them seem[ed] to know. So one poor soldier leaning on a stick came by & we asked him he took such trouble to find out for us, that we asked him to have tea with us when we found the place ...
(1 July 1915)

We will never know what Edie went on to say, for the next page of her letter is missing; but it was likely something her parents deemed to be socially inappropriate. Only two of Edie's letters are missing a page, and, in each instance, she is poised to say something that might reflect poorly on her or a family member. Whatever they censored, it clearly did not bother the Edie of Egypt.

10
IN THE LAND OF UNCERTAINTY

At the end of May HMAT *Kyarra* docked bearing more recruits, and twenty-eight AANS and four New Zealander nurses commenced duty at 1AGH and its auxiliaries including Luna Park. Ironically, Edie found she had preferred the activity and relative autonomy before the extra help arrived. Time dragged if she was idle: 'Too many nurses now on duty. Came off duty very tired' (Diary, 1 June 1915):

> [W]e are packing up to move to [Gordon H]ouse, nearer our work ... The nurses who arrived in Egypt by the SS *Kyarra* are living at Gordon House. I'm afraid we have not taken kindly to them. They want to take everything out of our hands, & of course we do not like being ordered around. (4 June 1915)

The new nurses arrived with the advantage of having known they were bound for Egypt. Hence they received their letters, precious lines of communication with family and friends, when they landed. Edie envied them: 'How I long for a letter, have not had one since Adelaide. It is only a fortnight since I wrote to Uncle to send mine on, but next week is six weeks since we landed, so hope to get some then' (4 June 1915). Week after week she committed her own letters to the mail steamers that toiled endlessly. It would be over two months after leaving Sydney before she received her first word from home.

In the land of uncertainty

> What do you think has just arrived – Queen's letter written on 14th April! Uncle Harry sent it on the 8th June. Queen did not say how Mum was, or anybody. So have been wondering. Nurse Swannell & I had been out & as we came into the Dining we were told that letters were put in our bedrooms – the two of us went up three flights of stairs, two steps at a time … the Post Office service here is very bad. The soldiers have a bad time here about the mail. All the mail goes to the Dardanelles before it comes here, then the men being moved to convalescent camp back to the Dardanelles or back to Australia causes delay in the mails. The mails follow but very seldom catch them. (19 June 1915)

Not only had the *Malwa* nurses not received any mail, but they were not paid for two months. Finally:

> Very much to our surprise we were paid yesterday by cheque. We got £16.0.8 for the two months pay. We are paid at the rate of £40 pa with 3/- per day for mess (food) & 3/- per day for rations & washing … I came to Egypt with £8. I have £1 left & was wondering if I would have to write to Uncle Harry for money, when the cheque arrived. Our [weekly] mess [is] 15/- & as our washing bill is 5/- a week we do not do too badly do we?

> … It is getting late & as all the doors are of opaque glass, allows the light to go through into Matron's bedroom, & I think she is getting figity [sic] & would like me to go to bed. She is a nice old thing & tries to do everything for our comfort, suppose I should be considerate. (4 June 1915)

If she resented sharing the work with the new nurses, Edie had no quibbles with the woman responsible for the division of labour. Formerly of Adelaide Hospital, now aged in her mid-fifties, Matron

Margaret Graham was in charge of Luna Park Auxiliary Hospital from April 1915 until July 1916. Speaking to the Adelaide *Register* newspaper in 1917, she showed the appreciation for her nurses that had been a hallmark of Miss Watson at the Coast, saying of Luna Park,

> [A]lthough not perfect ... [it] was as good as it could have been in the circumstances ... 'There was nothing to beat [the Australian nurses'] work. They were excellent. They had a great reputation, and have made just as good a name as the men have. They were always full of enthusiasm, and if there was anything to do they could do it'.[1]

Despite the socialising and sightseeing, Edie longed to escape Cairo's heat, and, as more and more nurses arrived, to be busy and feel useful at work:

> We are still in Heliopolis & still in the land of uncertainty. We were told to pack up on Thursday, we were ready to go & went on duty for further instructions, at 12 o'clock told we weren't going till Monday so here we are still waiting packed ready to go.

> We are to have Sunday off, tomorrow, the duty is ridiculous there are too many of us, think how hard we are working, I did nothing but fold a few bandages yesterday & talked to some of the patients ... The Kyarra brought 28 nurses to Heliopolis & the Mooltan 38, so of course there are too many of us, we haven't had a train of wounded for over a week ...

> I'm very sick of Egypt it is too hot. Friday Thursday the heat was terrific 122° [Fahrenheit] in the shade. I pitied the poor patients. My belt buckle badge & studs all seem to burn & if we went

into the sun, our clothes seem[ed] to scorch. Today is beautiful, the heat is something like the heat of Sydney in midsummer …

My blue silk has gone to pieces … But I'm going to rip it up for a pattern. Have bought some of that silk I sent on to you, so if I can will make a dress out of it probably two. Egypt is too hot to sew, my hands perspire so much, perspirations just drip & trickle down one's face & body. It is delightful to get into a cold bath & stop there … (19 June 1915)

Before she finished her letter, the news they were waiting for came through:

We were told today that our destination is Alexandria … I'm afraid I shall remain in Alexandria till the Dardanelles campaign is over. At any rate the nursing is better there, as the cases are the severest. No 17 is the biggest. Ten of us are to go to 17 & five to go to 15. The heat is not so great at Alex, besides there is surf bathing. (19 June 1915)

Edie went to Ghezireh to say goodbye to her friends Clarice Dickson, Dorothy Cawood and Dr Fletcher. On Sunday she packed her bags then went out to take photos of places she had already seen, because she might never see them again. On Monday, 21 June 1915 the Coasters met Nurse Dickson at Groppi's for tea, then caught the midday train to Alexandria.

11

CULTURE SHOCK

In the wards of 2AGH, Dr Mervyn Fletcher had tended wounded Australians. He defended them against early journalistic jibes about the well-paid, underworked men, writing that now 'we have plenty of real military work to do ... it is awfully heavy fighting over at the Dardanelles, and ... the so-called "Bob a day tourists" fight like tigers'.[1]

English war correspondent Ellis Ashmead-Bartlett's glowing article about the Australians who 'had been tried for the first time, and had not been found wanting' was printed in newspapers across the nation, and within ten days of its publication was reproduced in a pamphlet handed out in Australian schools.[2] Edie knew all about 25 April 1915: 'That memorable day, I do not know how often I have heard how the Australians effected a landing at Gallipoli' (1 July 1915).

Perhaps the observers breathed a sigh of relief, for they had not known how these citizen-soldiers would perform in battle. Out of the trenches, many were wont to disregard military expectations, swaggering around with collars unbuttoned, drinking too much, speaking informally to officers and failing to salute. Soldiers carried on in ways many never would have done at home. Cairo teemed with sex workers and the AIF refused pay for 'any period of absence from duty on account of [the] Venereal Disease' that was soon rife among the troops.[3]

The Australian Army's Routine and Regimental Orders offered a glimpse of the men's extra-curricular activities when they had to specifically prohibit and punish, among other things, drunkenness, gambling[4] and theft of motor cars.[5] Nor could the men ride on the roofs of tram cars[6]; purchase liquor from[7] or 'accost' 'natives'[8]; cut down villagers' trees[9]; travel in railway carriages reserved for veiled women[10]; urinate elsewhere than regimental latrines[11]; or 'interfere with Egyptian antiquities & monuments of any kind, by defacing or writing on them, or damaging them in any way ... this includes climbing on any part of the Sphinx'.[12] They once hung a nosebag on the statue of a revered Egyptian statesman seated on his horse.[13] Such disrespectful 'horseplay' was hardly new. Barely a decade earlier Edie's uncle Frank Blake had stopped in Egypt en route to the Boer War. A man was charging soldiers to view a mummy displayed in a tent. When the showman wasn't looking, Frank snapped off the mummy's hand and took it home, to Suffolk.

Edie had leapfrogged across the Empire – from the self-governing dominion Australia to the colony of Ceylon and the protectorates of Aden and Egypt. She saw them through the eyes of a white Australian of British origins, imbued with Imperial values. Racist language was inherent in her descriptions, and was typical of someone of her background, although attitudes also reflected class distinctions. When Britishers referred to the 'natives' they meant the Arab peasants (*felaheen*) and Bedouin – whom the troops collectively called 'Gyppos'[14] – rather than the Egyptian ruling classes (the *pasha, bey* and *effendi*).[15] From Ceylon she wrote,

> The only drawback are [sic] the natives ... They are dreadful beggars, & dreadful liars. Give them anything & you cannot get rid of them, they will run miles behind a rickshaw or carriage asking for alms. Walk along the street a dozen of them will come around you sticking their grubby hands under your nose on their wares. The curios they sell they will ask ten times too much, but you can always beat them down ... [In the Temple of the Tooth] things seem to be tawdry, & not at all genuine ... the hyroglyphics [sic] are all freshly painted, which looked less genuine than ever. (23 April 1915)

The Coasters were rightly suspicious of street hawkers, though, for souvenirs were generally only worth the pittance paid for them. This provided some light relief in Cairo:

> [Graham & Copeman] went to see the Museum last Wednesday. On coming out, they were pestered as usual with beggars, who wanted to sell miniature Sphinx's at 2/- & 4/- each. They beat them down to a piastre each (2 ½ in English money). When they came home & showed me their purchases, I remarked on the smell of them, so they thought they would wash them, so put them in the wash basin while they went to dinner, & when they came up, the Sphinx had turned to mud, & the odour was abominable. I laughed & they got cross & they had awful difficulty in getting the mud down the sink! (4 June 1915)

Egypt inspired in Edie a confusion of awe and disgust. She leapt at every chance to see its ancient wonders but suffered a visceral reaction to Cairo and found the assault on her senses intolerable the first time she visited the mouski:

> [T]hree of us went to the mouski (probably incorrect spelling) or native bazaar. We went in a garry [gharry] (carriage) to the place. You cannot conceive what it is like. The streets are narrow, mucky, crowded with dirty people, they display their wares out into the footpath, which is about 2 feet wide. The traffic is dense, containing mostly donkeys, camels & garries, they go anywhere, on the footpath, no such thing as traffic regulations. The noise is deafening & the smell is too awful for words. I felt like holding my nose.
>
> A man got on to our garry & insisted taking [us] to his shop, didn't matter how we protested. He wanted to take us into a side lane, but we would not go, & went to the native police for

Culture shock

> information, they told us we were in the Turkish Quarter. We soon got out of it, for I felt scared. Twice I found a donkey's nose up against my back. It was so hard dodging the traffic. How glad I was to get out.
>
> I hate eastern things, the more I see of them the more I hate them. I do not know how people can say they like to see how the Arabs live. I think they live disgustingly. They suffer very much from sore eyes. The flies swarm around their eyes & in the mouths & nostrils, & they make no attempt to dislodge them. The flies are like leeches here, you almost have to pull them off. I don't think that the mouski will see me again. (12 June 1915)

For her, local displays of feelings were bemusing histrionics, foreign to the public reserve and emotional restraint that were valued not only by Edie's culture and class, but by her profession.

> Coming home [from the pyramids] we had a mishap. There is a long avenue of trees leading from Mena House. A little Arab child ran towards the car with outstretched arms, the driver tried to get out of its way, but the kid would come forward consequently it was knocked over, we picked it up unconscious & took it to a hospital in Cairo, could not find much the matter with it. Suppose there will be an inquiry. It was not careless driving the child was knocked over, it was simply the child's fault. But the Arabs around made a dreadful fuss, screaming & crying. After we picked up the child, we passed a funeral, the coffin was white also the hearse. There were ever so many people following it on foot making a most mournful sound. (16 May 1915)[16]

Edie had little sympathy for the local people. The dust and dirt and cacophony of noise and emotion offended her sensibilities, and she struggled to equate the living conditions with the poverty-stricken of her own culture:

> I hear others speak as if they enjoyed the smells, squalor, filth of the people & their hovels. I have seen how they live, & I don't want to see them anymore. I am not a good Christian as you see, for I couldn't be a missionary for all the tea in China. (1 August 1915)

12

ARRIVAL IN ALEXANDRIA

The train journey to Alexandria took a little over three hours. After snaking over 4000 miles from the river's sources, the Nile Delta bloomed northwards from Cairo like a lotus opening its face to the sun, extending from Alexandria in the west to Port Said in the east. Beyond the fertile limits of the Nile's annual inundation stretched hundreds of miles of desert. Reputedly founded in around 332–331BC by Alexander the Great, Alexandria had a population of perhaps 400 000, roughly half that of Cairo or Sydney. A centre for commerce, the city had been inhabited by many peoples over thousands of years. The thriving cosmopolitan hub barely felt Egyptian compared with Cairo. Edie later observed, 'No-one knows who's who here. There are French Italians Greeks Assyrians, Arabs & Soudanese [sic] ... The European residents speak all the languages' (11 June 1916).

The busy port was well placed to form a wartime medical base. Four hospital ships could disembark their patients simultaneously. Some patients were loaded on to ambulance trains bound for Cairo, but the most seriously wounded were sent to local hospitals.[1] It was to be Edie's home for some time to come.

> We are settled in a British hospital & I think for all time. The journey up or rather down to Alex is very pretty, all the banks of the Nile [are] cultivated by the fellaheen (Egyptian farmer). Mostly cotton plants. Here & there we came across a native village, & a mosque or minaret. The villages consist of low mud huts or hovels for they are filthy. The livestock live with them.

Each fellaheen has his own plot of ground, his wives (for they are allowed I believe 4 wives) & children all work in the field. They trust no-one so take their furniture with them. We saw numbers driving the goats, sheep, camels & donkeys before them. One man told us that they take everything away with them to the field. I didn't see any tables or chairs so came to the conclusion that [they] sit & dine off the floor.

We crossed & recrossed the Nile many times (and its branches).

We arrived at hospital 4pm, so was in time for afternoon tea. For dinner we went to a hotel called Beau Rivage, which means beautiful beach. We are right on the Mediterranean Sea. The house the government has commandeered has only beds & chairs in it. Today we got wardrobes. (25 June 1915)

Edie opted to join the 17th British General Hospital (17BGH):

Sister Swannell & I are at No 17 while Graham & Copeman are at No 15. At first I was to work with Copeman at 15, but asked to go with Swannell [although] Copeman has been very good to me & very companionable … Sister Solling is also at No 15 …

After Matron had taken our names, & addresses of our guardians, she allotted our places. Mine was the upper theatre, strange that I should be sent to the theatre. I was so glad that I had experience of the theatre at the Coast. For I may have had to refuse.

We will see much more nursing here than at Heliopolis but it is more depressing … Today I've seen ten operations for one theatre. There are two theatres going.

Arrival in Alexandria

We are very close to the beach, but I haven't seen it. I hear some of the girls say that they were going for donkey rides on the beach.

We get three hours a day off duty but it takes an hour to go into town & an hour to come back. Tomorrow I'm to have half day off duty, so is Swannell, so we are going to No 15 General Hospital to see Copeman & Graham for we are wondering how they are faring. (25 June 1915)

The two British general hospitals had been hurriedly established to support the Gallipoli campaign. Both were commandeered school buildings. 15th British General Hospital (15BGH), in the Abbasia Secondary School near the city centre, was ready on 25 April 1915.[2] Some 6 miles east, 17BGH had once been a large girls' school, the Victoria College, and was not fully equipped until mid-May. Within days of the RAMC inspecting the college on 12 April 1915 and declaring it suitable for a 600-bed general hospital, desks and chairs were removed and medical equipment brought up from the docks.[3] Dormitories became wards, each holding about 24 beds. Classrooms were also converted and marquees pitched to create extra wards.

On 23 April 1915, QAIMNS sister Mary Elsbeth Neville had reported as acting matron. Miss Neville had been serving in Egypt since Britain declared war on 4 August 1914, and would remain in Egypt until April 1919. On 29 April 1915 a handful of nurses arrived for duty, including nine AANS sisters despatched from Cairo in readiness for battle casualties.[4] The first convoy of patients arrived the next day, and they kept coming. A fortnight after it opened, 17BGH held almost 1000 patients.[5] The hospital was initially understaffed and underequipped. Even surgical cases were put up in the tents, where Sister Eveline Mary Vicars-Foote wrote that 'conditions … were terrible – overcrowded – no steriliser. We had to do the sterilising for this appalling lot of dreadful cases in a little saucepan'.⁶ Despite this, when the AANS were recalled to Cairo, Staff Nurse Elsie Cook was sorry to leave the hospital that she had helped pull up by its bootstraps into working order. 'Dear old No 17 ... from those awful first days after its creation, it has slowly emerged from chaos and muddle into its present orderly and cheerful state and now I have to go and leave it.'⁷

The 'orderly and cheerful state' handed to Edie in June included five large wards, sick officers' quarters, sisters' quarters, a pathological department, an X-ray department, the theatres, the post office, storerooms, the dispensary, and the quartermasters' and the sisters' sick room, all around a quadrangle (24 October 1915). There was a separate typhoid block and thirty tents that each held fourteen patients. The doctors and nurses also slept in tents. On a mast atop the central tower, a flag marked with a red cross flapped above the Union Jack. The 17th was less than half a mile from the beach, an easy walk for nurses used to getting around on foot. There was a large reserve near the hospital where troops camped, drilled and exercised their horses.

Edie was for the first time working in a British hospital under a British matron. Her sense of divergence from the AANS had been dulled by her time in Australian hospitals. The realisation she was staying in the British system, and not going to England, came as a shock: 'When we assembled in the morning at Matron's office she informed us that we are permanently on the staff. We all could have fallen through the floor with shock & disappointment. It seems that we shall not get to London' (25 June 1915).

Edie felt her Australianness keenly. Although welcomed by the English nurses, she detected a different national outlook, particularly among the patients. She later observed, 'Our Australians have sunny dispositions, & in comparison the English boys seem dull & heavy' (23 January 1916). Australians were characterised as being more upbeat and open, less class-bound than the British, from a recently federated nation that offered more opportunities to progress

Arrival in Alexandria

based on one's desires and abilities. Australia and New Zealand had even given women the right to vote. However, a byproduct was the indifferent attitude to authority found in some soldiers that had gained notoriety in Cairo: 'The Australians & New Zealanders have earned the name of being wild and unruly, therefore should be put down, according to English Doctors and Sisters. The Aust do not [like] the English Sisters, & I think our men should be nursed by Aust sisters' (18 July 1915). As it was, hospitals took in patients regardless of nationality.

Eager to mark herself out as an Australian, Edie asked her family to go into Sydney to obtain her ATNA badge:

> I am sorry I did not get one before I left. It is a mark of an Australian nurse, of which we are very proud. I can't have the Australian Army nursing badge which is the rising sun, as only Sisters of the Australian Hospitals can have it. Everybody knows the Southern Cross of the ATNA nurse. (23 July 1915)

She received the badge in October 1915.

Some were perplexed as to why Australians were even involved in the war:

> It was explained to me some time ago how the Australians rallied to the duty call quicker & better than the British. This man was an Englishman, & he says for the population of Australia, there are many more Australians, than English in comparison. This man asked me why the Colonials are so patriotic. (18 July 1915)

For many Australians this would be a strange question. Although thousands of miles from the mother country, Australia retained close political, emotional and familial ties to Great Britain. Britain's declaration of war had been seen as enough for Australia to be at war, too. And personal adherence to these values and affection for Britain had prompted many Australians to volunteer. Although they prided themselves on their lack of concern for class and authority, Australians were on the whole quite conservative in their desire to support their 'God, King and Empire'. Still, their insouciance was attractive. On the transport ship *Galeka*, QAIMNSR nurse Beryl Corfield bathed in the positive reputation they were forging. 'Australia everybody here adores even the word. I think after the Dardanelles to be an Australian is the greatest privilege one can have been born to. It is the same with the sisters too, all the Australians like us to nurse them & so do the English boys – they think we are such sports.'[8]

Edie appreciated, however, the organisational clarity of the British Army's medical service, and its well-trained orderlies. According to her, the water pressure at 17BGH was poor, and the orderlies often had to cart water up three flights of stairs. She concluded,

> The orderlies are very good. The one in the Upper theatre is a bit overbearing, but good orderlies are not to be sneezed at. So we let him have his own way. I do not work so hard here as I did at the Coast. The orderlies get the theatre ready & also clear it away. The sister helps the surgeon. (25 June 1915)

Initially placed in the upper theatre, with her Coast Hospital theatre experience she acquitted herself well and was soon placed in charge of the lower theatre:

> I'm getting more used [to] the consulting surgeon, he is a very nice man. Do not think I'm hard worked, we have a great number of operations, but I've excellent orderlies, & one is a medical student, & very interested in his work. The other orderlie is a man who has had a great deal to do with vet surgeons, so

isn't quite ignorant of medical work. He understands the use & care of instruments. (1 July 1915)

RAMC orderlies were almost as well trained as the nurses.[9] They helped transport patients, recording their names and units upon admission. They carried food, water, firewood and equipment, and ran baths. They washed, deloused and re-issued uniforms, and guarded and helped treat patients in isolation units. Some assisted during surgery.[10]

British orderlies were firmly ensconced in a military hierarchy in which they were obliged to follow the matron's orders. Their position was understood and valued. They received higher pay relative to their Australian counterparts, with the added incentive that they could earn efficiency stripes: additions to their uniforms that indicated their length of service and competence. In contrast, according to AANS principal matron Grace Wilson, Australian Army matrons were not given sufficient control over the orderlies and 'never knew from one day to the next what orderlies were available for nursing duties'. Matron Wilson said that ward work was unpopular in the AAMC: 'ward orderlies [were] often regarded as "Mugs" [by their peers]'.[11] She recounted an instance where a capable ward orderly was replaced by another, untrained person. No-one informed the matron. The untrained orderly accidentally burned a patient with a foment; the burn required surgery and many weeks' treatment.[12]

The Australian QAIMNS Reserves' ongoing lack of uniform accentuated their difference from their British counterparts:

I'm getting low down in clothes … the English nurses have no mufti [the military term for private dress] & we have no uniform … some of the nurses are growling … as their white frocks are still in use in the wards, & are beginning to wear. I'm so thankful I have my [Coast] uniform with me. (18 July 1915)

The Coasters were in Alexandria for more than a month before they received their second pay packet. Out of this, they had to pay for their uniforms, equipment and food. After the first fortnight, Edie wrote, 'I was asked for my payment of mess bills. I told the Sister I couldn't meet it. So she went over & told Matron, & I did not know then that everybody refused to pay' (18 July 1915). Once it was known that the nurses couldn't meet their bills, they were paid £10 in advance. In August 1915 they were paid about £28:

> This is including uniform & kit. We have to get three dresses & three capes, each dress costing £1-1 – exorbitant isn't it? ... Our kit I believe consists of a bed, mattress & stretcher, canvas bath, basin & bucket, iron kettle & spirit lamp, bed linen eiderdown & all sorts of other things I can't remember. I think we get £11 a month out of which we keep ourselves. Our mess bills last month amounted to £4.15. (7 August 1915)

The QAIMNS ward uniform was made of zephyr, a fine cashmere cloth. It was grey – a colour supposedly chosen by Florence Nightingale as it was calm and demure. Edie wasn't keen to purchase the heavier alpaca 'walking out' uniform until she got to England, but had no choice: 'Lord Methuen [the governor] of Malta has made a fuss I hear about the Sisters wearing mufti ... while off duty ... The outfit isn't conducive to beauty' (16 September 1915). This was no doubt the point.

The QAIMNS Reserves' cape was grey with a red border, while the Regulars wore a red cape. This meant that it was difficult to distinguish a senior British nurse from any mere Australian.

Edie took malicious pleasure in this turn of events: 'The indignation of the regulars was rather acute, when they learnt that Australian Army sisters wore the all red capes' (16 September 1915).

13

FLIES, FAECES AND FOOD

The operating theatre at 17BGH revealed the savagery of the frontline: 'When I see eyes taken out, legs amputated, you wonder what sort of existence that these poor men will lead as time goes on. It is far better to hear of them being killed, than maimed for life' (25 June 1915).

Edie's words were harsh, but many experienced nurses recoiled at the shocking wounds. Some soldiers were so damaged and deformed that it was difficult to conceive how they could live with their scars.[1] On a hospital ship anchored off Cape Helles, nurse Beryl Corfield cried:

> Oh Lizzie you have not the faintest idea of what war is like, you don't know what we have been through – to sit & hear the firing & see the dust & smoke & to know that in a few hours the wounded will be brought in from that very shell. Of the ones that are killed & that are so bad that they don't bring them to us we hear nothing. If I were a soldier I should pray day & night to be killed right out, but to see men come into your ward with legs off, arms off – mouth & tongue or lower jaw blown off – you would wonder what it is all for & with whom the great reckoning will be.[2]

At Cape Helles the high ground of Achi Baba remained out of reach, despite it having been an objective of the first day. Another attempt on it was launched on 12 July 1915. Edie wrote,

[D]o not expect a letter next mail, nor perhaps the next for it may take a fortnight to bring the wounded back, for they are expecting a big slaughter at Ac[h]i Baba that hill at Gallipoli that is to be taken at all costs. (18 July 1915)

Found work very hard. Patients difficult to manage, wounds very bad. (Diary, 20 July 1915)

On several occasions Edie was the only theatre assistant: checking instruments, retracting, swabbing, holding artery forceps while the surgeon, Mr Waddy or Mr Bourne, tied off, then cleaning and dressing once the surgeon was finished. What she witnessed there was often appalling, yet it was the work she found most stimulating and the only work detailed in her diary. Some afflictions were familiar from the Coast, such as appendectomies or mastoid surgery; others were the results of a violence rarely seen except in a theatre of war. They included trephine operations (where the surgeon manually drilled into the patient's skull, as if coring an apple, to relieve pressure from swelling or to remove a bullet), wiring teeth and shattered jaws, and surgery to extract splinters of glass from rifle periscopes, shrapnel or rock from eyes (at worst, removing an irreparably damaged orb in its entirety).

On 25 June 1915 Edie assisted in amputating a soldier's leg halfway up his thigh. Nurses and orderlies were known to pin down a limb as it was amputated, and, in time, to administer ether or chloroform anaesthetic. Removal of a shattered or gangrenous limb was often the only means of saving its owner's life; but where the extremity might be preserved the surgeon was willing to try. On 27 June 1915 Edie noted in her diary: 'Haemorrhea secondary from brachial [main upper arm] artery; was stitched & ligatured & many other incisions made. Arm very offensive. Patient very sick'. To heal such a complex infected wound required 'snakes', which Queenie later queried. Edie explained,

Flies, faeces and food

Well Queen, what would you think we would be doing with snakes in an operating theatre? Sometimes when opening into a cavity in the body a rubber tube is put in to take away pus or matter, which is injurious, these tubes are something like a garden hose, some almost as big & grading in size to so small a tube that a needle can hardly pass. The tubing is boiled & kept in boiled water or some antiseptic. (24 October 1915)

And so the month went on, recorded in her diary:

Tuesday, 29 June 1915: Big operation in morning, excision of rectum. Commenced 10am finished 1pm. Two operations this afternoon. Further amputation of left humerus. The second was emphysema.

Thursday, 1 July: Several ops this morning. One this afternoon just as I was going off duty, cellulitis.

Sunday, 4 July: On duty this afternoon had trephine, piece of shrapnel taken from frontal region. Went to dinner. Called back on duty nine pm. Mastoid operation.

Monday, 12 July: Six operations. Two Laminectomies, to relieve pressure on the spinal cord.

Tuesday, 13 July: Six operations today. Mostly removal of bullets.

The work was satisfying. 'The month I've been here ... I've learnt a great deal, & I have been happy in it & do not think Mr Bourne (the consulting surgeon) was displeased with me.' (15 July 1915)

After her time in theatre, Edie was given 'special duty': one-to-one care of a patient with tetanus. 'Wound very dirty & large. Wound through thigh, very bad fracture' (Diary, 21 July 1915).

Her 'special' was in a bad way. No effective vaccination existed for 'lockjaw', but on the peninsula an antiserum was administered to very dirty wounds (and, from July, to all shell and shrapnel wounds)[3] in the hope of halting the deadly toxins. It was mostly effective. This man would have been placed in a darkened room where Edie could apply wet towels to keep him cool, check his pulse regularly and watch for signs that his nervous system was affected. She had to go about her work gently, to avoid triggering the spasms that would retract his lips in a rictus grin and agonisingly arch his back and neck, requiring morphia, chloroform and paraldehyde enemas to try to relax the clenched muscles.[4]

Spasms would also increase the risks posed by the poor man's fractured femur. He was lucky to have made it in alive – at the war's outset, 80 per cent of those who fractured a femur or sustained a compound fracture on the battlefield died from complications such as blood loss, blood clots and infection. During 1915 the need for amputations reduced dramatically and the mortality rate dropped to around 20 per cent (and continued to decrease throughout the war) as stretcher-bearers and medics were trained to apply a Thomas splint (designed so long rods were strapped over clothing and boot, and the limb suspended from a frame) to immobilise the leg for the jolting journey to the rear of the lines.[5]

Edie's 'special' improved under her care. Within a week he was well enough to be X-rayed and his leg set: 'Anaesthetic given. Leg put into Balkan extension [a traction frame]' (Diary, 27 July 1915). There was hope, for he was still alive when she last mentioned him at the end of the month.

Soon after, 'a sister came to tell me that a very scotty looking man wanted to see me' (1 August 1915). It was Dr Millard, back from the peninsula, taking the time to check on his Coasters. He visited nurses Graham and Copeman at 15BGH, and the next day, according to his diary, he travelled

some 6 miles or so by tram along the sea coast to the east of
Alex. There saw ... Sister Blake of the Coast Hospital who
seemed delighted to see someone she really knew. She has been
there about 3 months I think, and is a good deal thinner than
she used to be. Sister Swannell also of the Coast is on duty at the
hospital but on night duty so I did not see her.[6]

Edie *was* delighted:

I came from behind the screen where I was doing a dressing &
found the scotty looking man to be Dr Millard or rather Major
Millard ... he was the superintendent at the Coast. It was a great
pleasure to see him & I felt a bit flattered when he informed me
he came specially to see me. He belongs to the First Australian
Field Ambulance & has been over on the beach of Gaba Tepe in
Gallipoli. I quite forgot he was a Major, which is a high position
in the army & I also forgot he was the 'super' at the Coast. We
talked as if we were old friends for quite half an hour. (1 August
1915)

Dr Millard had detected a vulnerability. Edie never dwelt on feeling homesick or lonely, but a wistful note sometimes crept in:

I wish I could come in an aeroplane one night, or come 'via
wireless', I would love to see you all again. I have been wondering
what has been happening. I think all our letters are censored by
holding them back a fortnight. The letters are dated 6 weeks ago.
The English letters 2 months behind. (18 July 1915)

Everyone was hungry for news from home. Edie's letters invariably commenced with a report concerning the status of her mail, and she revelled in becoming a link between the Blakes of Sydney and England:

It is now two weeks since I've had a home letter. Uncle hasn't sent your letter on. I got quite a budget yesterday, from London. Two from the Coast great long ones. Two had been written from Egypt. Sister Dickson & Dr Fletcher wrote, sent them to Australia. Sister Brown from the Coast sent them to London & Uncle sent them on to me. Sister or Dr never dreamt that their letters would be read in Egypt. (9 July 1915)

Had a letter from Aunt Alice this morning & she tells me that Grandfather has been very ill. They thought he was going to die. He was to be operated upon, but [they] decided not to do him. He is better now. Joyce Uncle Frank's daughter met with an accident, was thrown from her pony & fractured her elbow so badly that they are afraid that she will not be able to use the joint. Aunty does not give other news. (15 July 1915)

Joyce's badly damaged right arm withered and her fingers became 'dithery' so that she had limited use of the limb for the rest of her life.[7]

I received a letter from London. I didn't know the writing, the address on the paper, printed telephone number and all, is 165 Melrose Avenue, Cricklewood N.W. ... I suppose you can guess who it was from. Uncle Will. I was very surprised. The letter was an extremely nice one. He says he has experienced being 1000's of miles away from anyone, & knows what it is to get letters so thought he would write to me, to let me know that I had a sympathizer, also to tender his compliments to me on coming to nurse the sick & wounded ...

It is now three weeks ago since I had a letter from any of you, have been wondering where they go to. I have had five, so there must be many roaming about ... I wish there could be a telephone across the water & I would ring 576 Kog & have a good old talk. Perhaps one day we may be able to talk 'via wireless'. (1 August 1915)

The Allies held on at the Dardanelles. Engineers constructed piers at Anzac Cove and Cape Helles for boats to remove sick and wounded and bring in fresh troops and stores. The beach resembled a warehouse. Weathered gullies were pockmarked with dugouts and tarpaulin-clad lean-tos, sandbagged to protect against mortars and shrapnel shells.

As the summer wore on, the soldiers struggled in the heat. The Anzacs stripped off their shirts and cut their breeches into shorts. Clean drinking water was in short supply. What streams there were, were contaminated by corpses. Potable water was brought in by barges and guarded. Each man's standard ration was a third of a gallon of water per day for drinking and washing, but many times they received far less. A rare bath or shave was generally accomplished in the mess tin from which a soldier ate and brewed his tea.[8] At Anzac Cove men on fatigue duty hauled kerosene tins full of water up steep tracks to the trenches, straining as the ropes connecting the tins cut into their shoulders and bullets whizzed by – some said it was harder than the fighting.[9]

The diggers' diet chiefly consisted of canned bully beef, dehydrated vegetables, jam, and biscuits called 'hard tack' because men broke teeth on them. These had to be soaked in tea or water or grated to be edible. Fatty corned beef and occasional bacon and cheese rations grew greasy and rancid, the saltiness compounding the soldiers' thirst.[10] Indian and French troops fared better as their diets incorporated more vegetables, but those used to the English diet stuck with what they knew no matter how bad it got.[11] (The French garrison at Kum Kale received a 1-pint daily red wine ration, which was rough quality, but at least it didn't spoil.)

At Anzac Cove there was almost no natural shade: any respite from the relentless sun came from dugouts, makeshift covers and the men's hats. When possible, men bathed naked in the sea for the sheer pleasure of it. They were clean, free and momentarily closer to home, diving and splashing as they had on the beaches or in the cold country creeks of Australia and New Zealand. A swim was worth the risk, though some were killed doing it.

Lice and ticks crawled through scrub and trenches, infesting uniforms and bedding.[12] Worst of all were the flies. By June they were in plague proportions, tormenting the men day and night. Foul sticky swarms that were one moment breeding in decomposing bodies and crawling over open latrines were the next in their faces, their food, their mouths. Dysentery and diarrhoea became endemic. The men had all sorts of names for these conditions: The runs. The shits. Turkey trot. Gallipoli gallop.

If the troops knew the mantra 'Flies, faeces and food equals typhoid', they couldn't do much about it. Obeying the medical Standing Orders for Sanitation – which called for infective matter and refuse to be incinerated or disinfected, clothing to be washed, and unfiltered water to be boiled – was well-nigh impossible.[13] The men stewed in their own juices and lived in their own muck.

By July almost every man had a stomach upset and evacuations of the seriously ill from Anzac increased.[14] Typhoid cases were sent to Egypt, and other illnesses, including influenza and jaundice, to Lemnos.[15] Due to the persuasion of Oxford University professor of medicine, Sir William Osler, army commanders ensured the vast majority of the troops were vaccinated against typhoid, halving the mortality rate.[16] AIF troops were vaccinated against smallpox, cholera (there were no cases at Gallipoli)[17] and typhoid – against which Edie was 'done' at the Coast and again eighteen months later (9 May 1916).

A few still fell ill with typhoid, and ten times as many with paratyphoid.[18] These had similar symptoms and together were called

Flies, faeces and food

'enteric fever'. The first symptoms weren't obvious. Headaches, fever and tiredness could have had any number of causes. When rose-coloured spots developed in the second week, doctors could diagnose it and order the victim off the peninsula. By then the bacterium had inflamed the intestines and he had to be handled carefully when loaded on to the barge and up into the hospital ship, for bumps could cause deadly haemorrhaging or perforation of the bowel and peritonitis.[19] Often by the time he reached a hospital he was at a crossroads: he either improved, or worsened into the semi-comatose 'typhoid state', tongue furred and brown, breathing ragged, pulse fast and shallow. From here might follow delirium and death, or, if he was lucky, many months' recuperation; and, if he was even luckier, no heart trouble or other ongoing problems.[20]

The Dardanelles campaign had become a drawn-out, disease-ridden stalemate, and the men were becoming dispirited. By the end of July, only a fraction of the force was truly 'fighting fit'.[21] Something had to give. It was the Allies' turn to see if they could break the deadlock and make something of this failing campaign.

14

NOT ONE WHOLE MAN

The 17BGH war diary recorded the constant churn of admissions and transfers of patients and staff to convalescent camps, hospital ships and other hospitals. Nurses could be swept up almost without warning:

> There was great excitement in the home this afternoon, two of our nurses were sent to Lemnos Island. I believe there is a hospital there. I'm so glad I hadn't to go. These two girls had only a few minutes to go. I saw them at 4.30 & at 6pm they were gone. They did not know till 5pm. (1 July 1915)

It looked at one point as if Edie was about to go too:

> I'm writing in a great hurry for I've just received notice to pack up & go on transport duty. Whether to England or to the Dardanelles I do not know ... I am just the luckiest woman possible ... Now if I go to the Dardanelles I shall do the work for the patients as they come off the field. (15 July 1915)

> I'm still packed to go. It seems every hospital is sending 10 sisters & 6 doctors besides 40 orderlies to equip a ship ... We are I believe to go to Lemnos Island where there is a clearing hospital. Only the worst cases are to come to Alexandria, the rest to go to England ... going to Lemnos Island will mean no submarines, or any danger like that. (18 July 1915)

Not one whole man

You can see by the above address that I haven't gone on transport duty yet. It seems to me that that hospital ship is all froth & bubble. I heard one of the Doctors say a few days ago he thought that the scheme had fizzled out. I still have my suitcase packed, it is rather a nuisance. (23 July 1915)

We haven't gone on transport yet & don't think we will, though it is still on the boards. I'm still packed up ready. I do hope it isn't cancelled. For I would like to see Turkey land (a bit of it). Wait till we get to Constantinople. Do you remember the No 3 Australian General Hospital. It went to London you know, but it is now in Alexandria en route to Lemnos Island. I think we are better off here than Lemnos. For I hear that all water will have to be carted. Though I have been told it is beautifully fertile. So perhaps the rumour about the water isn't true. (1 August 1915)

Within months of the landings at Gallipoli and Helles it was clear that the two sides were deadlocked. This was not a tenable situation for the Allies, who had a hold on only small pieces of the peninsula and were a long way from achieving any overarching objectives. It was determined that a new attempt to break the deadlock would take place in August, involving a British landing of 25 000 additional troops at Suvla Bay. This force was to seize the heights of the Sari Bair range in conjunction with an Anzac advance on the same. Diversionary attacks in the south of the Anzac sector at places like the Nek and Lone Pine, and further south at Cape Helles, were hoped to disguise the main thrust of the attack.

The August offensive involved 97 000 attackers.[1] The director of medical services estimated some 30 000 casualties over three days, which would prove accurate. Unfortunately, evacuation and hospital arrangements were based on General Hamilton's reduced estimate of 20 000.[2] The four stationary hospitals on Lemnos, two British and two Australian, were expanded in preparation for casualties from the renewed campaign. The No. 3 Australian General Hospital (3AGH), bound for England from Australia, had already been rerouted to Lemnos, and began arriving from late July. Lemnos would expand to 9000 beds, supported by thirty 'temporary' hospital ships, each 'equipped for 800 cases, for which a staff of 6 medical officers, 10 nurses, and 35 orderlies was requested'.[3] Edie's information was accurate.

'White' hospital ships (immune from enemy attack and able to wait offshore) would initially ferry the wounded 12 miles to Imbros. From there, the men who could return to action within a month would be treated 40 miles away at Lemnos. Worse cases would be sent to Alexandria or Malta on 'black ships' that were fitted as ambulance transports but not protected by the Hague Convention from capture or attack. One of these black ships, the British Steam Ship (SS) *Marquette*, was torpedoed and sunk in the Aegean on 23 October 1915 with the loss of 167 lives, including ten New Zealand nurses, being a legitimate target as a troopship that was carrying munitions as well as wounded men. Critics said that the nurses should not have been placed at risk aboard a transport, but hospital arrangements were such that there was little choice.

Hamilton insisted on such secrecy that even his senior commanders were not informed about the battle plans until late July, hampering their ability to prepare. It was also in vain, for the operation was not a surprise to the enemy. German General von Sanders had been gathering intelligence on the build-up of troops and ships at Lemnos since early July. He correctly surmised that an attack was imminent and deployed his troops accordingly.[4]

The August offensive was launched at 5.30 pm on 6 August 1915, when men of the 1st Australian Brigade attacked the Ottoman trenches at Lone Pine. This was a feint, designed to divert the Ottomans from the main attacks at Suvla Bay and the Sari Bair ridge. Having crossed no man's land, the men found many of the trenches roofed with pine logs; they were forced to rip these up with their hands before descending into the warren below. The soldiers fought with rifles, bombs, bayonets, even bare hands and teeth, trampling the bodies of the fallen during torrid hand-to-hand combat in the covered trench sections. The bomb fighting was intense. The Australians became adept at catching the Ottoman 'cricket ball' bombs and returning them, until the Ottomans learned to shorten the fuses.[5] The battle eventually involved six Australian battalions against many more defenders, but the Australians prevailed against all the odds, capturing the Ottoman position after four days in what would be the sole success of the campaign; but half of the attacking Australian force, some 2200 men, were killed or wounded.[6] The Ottomans lost twice as many.

Around the same time, the British launched another feint at Cape Helles which would become known as the battle of Krithia Vineyard. Three British brigades attacked a much larger Ottoman force, gaining only small parcels of ground, which were recaptured in vicious counterattacks. More than 4000 British soldiers became casualties over the week of fighting.

A little over five hours after the battle of Lone Pine began, the British landed at Suvla Bay, and the main offensive on the Sari Bair ridge commenced. While parts of the landing were successful, others had the boats grounded on reefs or landed in the wrong positions. The operation quickly stalled in the face of poor leadership and a strong Ottoman defence.

In order to support this operation, two Allied forces had moved north from Anzac Cove to attack high points in the Sari Bair range. On the left, a battalion of British and Gurkhas took the crest of Hill Q after a fierce bayonet battle. They saw the waters of the strait and vehicles on the road to Achi Baba, before they were shelled off – apparently by their own naval fire.[7]

To their right, the New Zealanders briefly took the advantageous heights of Chunuk Bair after nearly two days' ferocious fighting. Capturing the summit in the early hours of 8 August 1915, the Wellington Battalion of the New Zealand Infantry Brigade were forced off as the sunrise brought with it a torrent of Ottoman machine-gun and shell fire: one officer said the men 'left their outpost line about 750 strong at 4.15 am on the 8th and when relieved at midnight the same day they could barely muster the odd 50'.[8] Over two days, the New Zealanders had suffered some 2500 casualties with over 800 dead; of those who reached the top, some 90 per cent were wounded or killed.[9] The New Zealanders were relieved on the evening of 9 August 1915 by British soldiers who were soon forced off by a fierce counterattack led personally by Mustafa Kemal, the future 'Atatürk'.[10] The Ottomans charged the summit then drove the British down the other side, attracting strong fire from New Zealand machine-gunners. British troops in positions below, including a brigade of British New Army troops gathered at a plateau known as the Farm, were annihilated. After it was over, masses of Ottoman dead lay on the higher slopes, and for hundreds of yards below the ridges were strewn thick with the bodies of the British.[11]

Meanwhile, another diversionary attack took place further south at Anzac. The Australian charge at the Nek was intended to co-ordinate with Chunuk Bair. At dawn on 7 August 1915, men of the 8th and 10th Light Horse Regiments were ordered to attack Ottoman trenches on a hill dubbed Baby 700. Their way passed over a narrow saddle of land, around 30 yards wide at its narrowest point, known as the Nek. The operation was also supposed to co-ordinate with a naval bombardment and another attack from Steele's Post, but did not. The light horsemen, attacking with only their bayonets, were met by a hail of machine-gun and rifle fire. The attack was not called off until two more waves were sent forwards into what seemed to be certain death. The horror ended only after nearly two-thirds of the 600 attackers lay dead or dying.

The August offensive stretched the Allies to the limit, but Ottoman defenders had prevailed everywhere but Lone Pine. After a concerted effort that cost the lives and wellbeing of thousands of men, the Allies had done little more than see the sweeping panorama of the peninsula from atop the heights. They never reclaimed the peaks they had held so briefly.

At the very time the light horse were being slaughtered, an oblivious Edie wrote home,

> Have no special news this week. Nothing out of the way has happened. I have had an invitation to dine next week, somewhere [in] Sidi Gaber, with Mrs Carver an English woman I met a couple of weeks ago. A number of English & Irish nurses arrived last night, they are all sunburnt hot & tired. They are not like we pale washed out Australians, who have had two summers in succession … Suppose all the sweet peas are in bloom by this time. The daffodils snowdrops are all done. How is the fernery getting along … We haven't heard any more of our trip to the Dardos, I'm so disappointed about it. Of all the pictures I was going to take of Gallipoli when we got there. Oh! well we can't have everything we want in this world. (7 August 2015)

The next few days at 17BGH were quiet. Then the storm hit.

The first stage of medical intervention at Gallipoli was a man's field dressing kit. Troops were issued with bullet and shell dressings consisting of two bleached cotton bandages, each with a bleached cotton gauze pad stitched on, and a safety pin. Next was the regimental aid post, which accompanied the battalion into battle and stayed just behind the frontline. There at least one doctor assisted by two orderlies dressed light wounds with sulphur and boric ointment and administered a tetanus shot before the wounded man returned to the fray. If more was required, he received superficial treatment and morphine and was sent on to a field ambulance unit further behind the lines, which was equipped to hold a modest number of patients.

However, despite planning and April's example, in practice management of the casualties from the August offensive was almost as disorganised as the landings had been, because of the vast numbers of wounded men and congestion on narrow twisting tracks in inhospitable terrain. Getting to the CCS at the beach was tortuous and exhausting, and there weren't enough stretchers or bearers to meet the demand. On the first night fighting was so intense that bearers of one battalion were ordered not to carry wounded back but to bandage and leave them beside the track and move forwards with the column, and lone medical officers ventured out to tend groups of wounded where these were gathered in the lee of ravines and gullies, working ceaselessly by the light of hurricane lamps to arrest bleeding and dress wounds.[12]

Casualties piled up. In little more than two days 1st Australian Casualty Clearing Station (1ACCS) treated around 5000 men. In the early confusion lightly wounded were evacuated ahead of serious cases.[13] By evening on 7 August 1915 only one hospital ship, HMHS *Sicilia*, remained off Anzac, unable to take on more patients. The following day over 1000 men lay on the beach, freezing at night then baking in the sun with little water, wounds turning septic as they waited sometimes days for evacuation to a hospital ship that was understaffed for the inundation.[14]

It was always considered preferable to operate in a fully equipped base hospital. In the urgency, though, doctors, desperate to do what they could for dying men, operated at the peninsula or on hospital ships, sometimes with fatal results. Abdominal wounds were particularly difficult: sepsis meant they were often fatal under the best of circumstances, and so in the urgency and confusion severe wounds that might otherwise have been considered operable were often left untouched as a hopeless case.[15]

The hospitals on Lemnos were frantic. The new 3AGH was barely up and running; patients started arriving almost as soon as the nurses did.[16] Within four days, the hospital, which had only begun arriving on Lemnos a little over a week earlier, held more than 800 patients,[17] although most of its equipment hadn't arrived and would not for another week.[18] Nurses made do with what they carried in their kits, small spirit stoves and inadequate amounts of methylated spirits, cotton wool, bandages and a few instruments. Until tents arrived, wounded men were treated out in the open, and patients and medical staff alike slept on the rocky ground.[19]

The severely wounded were shipped to Alexandria, two to three days' voyage from Mudros, pouring in from 11 August 1915.[20] Within two days, the city's docks had received over 10 000 patients.[21] Convoys of ambulances trailed into 17BGH. Edie was on duty for days on end with barely a break in an endless whirl of flushing, draining, dressing, checking pulses, taking temperatures and administering morphine, which she summed up in a typical nurse's understatement: 'cases extremely heavy' (Diary, 14 August 1915).

The nurses had little concept of the battle strategy, but the scale of the horror was evident.

> There is no news especially to tell you except that the work is three times heavier, we only snatch an hour here & there off duty. The Dardanelles must be a large shamble, for the wounds are frightful. All the men in my ward have either lost an arm or leg, & their stumps are so painful ... We have about 1700 patients now in hospital No 17. (14 August 1915)

There was no respite:

> All the hospital ships have returned heavily laden with wounded. All the ships seemed to come together, the ambulances were seen coming up the road, one long line as far as you could see. I saw 15 cars coming at once. Oh! & how the poor wretches rolled in. No-one went off duty. Stretcher bearers worked till midnight. The whole of the hospital had been emptied as much as possible,

to be able to admit the convoy expected. In the ward I'm in there is not one whole man. They each have either leg or arm missing, some have shoulder shattered as well. You don't know how thankful I feel that we haven't a brother, to see these poor mangled men, would make one's heart ache. They are so hard to nurse. I've been in heavy wards and seen heavy cases, but never to equal this, nor so many. When they came in, I didn't know which to commence on. Several have died. I found it hard to tell which wounds were the most needful of attention. The nurse who was helping me went down to it & I for a few hours had the ward to myself. I do not know how I managed it. Last night Matron sent me off duty, & was continually asking if I was well, but goodness me, I never felt better, work has no effect on me whatever.
(20 August 1915)

Whether to reassure her family or to impress them, Edie glossed over the impact on her. Her diary told a different story:

Monday, 16 August 1915: On duty all day feeling very tired.

Tuesday, 17 August: Had an extremely hard day.

Tuesday, 24 August: Not feeling too well.

Wednesday, 25 August: Off all day sick.

The staff worked to exhaustion and were prone to catching illnesses from their patients – and other unwelcome conditions: 'Queenie said in one of her letters something about "fleaitis" – I think I've got in a chronic state for I've caught three fleas within the last ¼ hour. If Dad were here he would be rubbing himself up against every post he came across' (20 August 1915).

Hearing the half-truths and false hopes that were peddled freely in the wards, Edie was sceptical:

The rumour has it now the British have made such advance in Gallipoli that the Turks are surrounded, & all communications stopped. I hope this is true, for I would like to see this dreadful carnage stopped. The saying now amongst the men is 'wait till we get to Constantinople'. The men are always trying to make me believe that this hospital will go to the Sea of Marmara. Matron said the other day that two months will see the end of Egypt. I hope so. (14 August 1915)

In the wake of the August offensive, the British War Office sent a memorandum warning that medical officers and nurses on hospital ships and ambulance carriers 'have allowed themselves to become too seriously impressed' by the mens' naturally 'over-coloured' stories. It exhorted them to ensure that 'under all trials, they surround their sick and wounded with an atmosphere of enthusiasm and of invincible hope' for 'those who minister to the body diseased are best qualified at the same time to "Raze out the written troubles of the brain"'.[22]

Surrounded by human wreckage, the nurses knew that although their immediate duty was to minister to their patients' physical wounds, it was vital to keep up their spirits. To be washed clean, to have a sweet cup of tea – indeed, to be in a place where women existed – marked a return to civilisation after the privations of the trenches and the shock of fighting. The sheer presence of the sisters, with their firm but feminine voices and hands, often several years older than the boys in uniform, was comforting. The women were there in the quiet moments if the mask of bravado dropped. They were there too to laugh at the jokes and tall tales, cluck sympathetically at the hardships and nod reassuringly at the predictions for victory. The soldiers had gone to the Dardanelles seeming 'as happy as if going to a picnic' (Diary, 6 June 1915). Despite what they had been through, many would not admit to imagining their own demise: 'The boys who have been at the front tell us … [they] feel that [they] are always safe' (17 December 1916).

After the hard-fought losses of early August, the last major battle of the Gallipoli campaign was about to take place. General Hamilton believed that an attack with large reinforcements before the Ottomans built up sufficient defences was the only way they could succeed.[23] As it was, in an effort to link up the front in the time available, Hamilton proceeded with a force far smaller than he would have preferred.

On 21 August 1915, attacks were made at Hill 60 at Anzac and at Scimitar Hill near Suvla Bay in the hopes of linking the two areas. After two days' fighting the Australians captured a small area of ground towards the summit of Hill 60, while the British attack on Scimitar Hill failed in the face of strong Ottoman defence. Suvla and Anzac remained unlinked, despite a further attempt to take Hill 60 on 27 August. After three days, more than 1100 soldiers of the Australian 9th and 10th Light Horse were dead or wounded, and most of Hill 60 was still out of reach. There were no more orders to advance.

The August offensive was over. The Allies had gained little ground, and both sides had lost thousands of lives. In areas where they couldn't be reached, bodies of the dead lay in the open at the mercy of the flies. There they would stay until after the war. Soon it would become clear the Gallipoli campaign was futile.

Glenart Castle. Held up by the Germans at the outset of hostilities, she was rechristened and converted into a hospital ship in October 1914, damaged by a mine in March 1917, and finally sunk by a torpedo on 26 February 1918.

Source: *Australian War Memorial AWM PS1195*

The....
FEDERAL

COLLINS & KING STREETS,
MELBOURNE.

Close to Stations and Steamers.

LARGEST HOTEL or COFFEE PALACE IN AUSTRALASIA.

Refreshments can be obtained in Cafe at any time DAY or NIGHT.

Special Arrangements are made for ....
FAMILIES and PERMANENT BOARDERS.

Manager and Secretary,
H. PERCEVAL SMITH

Melbourne ____ 6 ____ 4 ____ 191 __
1915

Dear Mam and all at home.
    Arrived safely yesterday morning. We had a very nice trip. Of course couldn't sleep in the train it rocked as if we were at sea but didn't get as far as losing my tea. Some of the nurses did. The Victorian railways have a dining car. Of course we had dinner on the train. Dinner was very nice, but I did feel hungry. For the first time tasted clear soup to my mind it isn't appetising, a few pieces of carrots & peas floated in it. It seemed so strange to watch the passing scenery while eating. The Victorian country is fearfully dry did not see much of the New South Wales for it was 7 am when we arrived at Albury. This place is not too bad, it is a hotel without a bar. Meals very good. When we arrived in Melb there was no one to meet us, we were hanging about the dirty dingy station for about an hour

The first page of the first letter Edie wrote home, dated 6 April 1915.

Source: Blake, Edith, Papers, Australian War Memorial AWM PR 05423

No 17 British General.
Alexandria, Egypt.
August 14th 1915.

Dear Mum, Dad, Grace & Queen.

Another week has passed, & still no letters. What could have happened. Has all the mail boats been torpedoed. There is no news especially to tell you, except that the work is three times heavier, we only snatch an hour here & there off duty. The Dardanelles must be a large shamble, for the wounds are frightful. All the men in my ward has either lost an arm or leg, & their stumps are so painful. There isn't one whole man. We have about 1700 patients now in hospital no 17.

The rumour has it now the British have made such advance in Gallipoli that the Turks are surrounded, & all communication stopped. I hope this is true, for I would like to see this dreadful carnage stopped. The saying is now

A letter from Edie written as men wounded in the August Offensive at Gallipoli poured into 17 British General Hospital (17BGH) in Alexandria, dated 14 August 1915.

Source: Blake, Edith, Papers, Australian War Memorial AWM PR 05423

Blakes reunited when Charles brought his family to visit Suffolk in 1892.
Back: Will, Harry, Tilda, Andrew, Jim, Alice, Frank; Centre: Lily, Fanny,
Matilda, Catherine, Charles; Front: Louise, Edie, Grace.

Source: Author's personal collection

Grace, Charles, Alice (Queenie), Catherine and Edith Blake,
picnic at Long Nose Point circa 1900.

Source: Author's personal collection

The Coast Hospital at Little Bay, Sydney, early 1900s.

Source: NSW State Archives

Senior Coast Hospital medical staff, circa 1910. Back: Dr Donald Wallace, Dr John James, Dr Thomas Furber, Dr Thomas Frizell; Front: Matron Alice Watson, Medical Superintendent Dr Reginald Millard. All of these doctors bar Dr Wallace served in the war. Dr Frizell died of wounds suffered during the Battle of Passchendaele in 1917.

Source: Prince Henry Hospital Trained Nurses' Association Museum

Edie in Coast Hospital uniform, middle row left. It is believed to be Grace standing next to her, and Queenie and nurse Clarice Dickson at the back, perhaps when 'we had tea on the beach that time' (17 February 1917).

Source: Author's personal collection

Contingent of Australian Army nurses from New South Wales who embarked on the *Kyarra* with the second convoy in November 1914. Edie's Coast Hospital colleagues Clarice Dickson and Dorothy Cawood are in the front row, fourth and third from right. Dickson received the Royal Red Cross for her exceptional service, while Cawood was one of eight Australian nurses awarded the Military Medal for heroism after casualty clearing stations were shelled in France.

Source: Australasian Nurses Journal, 15 December 1914, State Library of New South Wales

Mildred Crocker Brown, Edie's Coast Hospital colleague, who served with the Australian Army. They attended a play together in London days before HMHS *Glenart Castle* was sunk.

Source: Courtesy of Robert Cull

Evelyn Ellen Swannell. She and Edie served together for almost two years in Egypt and on HMHS *Essequibo*.

Source: Courtesy of Robyn Atherton

Dr Wallis Mervyn Alfred Fletcher, Edie's former Coast Hospital colleague. He contracted enteric fever at Gallipoli and was wounded while tending troops in France, where he was mentioned in despatches.

Source: University of Sydney Archives, Book of remembrance research files, G14/12, Dr Wallis Mervyn Alfred Fletcher

The Heliopolis Palace Hotel, Cairo, occupied by No. 1 Australian General Hospital.

Source: Australian War Memorial, AWM A03074

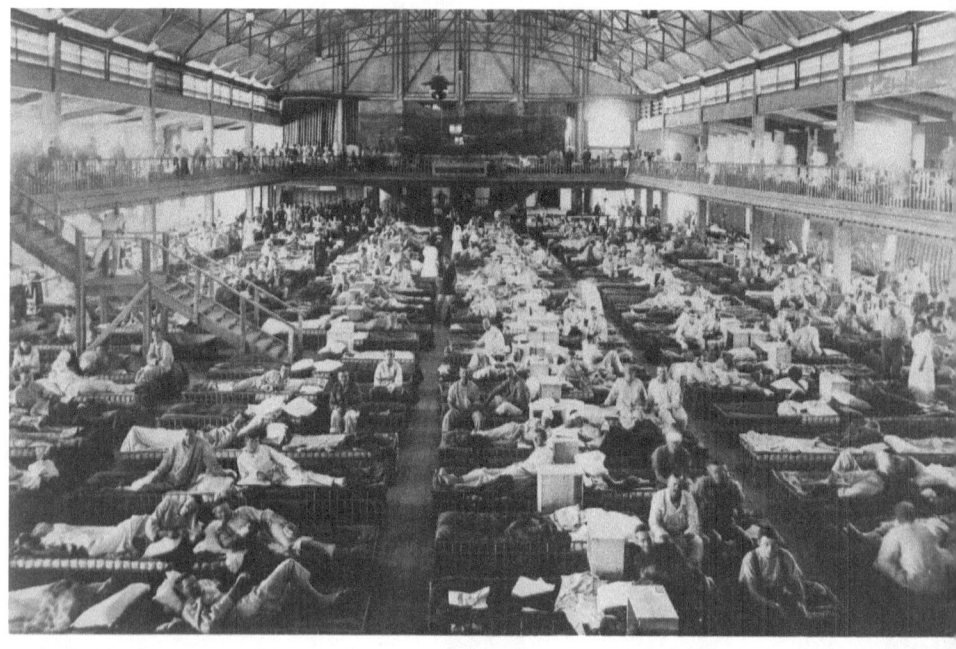

Wounded men in a ward at Luna Park Auxiliary Hospital, Cairo, which was taken over by 1AGH in April 1915.

Source: Australian War Memorial, AWM P11554.002

Edie in a group by the Sphinx: 'Do you recognise me under the chin?' (23 May 1915).

Source: *Australian War Memorial, AWM P11193.003*

17BGH, Alexandria. Edie is in the middle of the second row,
behind the second seated officer.

Source: Australian War Memorial, AWM P11193.001

Edie at 17BGH, in 'a snap one of the VADs took of the ward' (9 January 1916).

Source: Australian War Memorial, AWM P11193.006

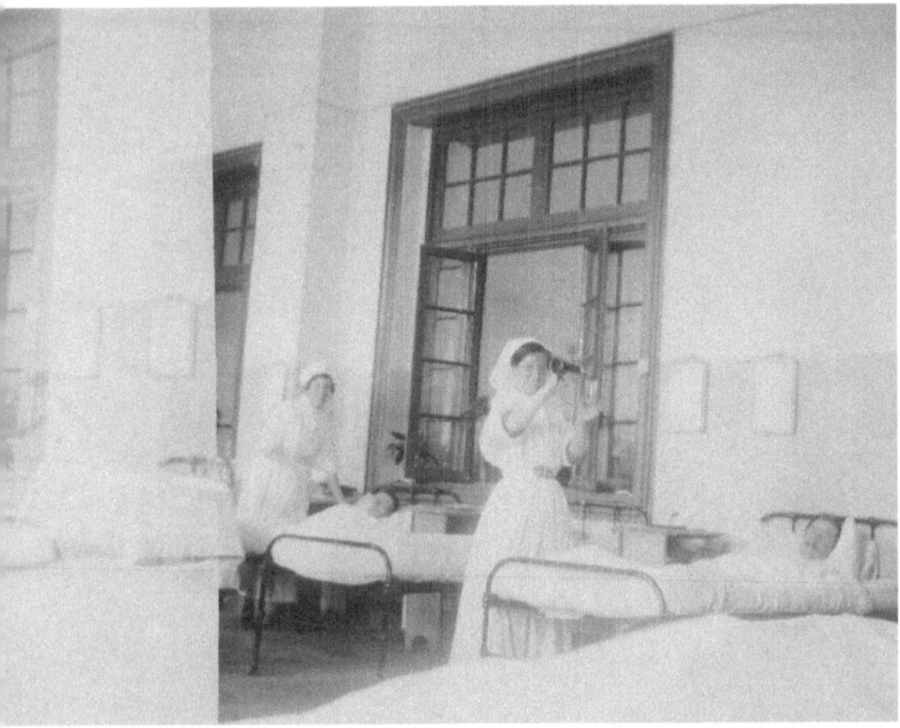

Tent wards at 17BGH: 'walking from one to another is worse than walking on Manly beach sand. It makes me so tired' (1 September 1915).

Source: Australian War Memorial, AWM H00871

Belmont workhouse, Surrey, viewed from the east, early 1900s.
It was converted into a hospital for German prisoners of war in May 1917.

Source: Peter Higginbotham Collection/Mary Evans Picture Library

Edie's cousin Charlie Blake, photographed when he was promoted to second lieutenant, Wiltshire Regiment, in November 1916, a few weeks before he was captured in December. Charlie was a prisoner of war in Germany until December 1918.

Source: Courtesy of Deborah Patten

Kapitänleutnant Wilhelm Kiesewetter, commander of UC-56, the German submarine that torpedoed HMHS *Glenart Castle*.

Source: *National Archives UK, German naval officers: information photographs, press cuttings, ADM 137/4352*

An artist's impression of the attack on HMHS *Glenart Castle* in *Graphic*, 9 March 1918.

Source: ©*Illustrated London News Ltd/ Mary Evans Picture Library*

Friends: photographs of Rebecca Rose Beresford and Edith Blake provided to the Imperial War Museum by their families after the loss of HMHS *Glenart Castle*.

Source: ©*Imperial War Museum, WWC H21-34, WWC H21-35*

Glenart Castle memorial, Hartland Point, Devon, after the centenary memorial service, 26 February 2018. Lundy Island is in the background.

Source: *Author's personal collection*

15

THE FORTUNES OF WAR

More than 22 000 wounded and sick were disembarked at Alexandria in August, and the worst stayed there, bringing Edie the heaviest and hardest cases she had ever been called on to nurse. Military historian Arthur G Butler's *Official History of the Australian Army Medical Services in the War of Alexandria, 1914–1918* records that 'medical arrangements were by now thoroughly efficient. The four British general hospitals – "among the best in the British Army" – were all equipped for dealing with large numbers of wounded'.[1]

Although the work remained heavy,[2] the staff were looked after: 'We are just as busy as ever. Matron insists that we should only work 12 hours or we have some time off each day. With a little time off each day, one doesn't mind how hard one works' (27 August 1915).

Before one evening shift there was a concert in the quadrangle: 'A sergeant sang, voice beautiful – was formerly a Covent Garden singer' (Diary, 29 August 1915).

At the start of September, Edie was given a month's night duty and professed herself not too pleased:

> [B]ut I'm on active service & must not grumble. There is one thing here that keeps Australian nurses up. Both Matron & the Doctors give Australian nurses unstinted praise. They say to us that they think we know how to work & to pioneer. Matron says she wishes she had more Australian nurses. (1 September 1915)

Edie's work at 17BGH, the former Victoria College, was split between the Ward III schoolroom block, which carried about sixty 'enterics', and her first duty in the tents (Diary, 4 Spetember 1915). Well drilled in the handling of infectious patients, Edie was 'very surprised' when told she had to do night duty in 'PQRS' tents, explaining, 'P&Q are surgical while R&S are medical, mostly dysentery cases' (Diary, 2 September 1915). The Coast would never have countenanced working in these wards at the same time due to the chance of cross-infection.

Nursing in the tents was hard going. 'The inside of the tents have boarded floors but the outside is heavy sand. Walking from one to another is worse than walking on Manly beach sand. It makes me so tired' (1 September 1915). She later asked her family to send her some ribbed stockings, the particular kind she liked: 'Having to walk in sand, thick stockings [are] best, besides they require less darning' (26 December 1915).

On night duty, Edie had time to sit by the lamplight and write long letters:

> Dad is a torment, he asks me if I would like a rabbit pie & baked potatoes, & when I go down to dinner we shall have either cold meat (very tough) or cold chicken (old fowl) with boiled potatoes, cut into slices [the] same way as Mum cuts up pears, a queer kind of vegetable, I don't know the name, but it looks like small cucumbers with white sauce ... then we have pudding. This is more English-like, nearly always milk pudding with Swallow & Ariels preserved fruits. Then comes the fruit. Grapes are in now ... We often have watermelon, it is not so nice as we have in Sydney. We often have a melon something like rockmelon, it is very nice. The oranges when we first came here, were delicious, the nicest I have ever tasted. After fruit comes Turkish coffee (black ie. without milk) which I can't drink. On Sundays we get ice cream instead of pudding. We have claret cup for dinner. After dinner we have a liqueur. Though I haven't signed the pledge, I do not partake of the last two. Sometimes we have

lollies, called Turkish delight. Our breakfast is not substantial. We always have fruit to commence with. Then some made up dish, as sardines & eggs on toast & such a tiny bit. Sometimes scrambled eggs mixed with ground rice flour which isn't nice. We always have toast & marmalade & tea. For lunch we have fish made into balls or souffle sometimes cudgery [kedgeree] sometimes liver curried with rice & haricot beans, [a] puzzle [to] find the liver. Milk pudding & tea. We have dinner 8.15pm finish at 9pm then go to bed. That is our day's meals. In between we work hard & when we have time off we write letters …

This month & next month is worst in the year so they say, there is absolute calm. Do not know what November & December are like, but January commences the rainy season. There seems to be no good news from Gallipoli, so I suppose we shall remain in Alexandria for a long time to come. It is now frightfully hot, & muggy …

Just now there is a brilliant sunset but there are no clouds about to soften it. It is too brilliant to look at. The afterglow is wonderful here. Some say it is the desert sand that causes the glow. A redness appears about the sky above the horizon until it is dark. (1 September 1915)

Sleep during the day was difficult until new accommodation was arranged:

[On] Sunday all night Sisters had to pack up & go & board at the Khedivial Hotel, which is in the heart of Alexandria & has been commandeered by the military for a nurses' home. Night nurses from all hospitals in Alex have to sleep here. There are 100 altogether. Only 14 come from No 17. The hotel is to hold 150 Sisters. This hotel [is] like all other big buildings

in Egypt, the floors, staircases are of marble (it may not be
marble, but looks very like it). Space in these big places is not a
consideration, there always seem[s] to be a waste of room. The
room I'm in has a tiny balcony, & is very quiet. I slept from 11
till 5pm today. Very good for a night nurse. We travel backwards
& forwards by ambulance, we go through Sidi Gaber, it is very
pretty. We do not live in Sidi Gaber, but some distance away.
The nurses in hospitals near the Hotels, are conveyed by mule
waggons, such slow old things. It takes half an hour stiff driving
to get to or from hospital. (21 September 1915)

When not on night duty, the sisters at 17BGH slept in quarters in the hospital grounds: 'The tents or marquees we sleep in are quite comfortable, the only drawbacks are the ants & the absence of bathrooms, we have to be contented with tubs. The Arab servants bring us water, they are now digging trenches round the outside in case of rain' (24 October 1915).

September brought the opportunity they had been waiting for, but with an unexpected outcome:

Sister Swannell came over to where I was sleeping today to tell
me that Matron had had a message to say that 10 nurses are to
go to England & the nurses [that] came by the *Malwa* were to
have the preference. There was great excitement. But we talked
it over, we all agreed that we were better off in Egypt, though
none of us liked the place. Still if the Dardanelles campaign
was over, or the hospital itself were to move along it would
be different. While in foreign service we are allowed Colonial
allowance, light & fuel allowance, board & lodging allowance
as well as pay, which amounts to £16.18 per month. We spend
out of that £5.0.0. So we are £11 to the good. All this would be
stopped in England, we would only get our pay & 15/- per week
for keep. We thought a few more months in Egypt would do us

no harm. Of course we hope to get to England later on, we shall
have more money to spend. At any rate most of us have refused.
Matron is very pleased. But some of us told her we would like
transport duty either to England or Dardanelles.

I suppose we are funny creatures, last week we all wanted to
go to England & now when we get the chance, we refuse. So
whether I shall live to regret this or not, will remain to be seen.
Of course I shall not let anyone know about this in England.
They would be hurt I suppose if they knew I refused to come to
England when I had the chance …

This letter has strange news in it. I wonder if you will think us
foolish in refusing the opportunity. (11 September 1915)

Ever practical, the nurses weighed up their options and judged that every penny saved was worth a few extra months of Egyptian heat and sand, especially while the fighting at the peninsula continued. Edie hoped that she might yet get transport duty:

This morning as I came off duty, I saw a dozen or so cars waiting
to take patients to the docks to embark for England. 170 went
from here. How I wish I were on transport. Matron says she will
put herself out to see that some of us will go, either to England
or Dardanelles. But there are a good many of us to get a chance,
& the chances are few. (16 September 1915)

Although eager to eventually be in England, Edie thrilled to news from and about Australia. Queenie described the first Australia Day, staged in cities, towns and villages across the country on 30 July 1915 to raise money for troops wounded at Gallipoli and encourage more men to enlist. Edie responded, 'What a day Australia Day must have been. What enthusiasm is shown. The Britishers here, I mean

Drs & Sisters, often speak of the patriotism of Aust. Both Doctors & Sisters speak well of our men as patients' (10 September 1915).

She was aware of, and sometimes bemused by, the new nation's cultural differences with England:

> I must tell you something, which will give you some idea of an Englishman's idea of an Australian. I hope it isn't an average Englishman's idea. I have 14 officers to look after. While I was in their room taking temperatures, one expressed great surprise to find out I was an Australian, & thought my English remarkably good for an Australian. (21 September 1915)

Or just amused:

> The other day an English nurse, just arrived, was passing a window [and] on looking out ran to one of the Australian sisters and said 'Oh Sister! I have just seen an ostrich led by an Arab with a rope tied to its mouth'. After a while she said to sister that she didn't think it was an ostrich, but perhaps it was a camel. A camel it was, for dozens of camels were carrying stone to the hospital. (21 September 1915)

And always keen to nurse Australians:

> I've been nursing officers. Well 10 of them went to England last week. One amongst them was an Australian Colonel. He asked me if I would like a trip to England, of course I thought he was joking. But the day he left he said he was sorry that it couldn't be managed … Of course I felt a bit flattered … The Australian officers who are going to Australia want me to go with them, but that is more unlikely as nurses in British Hospitals are not likely to go to Australia on transports …

The fortunes of war

> I got the Sydney mail this week. I noticed a piece in it about Australian nurses & men. About the English Sisters & Australian patients not getting on together in England. That more nurses should be sent to England. Here the English Sisters take more notice of our men than they do of their own. They tell me they would sooner nurse ours than their own. (8 October 1915)

Yet she held an affection for the British, respected her colleagues and was generally impressed by their military medical system:

> [A] Lemnos nurse [of 3AGH said in a letter] they were thinking of moving the hospital away from there, probably to Italy, & things were not well arranged. I am very thankful that I'm not at Lemnos Island, as things have turned out, the British nurse, or those in British hospitals get the best end of the stick. (24 September 1915)

October brought a letter from Edie's childhood friend Dot Dodd. Their fathers shared an English heritage and love of the water. Joe Dodd senior was a boat builder from Battersea Park by the Thames. Joe junior was three years older than Edie, and the youngest Dodds, Alice (Dot) and Bessie, were similar ages to Edie and Grace.[3] For now, young Joe remained in Australia, married and building boats. The Dodds had a pressing personal interest in war news, for Bessie had become engaged to Henry Bartrop shortly before he shipped out of Sydney in June.

Having enlisted only in May, Henry, a clerk from Balmain, had precious little time to train before shipping out and proceeding directly to Gallipoli for the August offensive, joining the 3rd Battalion on 4 August 1915.[4] Two days later he charged the Ottoman trenches at Lone Pine. Hearing nothing of his fate, Dot had written to Edie begging her to try to find out what had happened to her sister's fiancé. 'One of the officers is doing that for me, he knowing the man in charge at the depot. I feel sorry for Bessie, I can just imagine what she is like just now' (8 October 1915).

A week later, Edie had received some news and it was not good:

> In my last letter I told you I had a letter from Dot, asking me to find out about Bessie's fiancé. Well I have found out, he is still missing, poor fellow, since the 7th of August. He must either be a prisoner of war, or else dead & the Turks have his identification disc. I believe for every disc they take from a body they get so much money from their government. Still as far as I can hear, the Turks have not proved such devils as the Germans, they may probably treat the prisoners of war decently. I feel very sorry for Bess and I did hate sending that cable. I left it till the weekend (sending it under military expenses) as it wasn't good news. I will go occasionally to the records office to see if I can get different news. Though I suppose if I find any different news, the military will let them know. The records office told me they had inquired from the Battalion at Gallipoli if he was with them but no different report could be given. I want to write to Dot by this mail. (17 October 1915)

> Poor Bessie Dodd I feel very sorry for her. (19 November 1915)

In early December Edie wrote, 'We have a lot of N.S.[W. soldiers] in. Tell Dot when you see her that I have inquired again of Mr Bartrop, but he is still missing. The officer who first inquired for me, thinks there is very little hope' (6 December 1915).

There was indeed no hope for the young clerk, but it was a long and painful process to establish his fate. The fighting at Lone Pine had been so intense, uncertain and spread along extended areas of covered trench that many men who had been killed were recorded as missing. It took months of enquiries to determine the fate of many

The fortunes of war

of them – even if the most that could be discovered was that he wasn't in a hospital or prisoner of war (POW) camp. Investigations into Bartrop's disappearance turned up several witnesses who were interviewed by the Red Cross. Their accounts differed but none thought he had survived.[5]

The following February Edie told her family she had received a letter from Dot.

> [T]hey don't seem very hopeful now about Mr Bartrop. (13 February 1916)

> They tell me at the record office that only 40 Australians are prisoners, & they know who they are, so all those missing must be presumed dead. Such is the fortunes of war. (19 February 1916)

Henry Bartrop remained listed as 'missing' until a Court of Enquiry in June 1916 formally confirmed he was 'killed in action' between 7 and 12 August 1915.[6] His fiancée's hopes crumbled to dust. Bessie and Dot both survived into old age. Neither ever married.

16

NOTHING DOING ON THE PENINSULA

In mid-October Edie spent two days' leave in Cairo surrounded by Coasters.

> I took the midday train to Cairo, got there 3.15 pm & Crocker Brown was there to meet me ... Crock insisted that I should go to Sh[o]ubra ... where the infectious hospital is. I stopped there for the night ... The next day I went to Ghezireh Palace. Here I met Sister Williams (Billy), Sister Perkins ... & eight other Coast nurses. It was just like stepping into the Coast again seeing so many familiar faces. Most of them trained since I have, & worked under me in different wards ...
>
> In the evening Billy, a few others & myself went to Mena House (near the Pyramids) & saw a number of Australian boys. Dr Fletcher wanted to take us for a drive but Billy had already made arrangements to go to Mena. The next day went to Heliopolis, & visited my old home Luna Park [where 'great improvements' had been made: Diary, 13 October 1915] ...
>
> There are 20 Coast nurses in Cairo & 5 in Alexandria, I think in all there are 50 Coasters working under military authority ... The two days were extremely enjoyable ...

Nothing doing on the peninsula

> I felt while in Cairo that I would like to be amongst the Coast people again but comparing their hospitals to the British, I think we are better off here. There is no work to speak of in Cairo. I have had a fair amount of experience here. I can't grumble. (17 October 1915)

Everyone wondered what was next for the Dardanelles campaign – in fact, for the war – and what it meant for them:

> We hear very little news here, as I have said before, but rumours run riot amongst us in various shapes & forms. We know that Bulgaria is now fighting against us & Greece for us. We have also heard that the Dardanelles is impregnable & the Turks must be got at by another route, & that route we can only conjecture will be through Servia, though looking at the map, can't imagine how we can do it. At any rate Dame Rumour has it that some of us will go to Salonika (the sea port for Servia in Greece) & that No 17 is to go, how that can be I do not know, as No 17 is an Army Occupation Hospital. But rumour says that the Australian hospitals will take it over ...
>
> I would like to move on. Alexandria is very stale, though Salonika might be worse ...
>
> This trip has done me no harm. I feel just as well as I did in Sydney, but am much thinner. I have got into that way that I want to see everything I can, so if we go to Salonika I shall be pleased. Hard work never disagreed with me. (17 October 1915)

As quickly as they surfaced, rumours swirled away again. Edie wrote, 'They tell us there is nothing doing on the Peninsula ... Everything seems to be very quiet' (24 October 1915). Although sniping and shelling continued at the Dardanelles, neither side renewed the offensive on any meaningful scale. The best efforts of Hamilton's troops had achieved little, and it seemed increasingly unlikely that they could ever succeed.

The soldiers' health had deteriorated further in the height of summer. Since early August the number of Australians reporting in sick had tripled,[1] and at the start of September an estimated one-third of the available AIF fighting force was off sick or wounded.[2] In an effort to keep up troop numbers all medical units in Egypt were under instructions that A and B class men 'should be discharged from hospital regularly'.[3] They were not malingering; a combination of diet, death, decay and flies dragged down morale, and men who had summoned the shreds of their being together through sheer force of will felt them slip from their grasp. Even as they rotated through short respite spells on Lemnos and Imbros, they returned looking no better. Eight hundred AIF troops were being evacuated daily,[4] and most of those who remained were sick.[5] 17BGH received convoys of sick, and most of the deaths there for the remainder of 1915 were from enteric fever, typhoid fever and dysentery.[6]

Dysentery was brutal. Nurses were appalled by its capacity to transform golden youths into haggard old men, wasted and doubled in agony. On the peninsula sometimes all that could be done was tie a victim's trouser legs with string in order to catch the muck. Even in hospital, nurses could do little except clean the men, cool them, medicate them for the pain, quench the raging thirst, let them rest and inject 'emetine' (a drug also used to induce vomiting): it worked sometimes.[7] It transpired that emetine's anti-protozoal properties meant that it was effective only against amoebic dysentery, not the increasing number of bacillary (bacterial) cases. An urgent meeting of physicians convened in Alexandria in mid-October 1915 noted that most of the gravely ill were from Britain, Australia and New Zealand, who lacked immunity to the disease.[8] In hindsight, another factor was the British diet that favoured meat over fresh vegetables and was deficient in Vitamins C and B.[9]

The men clung on while the campaign's fate was discussed in London and Paris.[10] Even as General Hamilton and Lord Kitchener quietly weighed up the potential cost of evacuation, well-connected Australian war correspondent Keith Murdoch's 'Gallipoli Letter' was provided to British Prime Minister Asquith and Australian Prime Minister Fisher. The 8000-word letter damning the disastrous campaign was based on Murdoch's recollection of an original report written by Ellis Ashmead-Bartlett, who, after his initial hagiographic descriptions of the landings, was an eyewitness to the campaign; he had asked Murdoch to carry his uncensored view of the leadership failures and waste of life to Asquith. When Hamilton got wind of it, Murdoch was arrested by military police en route to London and the original report was confiscated. The result was that Hamilton was replaced by General Charles Monro, who inspected Suvla, Anzac and Cape Helles and immediately recommended the peninsula be evacuated, although he estimated that up to half of the more than 90 000 men to be got off could become casualties during the process.[11]

With little chance of success without significant reinforcement on Gallipoli (and not much chance even then), the battle over whether to evacuate or continue the campaign raged in the halls of power. Ignorant of such machinations, the people in Alexandria, including Edie, watched and speculated: 'We are all wondering what is going to happen. The place is full of British tommies, marching riding ... dragging guns with the aid of horses, driving ammunition waggons & service corps waggons etc ... Lord Kitchener is coming to Egypt too. They say they are expecting trouble on the Canal' (12 November 1915).

Kitchener visited Gallipoli in November 1915, declaring it 'an awful place' before recommending evacuation.[12] Having seen it with his own eyes, he realised that the campaign could not succeed, and in all likelihood never would have.

The question was still not settled when the weather broke in late November. Heavy rains drenched the battlefield and were followed by a blizzard which froze the ground and men alike. Alexandria felt it too:

> Just at present, it is blowing hard raining heavily & bitterly cold. It has turned like this all of a sudden. At night we are wakened with the canvas flapping above & around us. The first night I wondered if the tent would collapse. When we went on duty the next morning, we saw the Doctors with a very dejected air looking at their wrecked home. Three of their tents had fallen. All their possessions wet. They are sleeping all over the hospital anywhere they can. Some of the patients' tents have fallen down but they were soon rectified. I suppose I shall have to get gum boots ... The Sisters here wear mens socks over their own stockings then these gumboots. I must have a mackintosh also an umbrella. If we go to Salonika, must have a sou-wester. I have to see about these things tomorrow, as I have a half day off duty. (30 November 1915)

At Suvla men drowned as floodwaters gushed down gullies to the Salt Lake, and in the snowstorm that followed over 200 froze to death in their trenches.[13] At Helles, too, sentries froze to death at their posts. As many as 12 000 Allied soldiers were removed from the peninsula suffering frostbite and exposure resulting from the weather.[14] Within days the decision was at last made to evacuate.

The evacuation was in fact one part of the Gallipoli campaign that was well planned and executed. Various ruses were employed to disguise the Allied stratagem, and thousands of troops, animals and guns were gradually removed from Anzac Cove and Suvla Bay in the utmost secrecy. Stores were destroyed. Troops went around the little cemeteries, solemnly tidying up the graves. Even as Edie wrote 'There isn't much news nowadays. We hear nothing about war affairs' (19 December 1915), the last soldiers were leaving Anzac and Suvla, and within weeks all were gone from Helles, too. 'How lovely it is to think that the Australians evacuated Anzac, with so few casualties' (9 January 1916).

More than 40000 Allied troops died during the Dardanelles campaign, including some 8700 Australians. An estimated 87000 Ottomans died defending their homeland. The debacle had already cost Winston Churchill his position as first lord of the Admiralty. He had swapped his suit for a uniform and departed to the Western Front.

The campaign's failure was a bitter pill for the soldiers to swallow, but they could hold their heads high about the way they had fought against worthy adversaries. For many, the hardest part of evacuating the detested peninsula was leaving behind the mates who would never make it home.

17

SUCH A CHRISTMAS WE HAVE HAD

After the heavy work of August the hospitals had brought in more staff to be ready for the expected high casualties. Voluntary aid detachments (VADs) supplemented the work of trained nurses, and some were coming to Egypt. Edie had had doubts:

> I do not know if they will be much of a success, for we hear that 17 of the trained nurses here are to be sent away, where to, we do not know. If these people are coming out to do the work of the 17 nurses, I don't see how it will be a success, because nursing here is more difficult than in ordinary times. Then when trained nurses go off duty, someone responsible will have to be left in charge. (10 September 1915)

Two weeks later, the VADs had arrived:

> About 200 women arrived from England to help in the hospitals. These are untrained, they have gone in for ambulance work, & went into some hospital in England for one month. I have one on night duty with me. They are not [to] do dressing[s], serve medicines, take temperatures & do very little treatment. I suppose they are sent instead of trained nurses ... These women get £20 per year,[1] some of them have given up positions to come, but I believe most of them are stay-at-home girls. The one who is with me is a schoolteacher in Newcastle. (30 September 1915)

Such a Christmas we have had

Although VADs operated under the auspices of a Joint War Committee of the British Red Cross Society and the Order of St John, initially scepticism was widespread among registered nurses. In Britain, overwhelmingly working-class nurses saw what they perceived as untrained but motivated middle-class girls 'dabbling': carrying out mundane duties, but also reading to and writing letters for convalescents and having their families and friends bring the men sweets and gifts – things with which the professional could not, and should not, compete.[2] However, once the VADs arrived, Edie never complained about them. They, like her, had travelled far from home to help. Besides, they took on much of the drudgery, like the probationary nurses in civilian hospitals. Throughout the war, thousands of VADs diligently rendered assistance that allowed the trained nurses to concentrate on skilled work.[3] Their commandant-in-chief Katharine Furse, who had joined the Red Cross VAD system when it was founded in 1909 and led the first VAD unit sent to France in 1914, entreated them to be 'invariably courteous, unselfish and kind' and carry out their tasks in the spirit of the mottoes 'Willing to do anything' and 'The People give gladly'.[4] Perhaps the VADs were taken too much for granted, for after a dispute over their living conditions and her lack of power to introduce reforms, Furse resigned in 1917 and was appointed first director of the newly formed Women's Royal Naval Service.

Matrons tended to allow the nurses to pair up on overseas service, so that they could serve side by side, supporting each other as they transferred to different posts. Clarice Dickson and Dorothy Cawood, and Elsie Graham and Eena Copeman, became pairs. The latter had much in common: they were both around thirty-four, came from large rural families (Lismore and Narrabri respectively) and had brothers serving (Donald Graham was already at Gallipoli, and thirty-year-old Fred Copeman was in training, eventually to be assigned to the Camel Corps).⁵ All the while, the friendship between Edie and Evelyn Swannell deepened. Grace and Queenie had obviously noticed, as Edie responded to their enquiry about this nurse who was mentioned frequently in her letters:

> Yes, Sister Swannell is my friend here, so far she is a jolly good one, full of life, fun, & a great favourite, especially with Matron. She was trained at the Coast six years ago. She left a few months after I came to the Coast. I met her in Albury (NSW) & we have been friends ever since. Graham & Copeman are not exactly of the past, we do not see much of them, they are in another hospital some distance away. Occasionally we go & see them. (24 October 1915)

Sister Swannell became Edie's ally, confidante, sounding post, and friend on excursions when their leave overlapped:

> Swannell & I are both having one day off tomorrow, we keep planning how we shall spend it, we thought we would go for a picnic. Taking lunch & our spirit lamps, but we came to the conclusion that there would be only sand to sit on, & the palm trees, if they afford any shelter the Arabs will have it … [Instead w]e are having breakfast in bed. We each have spirit lamps & we have some tinned chicken, some tinned milk & some biscuits. Of course some breakfast will come over, but Oh dear! perhaps such a little, half an Egyptian egg (these eggs are a wee bit larger than a pigeon's egg) some bacon enough to fill a tablespoon, some toast marmalade & butter. So don't you think we will have rather a good breakfast? In the afternoon we are posting our presents & then going to the Nusia Gardens, then perhaps we will go & see Graham & Copeman. (6 November 1915)

Such a Christmas we have had

In November 1915 Evelyn Swannell was sent to Abou-Kir rest home for nurses and as soon as Edie had her half-day off duty she went to visit. The home was situated beside the beach some 8 miles east of 17BGH. It was bright and airy, with wide verandahs laid with rugs and cane tables and chairs. How the nurses must have relaxed, as zephyrs whispered through their hair, rattling palm fronds and carrying snatches of laughter and the clink of china teacups away over the ancient landscape. Local men in loose white tunics and trousers milked goats for the household and climbed the date palms that thrust out of the sands surrounding the house, using slings to carry down bundles of cut fruit.

> To get to [the house] from the train we had to go on donkeys. It was the first time I was on a donkey & my donkey boy would insist in keeping ahead of the others & made the donkey gallop, of course I was on sideways by not a side-saddle, so you could imagine how I stuck on. The donkey boy had hold of my leg. (These boys never leave their donkeys but always run alongside). But for all that I rather enjoyed it. After afternoon tea, we went for a sail it was glorious, the sun was setting & the afterglow was beautiful. I think I have told you about this afterglow before.

> When it was time to go the hostess ordered a cart to take us to the station, as some of the sisters were leaving & going back to work. You should have seen the cart. It is just wide enough between the wheels to hold two ordinary seat cushions ... on the floor of the cart. The wheels are extremely high, much higher than the sides of the cart. There are no springs. We crawled into the back of the cart. The last sister dangling her legs out the back. The driver walked alongside of the horse which was decorated with beads & bells. So I ended my pleasant afternoon

at Abou-Kir. I am and look very well, so don't think I shall be sent here, I would like it all the same for there is bathing.
(12 November 1915)

A month later Edie was sent to Abou-Kir. 'Matron thinks I look anaemic' (Diary, 23 November 1915). Besides, with the impasse at the Dardanelles and the arrival of VADs and nurses from England, the hospital was 'extremely slack' (30 November 1915).

> We are not expected to get up here till 9am breakfast, we have early morning tea in bed at 7. We are now waiting for the sailing boat to take us across the bay to the houseboat, where we are going to have a swim, it is a bit cold, but we must have a bath. We are only allowed drinking & tooth water, for washing all is salt. All fresh water is brought in tanks.
>
> Sister Swannell has the 1/2 day off duty, so is coming here to spend the time with me …
>
> [M]any of us had a swim. Th[e house]boat is very old & is historical. It was the provision boat for the ship engaged during the battle of the Nile. We are on the spot where the battle was fought. The boat is called Noah's Ark. Small guns are still on her, pictures of the battle, & accounts in newspaper framed on the walls. The battle of Abou-Kir on the Nile was fought between Napoleon & Nelson, Nelson being victorious. We went for a sail in the afternoon & took some snaps. Then we went for a donkey ride. One of our party was thrown, but I managed to stick on. My donkey would be ahead, & if any other tried to get ahead, he just galloped. I went to bed tired, can you wonder.
> (6 December 1915)

Such a Christmas we have had

Ironically, Edie returned to 17BGH with a cold and was sent to bed with a temperature. After a day's bed-rest she was on duty again, busy with 'some very sick cases' (Diary, 12–13 December 1915).

On her first day at Abou-Kir, Edie had caught the train into Alexandria to visit her friends on the HMHS *Assaye*:

> Sisters Dickson & Caywood [sic] … are on transport duty. How I envy them. They have been to London … Surrey [and] Llandudno in North Wales. On the return trip they went to Malta, Salonika, Mudros, Anzac, Cape Helles, Lemnos & finally to Alex. Can you wonder how I envy them. I went over the hospital ship yesterday. Everything is so compact & so convenient. I met on board two doctors that I knew. One was at the Coast. I spent a most enjoyable morning. Had lunch on board. When leaving the ship I had to get on a felucca (native boat). An officer came with me, then he took me in a felucca to the Bourse (Alexandria Exchange) then I sent telegrams & posted letters for the people on the hospital ship, for they went away unexpectedly. (6 December 1915)

Edie failed to identify the 'Coast doctor' in that letter. According to her diary, it was Dr Fletcher, for whom she sent a telegram and in so doing missed her train back to Abou-Kir and had to wait over three hours for the next. The *Assaye* took Dr Fletcher to Lemnos, and from there he went to Anzac Cove. Edie watched enviously again as a ship carried Sisters Dickson and Cawood and Dr Fletcher away. Although keen to get transport duty herself, she was pragmatic:

> Swannell & I have asked for that duty but Matron has asked Swannell, while I was away, to stay back till after Christmas. For my part I would rather stay back till the spring. The weather will be better. Now it is pretty rough I believe. On board hospital ship we will only get £40.0.0 per year. But we are anxious to

see a little more of the world. I have £30 in the bank here & presents for everybody except those in Dallinghoo. I don't much care about the pay now. (10 December 1915)

As 1915 drew to a close, thoughts turned to Christmas. Nothing underscored the dismal realities of a world at war more than the monotony of their diets. Nostalgia for the kitchen at Sans Souci suffused Edie's thoughts:

Tomorrow I must post this, or else you shall not get this in time for Christmas. I wish I could come by wireless while you are reading this. I could descend into the kitchen while you are having afternoon tea, & have some nice tea with hot scones & butter, or soda biscuits & butter. Just at present I should love some tea & hot scones. Well never mind, you can imagine me eating some of Queenie's Christmas cake. I do hope I get it … How beautiful it is to think I shall be able to eat something Australian. (23 November 1915)

I wish we could get some of Mum's dinners here. We never get a baked potato, & the butter is too sour to eat with it. (19 December 1915)

By mid-December the withdrawal from the Dardanelles was in full swing and 20 000 boxes containing handkerchiefs, cigars, cigarettes and matches were distributed to the men by the Australian Comforts Fund. Edie received letters from Grandfather, Aunt Tilda, Aunt Alice, Uncle Will and her cousin Lily and even 'a very nice card from Matron at the Coast & one from Doctor Wallace … telling me he had received my letter & that he missed me, but was glad for the men's sake. (Rather an unusual thing for Doctor Wallace to say. I feel a wee bit flattered)' (31 December 1915).

From home there were letters and a parcel containing Queen's

Such a Christmas we have had

cake and a dress made by Gracie that Edie had been too late to head off after writing more than a month earlier, 'I do hope Grace hasn't made up the silk I sent yet, we are not allowed to wear anything but uniform. I wish I could send back all my private clothes' (12 November 1915).

> Christmas is over. Such a Christmas we have had & how tired we all were. No one going off duty …
>
> Christmas Eve we had carols without the waits (by the bye I don't know what 'waits' mean, but I hear the English girls talking about them).[6] We all procured lamps, mostly coloured & at half-past eight sallied forth from the Church tent with our lighted lamps, the night was perfect, the moon on the wane, & we made, I thought a pretty sight, with our coloured lanterns. We sang in different parts of the grounds of the hospital. The English girls said it wanted snow, to make it like Christmas. For me it was all new, & I thoroughly enjoyed it. We made tea in our tent afterwards, & ate a good part of your cake. It was delicious it came 3 days before without a dent or scratch. Tell Grace the dress fits beautifully. I'm so sorry I can't wear it. I'm afraid I shall have to wait till after the war is over. (26 December 1915)

The OC recorded in the war diary of 17BGH: 'Xmas Day. 1 officer [patient] received from Docks. Brig Gen Boyle commanding the troops in Alex visited.' There were concerts for the patients and staff, and a 'Message from His Majesty the King … The patients enjoyed their meals immensely & the concerts were very much appreciated. The weather unfortunately was wet & windy'. Edie wrote,

> [On Christmas Day w]e were not allowed to decorate the wards, but we decorated the tables. The men had a jolly good time. All the week we were shopping. We gave each man a parcel, the Red

Cross gave one too. We encouraged the men to hang up their socks. We hired cups & saucers, made sandwiches of egg, bought cake & fruit & nuts. Men pulled bonbons & had fireworks from them, & the Doctor gave each man a cigar, which was thoroughly enjoyed & appreciated. Dinner was excellent turkey & plum pudding, very nicely cooked. They had also ale. After 8pm we went over to the gatehouse & had our dinner. The room was beautifully decorated. The usual turkey & plum pudding, which was served in blazing brandy, sweets fruit, bonbons, claret cup & liquor, we rose from table 10.30pm & danced till 11pm. You can imagine we wanted to sleep in in the morning …

In spite of active service & in spite of being in Egypt, we all had a jolly time. Hope you people had the same. (26 December 1915)

18

DON'T THINK THAT I'VE LOST MY HEART

The close of 1915 brought concerts every afternoon to the hospital, performed by patients, sisters and medical officers. They sang jaunty ditties such as 'Up from Somerset' and wistful ballads like 'When We Go Down the Vale' and 'That's How They Bid Goodbye to England', but performances always concluded with a rousing rendition of 'God Save the King'.[1] On New Year's Eve, Edie and Evelyn Swannell went to a nurses' home for a night of games and songs. 'Auld Lang Syne [was] sung at midnight. The usual toasting & cheering' (Diary, 31 December 1915).

On New Year's Day Matron sent thirty-six bags of New Year presents up to the ward for the patients:

> As the patients are enterics & can't eat food indiscriminately, we had to open them all. We found out that they were from Australia. Books, smokes, writing material, chocolates, sweets, cakes, nuts ... Many of the parcels had a label marked 'A present for your nurse'. These contained all manner of things suitable for girls. There were some very funny letters, evidently written by children but they all expected the recipient to write ... I must stop now. I have many letters to answer, my Christmas mail was a nice big fat one. (2 January 1916)

For now, she said, work in Egypt was 'frightfully slack ... The 17th Gen has only 200 patients ... [but] 2500 ... beds' (7 January 1916).

The season, combined with the end of the campaign, raised everyone's spirits. Concerned that standards were slipping, on Boxing Day 'Headquarters Alexandria [issued orders to hospitals] that soldiers should on all occasions salute officers, this order is in many cases not observed by the men, especially the Colonials who rarely salute anybody'.[2] Staff drank and socialised. It caused comment:

> I am very glad to think that the Australian sisters here have caused no trouble here. The English girls have made the place pretty hot. They have been seen with officers smoking & drinking in public. They came so much in the public eye, that some busybody wrote to Miss Oram complaining of unseemly behaviour & from what I can gather, it is [due to] the trouble these girls have caused that allowances have been stopped. When there were only a few of us, with a great deal of work to do, there was less trouble, but since there are so many sisters here doing nothing, also officers, they have been getting into mischief. It is a pleasure to think that the Australian girls here, have not come under public notice. (2 January 1916)

Edie had described similar behaviour in Cairo – natural, but against the rules that forbid fraternisation. For a military nurse perception mattered, and with her uniform came expectations about propriety. The 'busybody' Edie mentioned would have been concerned not just by the interaction of the sexes but by the drinking and smoking; the latter had once been associated with 'fast' women – even though it was now an affectation of upper-class women like the ladies in the *Malwa*'s First Class. For the men, smoking was not only acceptable but expected. Tobacco was often part of a soldier's rations and comfort packages. A long drag on a roll-your-own was an almost obligatory form of relaxation in the trenches. It was also popular in the hospital tents of 17BGH, where smoking was banned: an order to this effect had to be published – and published again.[3]

Much of Edie's socialising was with Australians, and the patients she wrote about were mostly Australians, with whom she reminisced about home and enjoyed the fellowship of generally shared origins and a similar world view. She understood them and was comfortable with them. She wrote warmly about Private Alfred Parkins, 'a very nice boy, only 23 years old'. Parkins had been shot while serving with the 2nd Battalion as a despatch rider on the peninsula and was to be invalided home. He was eager and upbeat, but perhaps his best feature was that he was from Sans Souci[4]: 'He is leaving here for Port Said for Aust on Thursday. So asked me today if there were any messages he could take, so I gave him a letter of introduction to you people. So you must expect him to call' (30 November 1915). This he did and Edie, on hearing the news, wrote: 'I am so glad that young Parkins has come to see you. He would keep you entertained for hours as he did me, while in hospital. I didn't think he would be shy … I got several letters from him from Port Said' (26 March 1916).[5]

It was not unusual for patients to write to the nurses who had tended them and offered a sympathetic ear. In the wards Edie was confident and at ease, particularly with the Australians:

> I think in my usual big headedness, that the patients who walk into my ward are very lucky to have me to talk to! (31 October 1915)

> I don't think I have forgotten any of [the] Aust men with whom I have [had] anything to do. (6 December 1915)

She listened eagerly to their descriptions of the front:

> The nicest of all [in my ward now] is a Melbourne boy, who knows how to describe things on the Peninsula, I could listen to him all day long. (31 October 1915)

> When I get the Sydney Mail, I have only had four, I pass it round to the Aust boys & any Gallipoli pictures they describe & make it very interesting for me. I do not know what we would do without them. They are so much brighter than the British. Though in the last convoy, the British boys we got were from the better classes in England. They are extremely nice & well-behaved boys. (19 November 1915)
>
> Last Tuesday 22 Australian boys went to Port Said en route to Aust. How I missed them all, they made things very pleasant for me in the ward. My arm ached when I had said goodbye to them all. I had taken a snap of them all, so of course I must send them each one … Don't think that I've lost my heart to any of them, I'm afraid there were too many, & they all range between 20 & 22 years old. We have a few Aust boys in now, but these are not so nice as the others. We are working pretty heavy now, the boys we got in by the last convoy are very sick, so sick that they take up all my time. (19 December 1915)

Like many nurses, Edie wrote warmly and almost maternally about the 'boys':

> I was very impressed at a British Tommie the other day. He told me he had a letter from an Australian girl, who wanted him to write to her. This boy (whom I call 'the boy', he says he is 20 but I'm sure he is only 16) went to the Red Cross ladies for a bag to keep his things in, for he had lost most of his kit in Gallipoli. In the bag was a sprig of wattle & a letter, he gave me the letter to read, it began with 'dear Tommie' & ended with Flossie & her address somewhere in Melbourne. All the other men want bags now with sprigs of wattle & letters from Flossies. (30 September 1915)

Edie was generally more at ease with youthful 'other ranks' than with officers, later declaring, 'I do not like nursing officers, I would far sooner nurse the tommies' (31 December 1916). Perhaps she found the officers' class and privilege off-putting, or perceived an irksome sense of entitlement ingrained by a military hierarchy that resolutely divided them from other ranks in all things, from awards and decorations to the messes in which they ate and the quarters in which they slept. On land and at sea, officers had separate wards.

Deference was also shown in hospitals. While men were not obliged to salute nurses, Edie reported they often did so voluntarily.

> This morning we were wakened with sounds of music, a brass band. On getting up & looking out of [the] tents we saw soldiers passing, thousands of them … The sentry presented arms at the gate, so as the men passed they saluted the sentry. An officer would give the order 'Eyes left' & another order 'Eyes front' that is the salute. There were some sisters at the gate & the officers saluted them. Of course a soldier need not salute a woman except the Queen, but we are always saluted out of courtesy. Some 'big dogs', or 'bigs' or 'top dogs' as the slang goes came to visit the hospital yesterday. I was on duty. To my surprize, as they passed through the ward they saluted me by touching the peak of their caps. (12 November 1915)

Edie had turned thirty in September, a milestone she did not acknowledge. Her diary merely said, 'Nothing of importance happened'. Only once did she ponder her single status:

> [An Australian Army Nurse friend] asked me out to dinner … telling me she wanted me to meet a British officer aged 19 years, who is very lonely. He is training in a camp very close to us. I went to dinner & met the gentleman. To whom I couldn't take a fancy, he is only as high as six penneth of coppers. I cannot

understand why I do not take pleasure in men's company. In the ward I can please myself whether I will talk to the men or not, & it is always in the ward I can take any pleasure at all in their company. But outside of the ward, when a man's company is thrust upon me, I find it often a distinct displeasure. I'm afraid I'm doomed to the solitude of an old maid, but mylashe (Arabic for never mind) so far the life of an old maid is anything but unpleasant, but of course I cannot tell what life will present in another 10 or 15 years. (27 February 1916)

What, then, of Dr Fletcher? After embarking on HMHS *Assaye* in early December, he was stationed at Anzac Cove hardly more than a week before contracting enteric fever and passing a fitful Christmas on Lemnos in 3AGH: 'Dr Fletcher (the one Gracie thinks I've lost my heart to) is sick with enteric fever. He is coming to Alex' (23 January 1916). In fact, after a month in St Andrew's Hospital in Malta he spent months recuperating in 1AGH. 'Dr Fletcher [has] heart trouble following paratyphoid. Poor beggar I must go & see him when in Cairo. He has been very good to me. Please don't think he is the one please though I am going to see him' (13 March 1916).

Perhaps Edie had known that his heart was already taken. She did see him in Cairo and Alexandria in April, but when he was well enough in June 1916, he left to join his unit in France, and by May the following year he was formally engaged to his girl at home in Sydney.[6] Edie never saw or mentioned Dr Fletcher again.

19

WAITING FOR THE NEXT MOVE

The failure of the Gallipoli campaign did not seem to dent Edie's confidence that the war could not last much longer or that the Allies must win.

> Now something has happened that will make you wonder … Matron got notice two days ago saying that if any sister will sign for the duration of war & go where she is sent, she will be entitled for £20 extra per year. Well war will only last another 12 months why not sign on & get the extra money? We are to do so in England, so I have time to think about it. If I had been in an Australian Hospital instead of a British I would have had to sign on for duration before leaving Sydney … So I think I shall do it. I'm not tired of war work yet, though I wish they would let us transport back to Australia by way of change. Though none of us bargained to be away so long as we have been now. But surely another 12 months will see it all ended. Don't you [think]? (7 January 1916)

Again she speculated on her future, saying, 'We think we are sailing for England on the 14th … I wonder if we will' (7 January 1916). They didn't:

> Another week has passed, & nearly one month of the year has gone. I wonder how long all this will last. There seems to be millions of troops in Alex. But nary an Australian do we see. There seems to be no fighting going on, & all seem to be

waiting for the next move, wondering what the future will bring. A number of Sisters are going to Salonica tomorrow but I'm not amongst the number. I feel I would like to be amongst the number, I would like a change. Though we are told, the change would not be for the better. Most of the Australian patients are going to Cairo tomorrow & we don't think we shall get any more. We are sad indeed … On Thursday last I went to the station to see Dick & Cay off. They have left the ship & have been sent back to their unit. I feel down in the dumps at this, as I used to look forward for their ship to come to Alex. (23 January 1916)

I'm afraid No 17 is too busy [for us] to be sent away. We are the only hospital that has any work to speak about. We are surrounded by camps & we get many patients in from these places … I wonder how long it will last, by the Egyptian gazette this morning it said that Germany will not attack Egypt but that may be bluff. (13 February 1916)

Yesterday Matron came asking the sisters if they would care to volunteer for Mesopotamia … Only those who have spent a summer in Egypt are allowed to go. Each sister has to go through a medical test, which is very severe. I hear that many who have volunteered have been turned down. I would prefer much to go to British East Africa, a hospital goes there today. It seems to me that we have to stick to 17th. I believe Matron does not care to lose her staff, so I suppose we should take it as a compliment. (19 February 1916)

The end of war is not yet within sight, & goodness knows how long that it will be in sight. Perhaps another couple of years. Lord Kitchener is in Egypt now so I wonder how things will turn. Would it not be lovely if the war ended now, then in May

we would be in England then have 4 months furlough there &
be in Sydney next October. But it is of no use building castles in
the air, they have no foundation. (27 February 1916)

While the Australian hospitals were still in Egypt, Edie's precious
network of Coasters cheered her up and staved off homesickness:

> Last week two Australian Sisters who came from the Coast
> came to see me, I spent my half day with them ... They had hired
> a car & drove me round Alex ... They afterwards insisted that I
> should stay & have dinner. Then the next day, Crocker Brown ...
> rang me up, she has furlough [and] insisted that I should have
> dinner with her. So that was two evenings out in one week. So
> this is what we call active service. (13 February 1916)

Also cheering was the gift of a 'huge billy' from three Coasters in
Australia containing a cake, pudding, tin of cheese, toffee, bonbons
and nuts. The can was soldered down, but almost the best bit was
the packaging, which showed that Edith Blake was in the thoughts
of Sisters Hawdon, Neal and Athol: '[M]y name was written on it
three times, each of the girls had written on it ... I recognised each
handwriting. I think it awfully good of them don't you?' (23 January
1916). This was followed by a Women of Australia box for each
Australian nurse from the subscribers of Lady Bridges' Appeal to
'show them that Australia remembers, and sends greetings, not
only to her sons, but to her daughters also'.[1] Lady Bridges' husband,
Major General Sir William Bridges, was a career soldier who had
commanded the 1st Australian Division on Gallipoli, but had died
of wounds a little over three weeks after the landing.

> My box contained a pair of good black cashmere stockings, a
> bottle of eau-de-cologne ... [myriad toiletries, sewing things,
> biscuits] and a little red cross, nicely enamelled with 1915

on the back ... We all like the little pendant, & go about the hospital [with it] pinned on us. The English girls say we swank with it (the pendant). It is so nice to think that the Australian Women were the only women who thought of the nurses.
(6 February 1916)

Everybody was waiting for the next move. After returning from the Dardanelles, some 30 000 experienced Australian troops were sent to a vast camp near the Suez Canal, ready to help defend Egypt against Ottoman forces now freed up from Gallipoli. Just as many Australian recruits swarmed over Cairo while they trained and waited to join units. Prime Minister Billy Hughes' government had promised more forces, which would effectively double the current size of the AIF.[2] The AIF's two infantry divisions were expanded to five. The two evacuated from Gallipoli were expanded to four in Egypt, while one was raised in Australia that would go directly to Britain to complete its training.

In late February 1916, the Germans launched a massive attack on the Western Front. Edie wrote, 'There has been a great deal of fighting round Verdun according to the papers' (5 March 1916). The French were obliged to focus on the defence of Verdun, while the British took over much of the conduct of the planned joint offensive on the Somme for that summer. The Australian infantry battalions and much of the AIF's artillery decamped to the Western Front to take part, while the light horse remained behind to fight the Ottomans in Sinai and Palestine.

Edie suspected that her time with the Australians was coming to a close. It seemed likely that the Australian hospitals would follow the AIF to France[3]: 'I hear that the Australian Sisters have asked to go to France. They will be lucky dogs if they get there, away from the burning heat of Egypt' (27 February 1916). In contrast, Britain had so many interests in the war, Edie felt she could be sent anywhere:

No 2 Australian Gen Hosp has gone to Marseilles in France, the No 1 is to go next week. Oh Dear! Why am I not in an Australian hospital? I hope we soon get to England, & then to France I hope. (26 March 1916)

On Friday the No 1 Australian Hospital left Alexandria. They were going to Marseilles. I went down to the boat & saw a lot of the Coast girls, how I envied them. (2 April 1916)

At this time, Edie received a newspaper cutting about riots near Liverpool, New South Wales, on Valentine's Day after new recruits objected to increased drill hours. The *Sydney Morning Herald* called it 'an orgy [of violence] of the wildest and most disgraceful kind that ever occurred in Australia'.[4] Edie wrote,

> When Swannell & I read it, we tore it into shreds, we felt so ashamed of them. If they think they are going to do the same in Egypt, I hope I shall be out of this place when they arrive here … When you see our boys in the streets here they look so spick & span & in every way superior in appearance to the British tommy, who looks dirty stumpy & heavy, & yet the Australians are proving a rabble. It makes one feel disgusted. I hope the boys will do something for themselves in France. (2 April 1916)

Charles Bean wrote that the Australians were warmly welcomed in France.[5] They had distinguished themselves at Gallipoli. They would do so again on the Western Front, where over 295 000 would serve: 130 000 would be wounded, and 46 000 of them would die.

20

IT IS AN EDUCATION

Edie had to decide whether to re-enlist when her twelve-month contract expired in April 1916. In January she and Evelyn Swannell were already thinking about what to do: 'Some of the Australians who joined up under British authority, are getting discontented, & want a transfer to the Australians. I don't think I'm discontented, the British have been very good to us, we have no room to grumble, have we?' (9 January 1916).

Only a handful of the Australians allocated to the QAIMNS Reserve transferred to the AANS.[1] Even if Edie felt so inclined, a transfer might not have been simple to arrange, especially considering how disorganised things had been a year before. So, that was that; she would commit to the British:

> On Tuesday next Sister Swannell & I are signing on for another 12 months service ... I feel quite capable of going on for another 12 months ... I'm not at all tired of active service. (2 April 1916)

> I have signed on for another year. I shall then see how I shall feel ... I don't think it will be 5 years before I return. (14 April 1916)

By now, Edie had become less hostile to Egypt. Having always appreciated the beauty of the place, she became more open to Arab culture.

> One Sunday at lunch we heard what we thought was a drum & fife band. Sometimes the soldiers march past playing in a band,

hearing this we all ran out to see them pass. But to our surprise we only saw Arabs. One was dressed in a bright yellow satin vest, very white baggy trousers, dancing in a ridiculous fashion with another Arab robed in grey. The first man was the bridegroom. Following on was a gaily decorated camel, with a large canopy of red blue & yellow striped woolly material, the bride was in under the canopy completely covered. Following on were many camels carrying the bridesmaids & guests, do not know which were which. A great number of Arab women followed on making a peculiar loud noise they call 'the cry of joy'. I did not see the band instruments, but as they passed the hospital they played 'Tipperary' tunefully enough. I believe when they get to the house the bride when taken off the camel is enveloped in black, so as she won't be seen, she then forever wears a veil. The lower classes they wear black veils, with a brass ridged tube on the nose. The eyes only are seen and as they suffer so much from eye diseases, the eyes are not good to look upon. The higher class women wear white veils no brass tubes & the veils are very thin seeing the features behind the veil. These women are often nice looking, have seen many really beautiful ones. The eyes in these women are evidently carefully looked after, they are all well shaped & large, & of course black. (30 November 1915)

She also added Arabic words to her vocabulary. One Wednesday afternoon,

> Swannell & I had the 1/2 day off duty, so we took a garry [gharry] or arabya (Egyptian cab), & went along the Mahmoudieh Canal. It is pretty in places, but the water is dirty, one spot there were a lot of palm trees & these reflected in the water so I took a snap, I also took a [snap of a] native village … Then we went to the Empire nurses club. The place just opened the day before. We became members and paid down our 10

> piastres & had afternoon tea. In this place there are writing rooms, reading rooms, also lounge rooms ... I heard one sister remark that she could come & write letters & use backsheshe [baksheesh] writing paper & envelopes. Backsheshe is an Arabic word meaning alms, or to give or get something for nothing. The Arabic children are brought up, most of them, to ask for backsheshe ...
>
> That is a good afternoon's pleasure, don't you think? (27 February 1916)

Edie and Sister Swannell had been determined for a long time to see Karnak, 'the beauty spot of Egypt' (1 August 1915). In March, they were granted leave.

> Unfortunately this is the month for the campseens [khamseen: 'wind of fifty days'], these are sandstorms, when you can't breathe without getting sand down your throat. I hope one won't be blowing when we get to Luxor. Unfortunately too, it will be hotter there than here. But mylash ('never mind'. I love this Arabic word it is so soft sounding, very few Arabic words are) we are looking forward to a good time. (5 March 1916)

In the event, Edie declared their holiday the most interesting four days she had ever spent.

> We arrived in Luxor at 9 am very tired dirty & dusty. It takes 18 hours from Alex. It took us 22 as we stayed 4 hours in Cairo.
>
> We visited ruins of temples of which the principal are at Luxor or ancient Thebes ... Another time we went across the Nile & visited the tombs of these ancient Pharaohs & their Queens ...

It is an education

To get to the tombs we rode donkeys, the first part through the fields. The natives were tending & irrigating their ground in exactly the same manner as they did in the time of the Pharaohs. They have made no progress whatever. You have seen pictures from the bible haven't you? Well these people dress in the same way. One shepherd was driving his flock & carrying a lamb in his arms. The scene is exactly the same as the story of the lost sheep in the New Testament. The Arabs with their dress often make me think of the bible …

While we were staying in Luxor the weather was perfect, not too hot, always a breeze blowing, it was full moon, so one night we went up the Nile. I will leave it to your imagination as to what it was like. The peacefulness of the scene, the dress of the Arab, made one feel the ancient things and how close & yet so far away from the ancient people … it was hard to realise that there is a great war going on.

One night we went up to the top of the ruins of Karnak. These pillars and statues are wonderful by day, but they are awe-inspiring by night, & the moon showing up the shadows cast the writing in relief.

Yesterday we went four miles up the Nile & visited the orange groves. The perfume from the orange blossom was delicious. I didn't want to come out …

The whole trip cost a little under £9.0.0. But still I wouldn't for all the world have missed it. It is an education. (19 March 1916)

Edie began framing her descriptions of Arab life and culture with more appreciation and less judgment.

The police here are very different to ours. They wear white suits with red bands round the waist & red tarbouche (hat shaped like this with a black tassel). The Turks wear the same kind of hat, they call theirs a fez. The Arab servants here look very nice. They wear long white gowns with the red tarbouche, red belt & red babouche (the last mentioned is a red morocco shoe with pointed slightly turned up toes). The white & red against their black or almost black skins look very well. (11 June 1916)

One night she 'was restless, so didn't go to sleep', and

at midnight I heard reports I thought of bombardment but put the idea out of my head, as I thought a bombardment would make a great deal more sound. But reports continued & became more frequent, so I thought I would get up & look out of the window. Then I suddenly remembered it was the end of Ramadan. Fireworks were being fired into the air, they were very pretty. The rockets would shoot into the air & then would come down in different coloured stars or float in the air. This lasted for half an hour.

The Ramadan is a Moslem [sic] religious ceremony. It is like our lent. I have been told that Mahomet is supposed to have received the wisdom & power to write the Koran (the Mahomet Bible). The Mahommedans celebrate the month of July or Ramadan by fasting. They do not carry it out the same way as we do. They do not eat while the sun shines … This is carried out for a luna[r] month. At the end of the month they feast, this is called the feast of Byram [Bayram]. They often become uncontrollable & cause disturbances. It isn't safe for us to be out after dark. So no one is going out till Wednesday when the feasting will be over. During the Ramadan the Arabs are often quarrelsome. Perhaps they [are] out of condition caused by the fasting. (30 July 1916)

It is an education

When she returned from Luxor, Edie was placed on night duty, based in a hotel the British had taken for the 17BGH's night nurses 9 miles from Alexandria. '[It is] on the top of a hill & overlooking the sea. We shall be able to have sea baths' (5 March 1916). The Mediterranean dipped and danced, enticing them to beach walks and donkey rides. And to tragedy.

The khamseen had blown all night, rattling the shutters and whisking sand into every crevice and through their bedsheets. The winds whipped up the sea, perfect conditions to make the spouting rock, a little distance along the coast, cast up its spray.

> [W]e made up a party of 12 & took donkeys to the spouting rock ... The waves were much bigger than we expected. The Home Sister Miss Edith Butler & a VAD got too close to the edge. A huge wave came wetting us all, but took Miss Butler & knocked over the VAD. It was awful, there we all stood watching Miss Butler & none of us could help. Some officers & men came, but could do nothing. A life belt & rope was procured. Some of the party went back to hospital to tell Matron. Some went back with the VAD. Swannell, another Sister & myself stayed back, thinking perhaps that if the body was brought in we could try to resuscitate ... Sister had on a macintosh also a Sou-wester. All the time I saw her in the water, her head was under. I'm afraid the Sou-wester filled with water & kept her head down. All bathing has been stopped. I'm pleased about that, for the whole coast is treacherous & most seem to see no danger. We have done nothing but talk about it. (14 April 1916)

The accident shocked Edie in a way that the deaths of patients did not. Sister Butler had died in front of her. It had been so quick and, amid the churning water's push and pull, so quiet. It could have happened to any of them standing on the rocks. 'I cannot get the sight out of my mind' (14 April 1916).

Sister Butler's body was retrieved the next day by the Moutaza Coast Guard, several miles from where she had been washed away. Her appearance was said to be perfectly natural and calm except for one slight bruise on her face.[2] She was buried at Chatby Military Cemetery in Alexandria.

21

SUNBURN, SAND – AND SLACK

Edie was by now accustomed to the regimented routine of army life, which in many ways echoed the rhythms of the Coast Hospital, although certain aspects were distinctly military: 'The orderlies "fall in" bugle has just sounded, that is 8 o'clock, so I must go over to dinner' (9 January 1916).

Information about troop and consequential staff movements was necessarily kept close. The nurses carried out their everyday tasks conscientiously, but the bigger picture of the Great War and their places in it remained murky. They washed along like tiny leaves in a river of decisions made by governments and generals:

> Do you know it is nearly 12 months ago since we were told to present ourselves for examination. Oh Dear! how the time flies. I wonder where we will be this time next year. I think somehow I say this often in my letters for it is often on my mind.
> (5 March 1916)

> Something will have to be done soon, for it will be too much expense keeping hospitals in Alexandria with little or no work. We are just looking at one another now. If I were in Sydney I should enjoy it, but here it is miserable to have nothing to do, there is nowhere to go & no one to see. (26 March 1916)

In April, Elsie Graham and Eena Copeman went on transport duty. Edie was also 'down for hospital ship duty, but I do not know when I shall be put on. But I don't think somehow it will be soon.

Swannell & I are to go together & as Swannell is a favourite of Matron's probably we shall be left till somewhere near the last' (14 May 1916).

The easiest route out of their present situation was east to Mesopotamia; but Edie wanted to go west: 'I hope we go to France. It must be an awful expense keeping us here for practically nothing' (8 April 1916).

Although 1AGH and 2AGH had gone to France, 3AGH was at Abbassia on the outskirts of Cairo. Edie travelled there for the first anniversary of the landing at Anzac Cove, already dubbed 'Anzac Day', which was also marked at ceremonies in London and Australia. She wrote the next day on the stationery of the Grand Continental Hotel:

> You will be surprised when you receive this, how extravagant I have grown. Yes I have grown extravagant. But I don't think I shall let the fever of spending money get a hold on me. Though I don't suppose I shall come home with very much money after touring England. I can hear you say 'Oh she needn't stay in such a grand place as the Continental, for it is a grand place, the grandest in Egypt'. But I'm enjoying it. The Superintendent of the Coast Hospital [Dr Millard] is staying here. He is one of the 'top dogs' in the medical part of our regiment here. He doesn't forget any of his nurses.

> I came off night duty last Monday, & to our surprise we were given three days off duty so we came down here. We went to the Australian Gen Hosp No 3 yesterday. It was 'Anzac Day'. The anniversary of the landing of Gallipoli. There was a memorial service in the morning. In the afternoon there were sports & a concert in the evening. We enjoyed ourselves, as we met so many we knew. Lots of people from the Coast …

Sunburn, sand – and slack

Tomorrow we go back to Alex. It is frightfully hot here.
50 times hotter than Alexandria. It is giving us a taste of
what the summer will be like. I'm not looking forward to it a
bit. (26 April 1916)

Work was light, apart from two large intakes of wounded and sick.[1]
A British Army garrison of 8000 men was under siege in Kut Al
Amara, a town about 100 miles from Baghdad in Mesopotamia.
Most of Edie's patients came from the relief expeditions sent to help:

We are no longer slack. A large number of men came in
yesterday, if I mention names, as to where the men came from, it
will probably be crossed out. I'm working in tents & I don't like
it a bit, in this heat ... these last two days we have not been able
to think of the heat we have been too busy. But I came home to
dinner without a dry stitch on today. (14 May 1916)

Conditions in Egypt were uncomfortable for the medics, but in
Mesopotamia they were almost unbearable for the besieged soldiers
who had been reduced to eating their horses and mules. All of the
relief efforts sent to Kut had failed with heavy casualties, and the
survivors inside Kut were ultimately forced to surrender after nearly
five months. The remnants of the relief forces returned to Egypt.
'[W]e are all to be on duty [at 3.30 am] as the train is expected
from Suez at that hour. Poor beggars coming across the desert from
Suez in this heat. The hospital train has often to be shunted off from
place to place so as not to interrupt the general traffic' (9 July 1916).
Another summer under the implacable Egyptian sun was steadily
unfolding. 'Oh! how I hate ploughing through the sand!' (27 May
1916)

Edie was used to humidity, having grown up in Sydney.
Alexandria, though, was something else. Moisture hung above the

Mediterranean, smudging the horizon. Perspiration ran down her spine and dampened her armpits:

> It seems to get hotter & hotter each day. We never have a dry stitch on. I have taken to wearing white shoes & stockings, they are much easier to the feet than black in the sand. (30 June 1916)

> I am working in tents ... I shall be a nice 'Nut Browne Mayde' when I come home. I wear a hat all the time on duty to ... help to keep out the glare of the sand in one's eyes. (9 May 1916)

The summer of 1916 became one of swimming, sailing, sewing and reading; it could have been idyllic were it not occurring between shifts in a wartime hospital. Having initially dismissed the idea of bathing here as the sea and beach were 'so dirty' (5 March 1916), Edie now wrote that 'the people here have gone off their heads over swimming. They want me to every time I'm off duty ... Yesterday I went bathing & thoroughly enjoyed it' (25 June 1916). She made herself a swimming costume on a sewing machine in the Singer machine shop, which had been hired by the thoughtful women of the Red Cross for the nurses' use: 'It is a splendid little worker' (16 July 1916). Yet, even in a neck-to-knee costume, she managed to become sunburned, and felt exposed tiptoeing from beach cabins – also provided by the Red Cross – to the seashore. There were men everywhere. But how to cling to Matron Watson's primly conservative views on mixed bathing? As it turned out, the men were just enjoying the water too:

> Do you remember how much I was against continental bathing. Well I tried to get into the water before the doctors came. But of course they were in the water very soon after I was. But dear me they don't take much notice of us. It is our behaviour in the water if the men take an advantage. (19 August 1916)

Sunburn, sand – and slack

The mood of the Mediterranean was changeable. Every month or two the bodies of drowned soldiers were brought into the hospital: 'The [men] venture further out than we do. Though I go out a good way. But still, them being in the water makes it safer for us. When I have been in the water with a number of non-swimmers I always felt a bit nervous lest they should get out of their depth' (19 August 1916).

Edie and Evelyn Swannell shopped in town – 'it is just a nice [ride] on top of a tram for a piastre, only the tram takes an hour when a taxi takes 20 minutes' (25 June 1916) – and picnicked and sailed:

> Yesterday we went out for another sail. It was glorious, just enough wind to send us spinning through the water. The Home Sister was with us. She asked me if Sydney Harbour was at all like Port Alexandria. What a surprise she would get if she came to Sydney! Port Alexandria is one big open space with a breakwater, to make it a Port. There are no beautiful green cliffs, & no little inlets with sandy beaches. You can go round the harbour in little more than an hour. (30 June 1916)

All the while Edie speculated how, and when, she and Sister Swannell would move on. France, near the Australians and the action, sounded increasingly attractive. A hospital ship would do, but their prospects for leaving did not look bright:

> All our allowances have been taken off our cheques … As the time is up for many of the English girls, they are not signing on but sending in their resignations. As many as three a day have been sent in. So a notice went up to say that nurses are to reconsider their resignations [which seems to me, to be another way of saying the word 'conscript'. Full particulars are to be given why resignation is wanted. (30 July 1916)]. At any rate a lot have

managed to get their resignations through. They are to be sent to England on hospital ships. So these girls have to work their passage filling up the places we should be doing. Very few hospital ships come to Alex, so you see our chances are few. I don't want to go to England in November, I would sooner wait till the following April. When I hope war will be over. (6 August 1916)

In her summer of bathing and waiting, Edie never mentioned what was unfolding in France. Initially, she probably did not know.

I got two letters from France a few days ago. One from Dickson & Cawood. They are still in Marseilles with very little to do, expecting to go north any time. They are having a jolly good time sightseeing. The other letter is from a Coast Sister belonging to the No 1 AGHospital. That hospital is all split up & put amongst the British Hospitals. According to Sister's letter they are unhappy & do not understand how I put up with the English girls here. She is quite near the firing line & can hear the guns distinctly, though she says they are not busy. (19 June 1916)

As the year warmed into summer, so events on the Western Front picked up pace. The German attack on Verdun, launched in February 1916, had settled into a vicious battle of attrition, intended, in the words of German chief of general staff Erich von Falkenhayn, to 'bleed France white'. Verdun would become a drawn-out bloody campaign which cost each side as many as 400 000 casualties over the course of the year.

The French and the British had been planning a joint offensive on the Somme, but with much of the French Army being drawn in to service at Verdun, the British shouldered the burden of conducting the campaign. On 1 July 1916, the British Army launched the offensive to the north of Paris, in part to try to break the deadlock on the Western Front, and also to relieve the pressure on the French

Sunburn, sand – and slack

at Verdun. The first day of the battle of the Somme was disastrous, however. The preceding week's artillery bombardment had failed to destroy the German defences, and in many parts of the line the attacking infantry walked into unrestricted artillery and machine-gun fire. Nearly 60 000 British fell that day; almost 20 000 of them died.

Fresh to the Western Front, the Australians were soon called into the frontline. On 19 July 1916 the last of the Australian infantry to arrive on the Western Front became the first to enter battle when some battalions of the 5th Australian Division took part in a feint attack at Fromelles. Designed to draw German reserves away from the main battle on the Somme, Fromelles was a disaster, for both the Australians and the British 61st Division, which also took part in the attack. The 5th Australian Division suffered 5500 casualties, including nearly 2000 dead in twenty-four hours – a macabre record which remains Australia's worst ever twenty-four hours in war.

Four days later, to the south, the 1st Australian Division attacked the fortified village of Pozières on the left flank of the battle of the Somme. The village was successfully captured, but the 1st, 2nd and 4th Australian Divisions remained in the area, conducting attack after attack on German lines to the north of the village, and on the fortified farmstead known as Mouquet Farm. Their time on the Somme was in many respects characterised by the unending artillery bombardment that was unlike anything they had experienced at Gallipoli. Tens of thousands of shells screamed then exploded with a roar all along the line with little respite. The earth quaked and bulged and spewed forth great showers of soil that buried and reburied the living and the dead. The air choked with smoke, dust and gas and the stink of cordite. Pozières itself ceased to exist – all that was left was a large patch of brick dust. Men were killed by the concussion, ripped apart, obliterated. In six weeks, the AIF's losses were roughly equivalent to those they had suffered in the entire eight-month Gallipoli campaign.

Whatever war news Edie had, she expected her family to be as well, if not better, informed than she, particularly so far as the Australians were concerned: 'Dad must write & tell me what he thinks of the war, its duration & other things concerning the war & its effects on Australia, & anything about Australia & its trouble. You know, no one talks to us about Australia, it's always Blighty (tommies' name for home)' (22 July 1916).

Her thoughts kept circling back to what might happen to her:

> I have just received a telegram from Crocker Brown ... She is going to England on the hospital ship 'Essequibo' a boat we have been waiting for some time to come in ... & now we hear that the Australians are going on her instead of us ... Oh Dear! Crocker is the last friend I shall have in Egypt. I do not in the least like being left behind. (19 August 1916)

> Here we are again still in the 17th BGH. Still no sign of getting away ... Several wards are closed, now also several lines of tents. 200 patients went away on Friday to England, they had been waiting some of them for 2 mths. The latest rumour is that the Australian Sisters are to go to France, those who are working in British Hospitals. We often wonder who it is that puts rumours into existence, sometimes we wonder if there is a spice of truth in any rumour. (17 September 1916)

Just once in this frustrating time did Edie and Swannell have a difference, arising from the most unlikely of sources:

> At dinner hour Swannell brought a chameleon with her. When I found out that the horrid thing was to be our room mate I objected strongly, so strongly that Swannell got huffy & said that if I held my tongue that she would send it back to hospital by the mule ambulance driver which she has just done much to

Sunburn, sand – and slack

my relief. It has just struck me that you may not know what a chameleon is … It is the ugliest thing & most repulsive I've seen except an octopus. If you put a chameleon on some green leaves it will become green, hold it in your hand & it will become pink, put it on our grey frock & it will become grey. It is rather interesting to see it change colour. So much for a chameleon. (9 September 1916)

Then, at last, the wait was over:

Matron sent for me, to tell me I was to go on the hospital ship 'Essequibo' next Friday possibly. We may not go straight to England, but will probably go to Salonika & Malta. Swannell is to go too. How excited she is. I feel a bit doubtful about her. She is a very bad sailor. At any rate one can only hope for the best … I think I would sooner be on a ship than in Greece. In winter I believe Salonika is in mud up to your ankles. It isn't safe to go out. The nurses are like prisoners in the hospital grounds. So I think we are fortunate. We shall in all probability see Malta & Gibraltar. Next letter I hope I shall write on the Essequibo. I am writing to Uncle Harry now. (24 September 1916)

On 1 October 1916 Edie wrote her final letter from 17BGH in Alexandria:

Dear Mum Dad Grace & Queen

Writing this address for the last time. We are already packed waiting for the ambulance to take us to the wharf. After eighteen months of Egypt I wonder what is in store for us.

We are to embark on the Australian ship 'Wandilla' which will take us to Lemnos then we are to embark on the 'Essequibo' there.

Friday night they gave us a 'send off' … I will leave you to imagine our excitement. We have said Goodbye all round. Matron telling us that our work had been excellent while we were in Egypt … I will write to you as soon as we get to Mudros. Goodness knows where I shall be when you get this.

Much love to you all, hope you are well. Hope the warm weather won't bring Mum's headaches again. While you are sitting on the verandah admiring the sea, you can imagine me on a wintry sea & enjoying it.

Love from Edie

22

THE NICEST SHIP I HAVE BEEN ON

They left Alexandria on 1 October 1916 in the Australian hospital ship *Wandilla*, over a sea 'as smooth as glass' (31 December 1916), taking a great number of their patients from 17BGH. They were bound for Lemnos then Salonika, where Edie and Evelyn Swannell would join HMHS *Essequibo*. However, it would not be until December that Edie, always wary of the censor, felt able to tell her family about her experiences on the ships. Close to port in Egypt, she decided to write with freedom at last, saying, 'I am disobeying the censors. I don't know what harm I could do, for all the world knows what I write about' (17 December 1916).[1]

In two long letters she described her first two-and-a-half months at sea. She took great pleasure in matching the geography to what she knew of its history – augmented by information from the doctors, who were fully versed in the classics – starting with the *Wandilla*'s crossing to Lemnos:

> We found the Aegean Sea very interesting. The doctors seemed to know most of the islands & the history attached to them, one was [where] Homer was buried, another where St Paul preached … Most of the islands are barren & look uninhabitable. We arrived in Mudros harbour at midday Oct 3rd …
>
> The harbour looked a good one, but the shores looked barren like the islands we have passed. Mudros Harbour is a naval base now. As we entered we [passed between] two lines of buoys – it looked to me – called the 'booms'. These are stretched between

the shores of the entrance to the harbour to prevent submarines entering. There are two trawlers or mine-sweepers guarding the opening of the boom to let us through. We brought the patients to Mudros in order to tranship them to the hospital ship Britannic. There were many hospital ships in harbour all waiting for [her]. About three hours after we arrived the Britannic hoved in sight, a monster she looked. She was the biggest ship afloat except the German ships which are locked away in harbours of their own. The Britannic is 48 000 tons, imagine her size against the 'Essequibo' which is only 8000 tons. It is said that these big ships as the Aquitania [and] Mauretania are too big for most of our harbours such as Malta, Alex etc so the smaller ships have to come to these big ones to load up. She commenced to load up almost immediately she arrived. Two small ships unload at the same time, one on either side …

On the evening of the 3rd there was a most gorgeous sunset & when it became dark the hospital ships were lit up with their green lights & red crosses, they made a pretty sight indeed, and at 8pm the war ships, there were plenty of them, flashed their search lights … Some of the searchlights flashed along the water, presumably [looking] for periscopes, others lit up the ships in harbour while others searched the skies probably for aircraft. Imagine the ships being all lit up with their red & green lights … To me it seemed a wonderful display.

Wednesday evening we left for Salonika. On the following morning we woke up to find ourselves near Salonika harbour, we were just passing Mount Olympus. This mountain has some historical features. St Paul preached there. The old Greek gods, Queenie would know something about them[2] … are supposed to have had their games, battles & their laws & all the[ir] deeds … from this mountain, Jupiter Mars & those mythical people …

The nicest ship I have been on

on the 'Wandilla' the doctors would talk about the wanderings of St Paul in the Aegean. I found I could not always follow what they were talking about. (31 December 1916)

The Macedonian port of Salonika had become the base for an Allied attempt to aid Serbia, which was under attack by the Central Powers of Germany, Austria-Hungary and Bulgaria. It was connected to Belgrade by railway and would remain the centre of what was known as the Salonika front through the fall and eventual liberation of Serbia. When coming into the harbour, Edie observed that the city looked very pretty and interesting at a distance. Most houses were symmetrical blocks, painted pastel colours, with bright shutters and red-tiled roofs. However, up close the town was 'frightfully smelly, one would like to hold one's nose while walking through some of the streets' (12 November 1916). A group of thirteen nurses walked uphill beyond the crumbling ancient city walls and found themselves in a village:

> We saw some soldiers who couldn't speak English. We tried to make them understand the way back through the wall. They conducted [us] to a place which proved to be a prison, thinking we wanted to see the prison. The panorama was beautiful & mountain air was beautiful, we thoroughly enjoyed ourselves. (12 November 1916)

They had left Alexandria expecting to join HMHS *Essequibo* and were surprised and disappointed not to find her in Mudros:

> But imagine our dismay when we found she was not in Salonika. The ships officers on the 'Wandilla' began to tease us saying that 'Essequibo' didn't want us. Indeed, we began to think we should end up by finding ourselves in one of the Salonika hospitals. But we were very pleased to see the 'Essequibo' steam in at 10am.

We felt that we were in sight of our home at last. (31 December 1916)

Edie and Evelyn Swannell boarded her in the evening on 5 October 1916.

> The next morning, Friday morning, we were allotted our wards. I was given the officers ward ... It was rather strange the way Matron looked around us all & said she wanted one for the officers who would be firm & not fuss. I was chosen much to my astonishment. But still I haven't found them much trouble.
>
> That afternoon we began to load with patients. The patients were brought from the shore in a ferry boat very much like one of Watson's Bay boats.
>
> I had very few officers in my wards so two of them were taken up by tommies who thoroughly enjoyed the idea of being in an officer ward. They were as good as gold no trouble at all. (31 December 1916)

Almost every hospital ship was different because few were purpose-built. Britain had used dedicated hospital ships to support its navy at war since the 1600s, but the current demand was unprecedented and vessels of various configurations and sizes were converted to meet the need.

Once a ship was identified for conversion, its medical officer was responsible for fitting it out to meet the specifications of the Royal Navy's Medical Department.[3] Cabins or saloons should be used for officers' wards and the main deck for the men. The operating theatres, preparation rooms, galleys, bakeries and disinfector should be on the upper deck, for maximum light and ventilation. Any outpatients and dental departments were preferably near a gangway

The nicest ship I have been on

for easy access on and off the ship. The infectious wards, mortuary and laundry were to be located on the poop deck (the highest rear deck), from where foul air and steam would be carried away behind the ship.[4]

The *Essequibo* had been built for the Royal Mail Steam Packet Company, and was the perfect size for conversion to a hospital ship, after which she catered for eleven doctors, sixteen nurses, seventy-six other medical staff (mostly orderlies) and almost 600 patients.

On 6 October 1916, Edie had written her first carefully self-censored letter on board the *Essequibo*:

Dear Mum Dad Grace & Queen,

This is our first day on this ship. She will probably be my home now till April next. I can neither mention names of places or condition of patients. So there will be very little I can say.

This is the nicest ship I have been on. Our cabins are airy & convenient. We each have one to ourselves.

I am working in the officers ward. I have always escaped this before. I don't know that I shall like it.

I wonder when we shall get to England. I hope at Christmas time. I do hope in April that they will dump us in England & not back in Alex, for I shall not like another summer in Egypt. I think I've had enough.

Don't forget to address my letters to the Hospital Ship Essequibo GPO London. They will send our letters to us where ever we may be.

I shall not write every week, as I did before, & you mustn't be disappointed …

I must close now. Hope Mum & you all are well.

Much love from
Edie

From October to December they had criss-crossed the Mediterranean, making multiple journeys between Salonika and the hospitals on Malta. Edie knew it was the chaplain who pored over their letters, searching for any scraps of information that necessitated the attention of his blue censor's pencil or, at worst, destruction of the offending pages:

> The Padre when he censors this will smile when I say he is very like Dad to look at. I can't help looking at him (the Minister). He is darker than Dad & hasn't Dad's rosy complexion … He is, I should think, Dad's age.[5] He has lived some years in Turkey and was in Smyrna (Asia Minor) when war broke out. He is going to give us a small lecture about the Turks, their conditions of living & their attitude towards the Allies. We go to his services regularly. His sermons are very good! (28 October 1916)

She had limited her weekly letters to mysterious hints about where she was:

> It is the same cry all round. What are we going to write about? I wish I could write freely about our walk yesterday. There isn't much scope for exercise on the boat's promenade, & on the boat deck the lifeboats are all in the way for a vigorous walk.
> (12 November 1916)

The nicest ship I have been on

If ever I missed a mail would you think I was sick? It is terrible trying to write about nothing. If I were sick, you would soon hear it or if anything happened to us, so if I should miss one don't be alarmed. I can't say things on the sea are not interesting, they are, but I cannot write about them, but as Aunt Alice says in her last letter I can cherish my memory & unburden it when I see you all. (27 November 1916)

During this period Edie could at least describe a little of life on board:

Life at present is pleasant on [the] hospital ship. I am getting as soft as pap. We have had no work since we have been here. Still, it shows that the boys are not getting sick or wounded in great numbers. But I feel I'm not earning my salt. I used to think that I couldn't feel well, if I didn't work. But that is quite wrong. I sleep well, eat well & do nothing but laze & sew. I never get a headache or even an eye ache with all the sewing & reading I do. (22 October 1916)

Our last trip was rather a rough one, but I have found my sea legs & haven't been sick, our ship both pitched & rocked, sometimes I was toiling up the ward, & after a while I would run down it without stopping [and] find myself over a patient's bed. But somehow it doesn't make one bad-tempered. But the greatest thing is not being sick. (27 November 1916)

On Tuesday last the Orderlies of the ship got up sports & gave us a concert in the evening. Their sports were very funny. My sides ached with laughter. The sisters gave them a prize for the tug-of-war. Their first item was a pillow fight on a greasy pole. The next was a windsail race. The wrestling on horseback was rather dangerous … [I] wondered how many casualties but these boys can stand a lot. Then there was a jam & bun race … Oh dear! the state of their faces was very comical covered [with] splodges of jam. In the evening the concert was really very good. They gave skits on the doings of everybody on board from Captain Padre OC & down. No one except the sisters were left out. This was all given to celebrate the anniversary of the ship being made into a hospital ship.

Just at present the ship is rocking frightfully. Yesterday we were all sick, but today somehow I have got my sea legs. (8 December 1916)

After leaving Salonika the first time they steamed for Malta, arriving 'on Tuesday midday [10 October 1916]. It is very pretty when coming into harbour. We discharged our patients during the afternoon' (31 December 1916).

Established by the Knights of St John in the sixteenth century, Malta's capital, Valletta, seemed to emerge from the sea like a mythical Atlantis. The dense city skyline was dotted with church spires and dominated by the dome of St John's Cathedral. The *Essequibo* docked in an elegant harbour hewn from pale rock that reflected the changing light: almond in the morning, glaring white under the endless midday sky, rose gold at sunset. In summer it was suffocatingly hot and humid, although relief was available in crystal coves for bathers prepared to pick their way over the small island's jagged edges. Under a gentler autumn sun, Edie and Swannell explored Valletta's neat paved streets, purchased lace and marvelled at one of the most splendidly decorated cathedrals in Christendom:

Wednesday we had the day free. So we went ashore crossing the grand harbour to the customs house … When we got ashore we had to go up a lift to get to the top of the rock. The view of the harbour from the top is magnificent. At night time at this lift, the sight is really wonderful. The rowing boats on the harbour are very much the shape of a gondola in Venice. At the nose of these little boats is a single light. There are thousands of these boats or dhisers [dghajsas] the natives call them, with a single light they look like thousands of fireflies darting in all directions.

While on shore we visited the chapel of bones. This chapel is underground, & is decorated with the human bones of the Maltese men who defended the island against the Turks in 1576 … After leaving this chapel we went to St John's cathedral. The outside is unpretentious, but the inside gave us a pleasing surprise, for I was never in such a beautiful place before. It is Roman Catholic of course … One chapel has a gate of solid silver. Another has a sculptured figure of the Madonna & child. The expression of the Madonna was wonderful. How a sculptor can get such a human expression out of marble is beyond my power of imagination. (31 December 1916)

The next day they sailed back to Salonika, arriving on 14 October 1916.

There were seven other hospital ships besides ourselves. A tug belonging to the 'St Georges' the flag ship took us to the shore. We walked along the seafront. The streets & roads are of cobblestones which are extremely hard to walk upon especially [in] wet weather, as they are very slippery.

The heat was great, almost overpowered us, the smell & filth of the place is indescribable. We were so disgusted we took a garry [sic] back to the landing place & were glad to get back to the ship vowing & declaring we would never go again. But on Tuesday the Padre & the 3rd officer took four of us to the shore again, & we were conducted to an ancient church called

St Demetrius ... Beside this is a Russian bell. It is huge. Russia probably gave this bell to the church when Salonika became [a] Greek possession after the Balkan War ...

Salonika has been in the hands of the Turks for 500 years. On St Demetrius day Oct 26 1912 the city was restored to the Greeks. Which city we now use for troops to pass through. We saw today some Battalions of French reinforcements pass through. We went through some Greek bazaars. There was some Turkish curios, but the Padre, who has been in Turkey, said that the curios were of exorbitant price, so we didn't buy anything. Besides I was not particularly struck with anything I saw.

I hope I have made this interesting. It is hard to put into writing what interests one & make it interesting for others to read.
(31 December 1916)

23

PASSING THROUGH ALL DANGERS

'After our third trip to Malta, we had orders to go back to Salonika. We were a day out at sea when Matron came & told us that we were searching for the people who were in boats after the sinking of that P&O ship the "Arabia"' (17 December 1916). The RMS *Arabia* had been en route to England from Australia, carrying among other things more than 300 crew and 400 passengers, 20 tons of tin, 600 tons of flour, 619 bales of fine Australian wool and a large amount of Australian mail.[1] After leaving Port Said on 5 November 1916, the ship entered what passenger Mrs Paula Scotland, travelling to England to join her husband, a light horseman on sick leave, called 'the danger zone'. The ship was blacked out, portholes closed, lifeboats swung out in readiness. A 4.7-inch gun and three gunners had been taken aboard in Egypt and she had an escort of patrol boats until 9 pm on the second day out.[2] Paula Scotland remembered that the next morning broke calm and beautiful. 'The sea was too glassy. It seemed uncanny … About 11 am we were sitting on the deck on the starboard side, right against the railing. My baby was playing at my feet. "Here she comes." That loud exclamation and, almost simultaneously, we were thrown to the deck with the force of a terrific bump.'[3]

German submarine UB-43 torpedoed the liner around 100 nautical miles south of the Greek Peloponnese, killing several engine-room crew. In 'dreamlike calmness' people moved to the boat stations and watched as lifeboats were lowered, then climbed in. 'In 15 minutes all the living had left the vessel.'[4]

Aboard HMHS *Essequibo*, everyone sprang to action. Edie wrote, 'We went to all the preparation we could think of, such as hot water bags, hot blankets, stimulants, clothing etc for we knew that she (the Arabia) had left Sydney with women & children on board. The excitement was supreme on board' (17 December 1916).

No more lives were lost on the *Arabia*. Passengers and crew were safely scooped up within two hours by minesweepers and the SS *City of Marseilles*, all the while watching the 'weird sight' of the liner 'so huge and so helpless … settling slowly into the sea … [until] she seemed to give a deep groan. A puff of black smoke rose and she slipped down stern first'.[5] Edie lamented,

> We searched all day & we felt utterly miserable to think we couldn't find them. Later we heard that a cruiser had been before us & picked them up. Poor things they had been in the small boats for many hours. Strange to say we were very disappointed to think that someone had slipped in ahead of us. We all wanted a baby in our ward & wondered if there would be enough babies to go around. (17 December 1916)

Despite the risks, the Mediterranean seethed with traffic. Although the ocean-going courses offered better odds, there was no safe route to England, so shipping ran the gamut of the shorter run via the Suez Canal and safe harbours in Egypt, Malta and Gibraltar. It did not always pay off. The *Argus* reported, 'Since the war began the P and O Company has been carrying on its Australian service under great difficulties, owing to the diversion of so many of its steamers to other work, and to the losses suffered. The company has lost five vessels, four during the present year, [all bar one] directly or indirectly due to the war'.[6] Edie recognised the dangers faced by the commercial shipping companies:

Hope we shall get letters from Australia. But I wouldn't be at all surprised if they are all at the bottom of the sea. I can't explain further. Still it is much better for you to get my letters as I think the passage is pretty safe from Alex. Though it is not very safe till they get to Alex. So if you don't get my letters you can imagine them at the bottom of the sea. Being a hospital ship we are very safe, particularly the run we are doing just at present.
(12 November 1916)

Not long after this, however, Edie discovered even hospital ships were at risk.

> In due time we went to Salonika & brought patients back to Malta. Then we sailed again for Salonika. When we were amongst the islands of the Aegean Sea the terrible news came that the Hospital Ship Britannic had been torpedoed, we all seemed numbed at the news, we were not very far from where she had gone down. We had orders to go dead slow. We went so slow, that sometimes we wondered if we were going at all. At 8 in the morning we sighted the 'Braemar Castle'. To me she seemed as if she had stopped.
>
> We got to Salonika safely. I can truly say I did not feel frightened or nervous, I don't think any of us did. Somehow when one is on the sea & passing through all dangers without a hurt, we are inclined to feel that we are always safe. The boys who have been at the front tell us the same thing …
>
> We got to Salonika & received orders to go to Pyreus [Piraeus] a port near Athens to pick up the people of the 'Britannic'. Then the news came the 'Braemar Castle' had gone down. I cannot describe our feelings. We knew that the 'Braemar' was full of patients. (17 December 1916)

HMHS *Britannic* was one of the biggest ships on the planet. After her sister ship the RMS *Titanic* sank in 1912, the *Britannic*, still under construction in Belfast, benefitted from design changes including a section of double hull to protect the boiler and engine rooms, and five sets of motorised davits.[7]

On 21 November 1916 the great hospital ship was steaming for Lemnos with more than 1000 crew and medical personnel on board when an explosion shook the front starboard. A torpedo was suspected, though the damage was later blamed on one of the mines laid by German submarine U-73. The watertight doors were closed but damage meant that six compartments were filling with water regardless. Although built to float if up to six of her compartments were flooded, as she listed water poured in through portholes the nurses had opened against regulations in order to ventilate the wards. The *Britannic* was doomed.

An SOS was transmitted and the captain ordered the foundering ship towards the island of Kea, where he hoped to beach her. Passengers gathered their valuables and waited at their boat stations. Concerned by the way the ship was listing, crew lowered two lifeboats without orders to do so. The engines were stopped, but too late to prevent the lifeboats and their unfortunate passengers from being drawn into the churning propellers. Around forty-five minutes after the explosion the captain gave the order to abandon ship, which was achieved bare minutes before she pitched further starboard and dug her bow into the sea floor. Metal groaned as her stern reared skywards, pausing momentarily before crashing down, then slipping under. Fifty-five minutes after she was hit, the *Britannic* was gone. Within two hours all survivors had been plucked from the sea. Most of the thirty who died had been in the crushed lifeboats.

Edie subsequently met nurses who were saved from the *Britannic*. One told her,

[E]veryone with the exception of the stewards & some of the
crew, kept their heads. They were all at breakfast when the ship
was struck. All exclaimed 'What was that'. Then the commander
stood up asking all the ladies to be quiet as all was alright. They
then received orders to go to their cabins. Then the ship's siren
blew by which they knew they [were to] go to their boat stations.
The nurse who was telling us about this, said no sound was
made from the Sisters who were 80 in number. Everyone waited
for orders & did as they were told. When the roll was called
only one orderly was missing & he it seemed had gone to his
room just before the ship was struck. It is really wonderful what
discipline will do. Imagine 300 orderlies medical officers &
80 sisters being all saved without panic. (17 December 1916)

Two days after the *Britannic*'s demise, HMHS *Braemar Castle* was
bound for Malta with 400 patients boarded in Salonika when she
struck a mine south of Greece's Cape Sounion:

[O]ur orders were cancelled & we were sent to Syra one of
the islands in the Aegean Sea to pick up the patients of the
'Braemar' ... We had great difficulty getting these patients on,
the sea was very rough ... The people of the island nearly went
mad with excitement I believe. They couldn't do enough for
the patients. One poor fellow died, & almost all the populace
turned out to do homage. One patient I got in my ward had an
injured spine. He was no worse for the misfortune which shows
the discipline of the men in the hour of danger ... We got them
safely into Malta. (17 December 1916)

The *Essequibo* returned to Salonika on a route many miles out of
its course, no doubt to avoid what now appeared to be an extensive
minefield among the Greek islands.

We got into Salonika a little while before the Hospital Ship 'Letitia' came in, whose Matron was our home sister at the 17th. So Swannell sent a note over to the Letitia asking Matron to come & have tea with us. When she came over she told us of how the Letitia had picked up the people of two torpedoed passenger boats. One was French & the other was British. The British one, the 'City of Birmingham', was bound for India carrying cadets. Matron said she felt proud to think that she was English to see the order & preciseness of the people of the British ship. For the Frenchmen fought with one another to get on the Hospital Ship. They all seemed to have lost their heads. (17 December 1916)

The matron said a cadet on the British ship jumped into the water to rescue two babies who were being carried away on the waves of a rough sea. The boy held one 'in his teeth & the other under his arm'. Another 'little child of 5 years … finding herself safe after hours in the water, stood up & sang "God Save the King", the only way she could give vent to her gratitude' (17 December 1916).

Edie hung breathlessly on every word of the survivors' stories. The stoic heroism, and the confidence purposefully radiated by the *Essequibo*'s captain, instilled in her the faith that, if the moment came, their training would come into effect and calm fortitude would prevail:

> Hope you people are not anxious about me. We are all prepared for emergencies. I feel that nothing will happen to us. Even if we have our full complement of patients on board when an accident happens there is more boat accommodation than is actually necessary. The Captain says that all could & would be saved if when orders are [given they are followed] with coolness & precision. (8 December 1916)

After all her news of the dangers lurking in the Mediterranean, Edie reassured her family about their preparations for emergencies:

> If an accident happens we are to go to our wards if we have patients & help them with their belts. There is a special belt for me in the ward. Then I have to wait orders. When there are no patients we go to our cabins & get the belt that is there for us. When the ship's siren sounds we go to our boat stations. We all know our own boat. In each boat there is a number of the crew, several orderlies, a ship's officer & where there are sisters a medical officer. We have boat & fire drill every week. It is so arranged that the sisters who are friends go together & if possible the medical officer who is in that sister's ward. Swannell is with me & we have my medical officer, who is an awfully nice fellow. All the boats are slung out over the side of the ship ready to lower down. In the boat there is enough provisions & water to last a week. When I go up on the boatdeck I look in the boats, there are several pairs of oars, also a sail. There are lanterns & oil too. (17 December 1916)

She added, somewhat less reassuringly,

> While at sea, when going to bed [w]e have to wear pyjamas … we put in readiness our coat & dressing gown the sleeves of the latter inside the sleeves of the coat. In the pocket of my coat I have put several handkerchiefs, a pair [of] stocking[s], a silk scarf & a flask of Brandy …

> Must close now hope you are all well. I wonder where I shall spend next Christmas. May be at home. (17 December 1916)

24

THE WAR AT SEA

On the continent, millions of soldiers milled in and behind hundreds of miles of trench networks that, on the Western Front, twisted some 470 miles from the Belgian coast to the Swiss border, through battlefields with names by now well known to the Australian public: Flanders, the Somme, Aisne, Verdun. Theirs were the mud-stained faces of the war. But no matter how well trained and determined, they could not succeed if they were not transported to and from the battlefront and adequately fed and equipped, and, in this, the war at sea was critical. Everybody knew that the war must ultimately be won on the ground, but First World War German naval commander Vice Admiral Eberhard Weichold later wrote that Germany lost the war by failing to break British seapower,[1] and Winston Churchill observed that Admiral John Jellicoe, commander of the Royal Navy's Grand Fleet, was the one man who could lose the war in an afternoon.

The British Empire was founded on seapower. Since Tudor times English ships had sailed the world, establishing trade routes, carrying export items to the colonies and returning laden with all manner of goods: bullion, gems and fabrics from India, the Empire's jewel in the crown; tea and silk from China; minerals from Africa; sugar from the West Indies; spices from the East Indies; cotton from America; timber from Canada; wool and grain from Australia – the kinds of cargoes carried by the clippers that had borne apprentice seaman Charles Blake across the world. By 1914 Britain was one of the wealthiest nations on earth. It boasted the world's largest navy and approximately half the world's merchant tonnage.[2] (The size of fleets – and losses – was measured in tonnage. This was

The war at sea

a more useful indicator than the number of ships, for one 'ship' could be a fishing trawler crewed by a few men, or a leviathan like *Britannic* that could carry thousands of people, the loss of which represented a much greater impact on time, money and resources.) Britain's security depended on maintaining its superiority on the sea. This had been severely threatened by Germany's willingness to develop its own navy, and the ensuing naval race was an important factor in the outbreak of war in 1914.

Although they owned the greatest naval forces on earth, neither Britain nor Germany sought a direct confrontation. Britain would rather concentrate on trade, while Germany could not be certain its navy could win. When contact between surface vessels was unavoidable, the Germans almost invariably lost. In November 1914 SMS *Emden* was sunk by HMAS *Sydney* – the Australian ship using British technology and methods. In December 1914 German Admiral von Spee's East Asia Squadron was destroyed in the battle of the Falkland Islands, and in January 1915 the Germans lost one cruiser and had two more badly damaged in the battle of Dogger Bank.

These battles ensured that the bulk of the German fleet stayed in home waters, and Britain used its vast surface fleets to mount a naval blockade that would nullify any threat Germany's ships posed to global shipping routes. However, German submarines posed a considerable threat.

In 1909, age-old understandings of the rules of maritime law and war were formalised in the London Declaration Concerning the Laws of Naval War, to which both Great Britain and Germany were signatories. The declaration determined that merchant shipping should be given warning before being boarded or fired upon, and in fact seemed to try to do away with the capture of merchant shipping during war. Great Britain, for one, ended up not ratifying the declaration because it considered disrupting enemy supply lines a crucial strategy. One of the great deficiencies of the agreement was its failure to deal with submarines.

Both sides had submarines, but Germany's capabilities became devastatingly clear in September 1914 after three ageing Royal Navy light cruisers were torpedoed by the same U-boat in the North Sea. The cruisers had been lumbering straight ahead and abreast, in conditions thought too rough for submarines. They were easy pickings for U-9, which first attacked His Majesty's Ship (HMS) *Aboukir*, then the *Hogue* and *Cressy* as each, in turn, went to the aid of survivors. More than 1400 sailors died. The men of U-9 were all awarded the Iron Cross, a decoration for exceptional courage in the field.[3] The British public was shaken out of its complacency.

Unterseeboots ('undersea boats', widely known as U-boats) made quick hit-and-run attacks against much larger craft, and laid mines in busy shipping lanes – no matter that civilian or hospital ships could fall victim. Germany increased production as U-boats proved effective and cheaper to construct and man than warships.

The First World War did see one major naval engagement – the battle of Jutland on 31 May 1916. It had been one of the few snatches of specific war news Edie wrote home about: '[R]umour today that there has been a naval battle in the North Sea. Some say 14 British ships have sunk & 16 of the Germans. I wonder if it is true. What a tremendous amount of life must be lost' (4 June 1916).

This clash near the Danish coast was the only occasion on which the opposing battlefleets faced each other en masse. It was not the decisive battle the belligerents desired. Lacking a clear outcome, the British press was merciless and the public disappointed by the Grand Fleet's failure to deliver another 'Trafalgar'. Yet although Britain lost more ships (twice the tonnage and more than twice as many men[4]) and Germany's claim to victory hurt British pride, Jutland inflicted so much damage upon the smaller German fleet that it was unable to break the blockade and never challenged the British again. Germany's policy of avoiding such encounters was reinforced – the enemy was forced to revise its tactics.

The German approach to war at sea would soon have a

result that was truly shocking. In early June 1916 news broke that Lord Kitchener was dead.

The secretary of state for war had been the face of Britain's war effort. It was his image on the recruitment posters, with piercing eyes and sweeping moustache. It was his finger bursting forth from the page as he admonished, 'Britons, I want YOU', raising thousands, eventually millions, of New Army volunteers. He was the soldier who ultimately crushed the uprising in the Sudan with a barrage of western weaponry at the battle of Omdurman and took command of the problematic second phase of the Boer War, unflinchingly continuing a policy of scorched earth and concentration camps to counter the Boers' guerrilla tactics.[5] He was an autocrat who frustrated military and political leaders with his incorrigible indifference to administrative procedures. If his methods caused disquiet for some, and if politicians debated his performance in the House of Commons and attempted to sheet home to him a goodly part of the responsibility for the Gallipoli fiasco, it was of no moment to the people. They loved him. Earl Kitchener of Khartoum knew how to win.

Days after Jutland, Kitchener and his party had left London by train, heading for the sheltered waters of Scapa Flow in the Orkney Islands, where the Grand Fleet was at anchor. Kitchener boarded the armoured cruiser HMS *Hampshire*, which was to take him for secret talks with the Russians to discuss munitions and strategy, and hopefully provide the reassurance the tsar needed to reaffirm Russia's commitment to the war.

Due to storms the *Hampshire* had been ordered up the west coast of Orkney, rather than taking the usual route across the North Sea regularly patrolled by minesweepers. Around 7.30 pm on 5 June 1916, in the dim light of a long summer evening, the *Hampshire* hit a mine recently laid by U-75. As the ship began to sink bow-first, lashed by gale-force winds and driving rain, Kitchener was sighted on the starboard quarterdeck in his field marshal's uniform calmly talking to officers from his party. Within twenty minutes of the explosion the *Hampshire* was gone, coming to rest upside down on the sea floor. Although she sank just 1.5 miles from land, no lifeboats and only two Carley floats made shore; only a dozen of more than 650 men survived. Bodies washed up for days, but Lord Kitchener's was never recovered.[6]

Word that Lord Kitchener was drowned had reverberated across the Empire, and into the wards of 17BGH: 'The news was appalling, & one seems stunned. The men were fearfully depressed. They could talk of nothing else & also that the war was going to be lost. No one could believe it' (11 June 1916). In Kitchener's death the unthinkable had become conceivable.

After Jutland, German naval strategy centred around its submarines. A U-boat campaign was intended to force Britain into defeat, denying the island nation access to food and munitions imports; in turn it was thought that a British withdrawal from the war would force France to capitulate. In the autumn of 1916 losses from U-boat attacks and mines tripled to over 300 000 tons per month.[7] In December 1916 John Jellicoe was appointed first sea lord and instructed to defeat the U-boat menace.[8] The Royal Navy formed an Anti-Submarine Division, but could not know that things were about to change dramatically.

25

ENGLAND AT LAST

If the news of Lord Kitchener's death had been dispiriting, reports from the war of attrition on the Western Front were no more encouraging for the rest of 1916. The last battle of the Somme offensive finished in November. In little more than four months the British and French had suffered some 650 000 casualties and the Germans 450 000–500 000 (although the Allies believed they had inflicted more). The British had advanced the frontline perhaps 7 miles in a few places. The Battle of Verdun dragged on until December. When it ended, it had cost France and Germany together some 800 000 casualties.

In addition to perhaps 1.9 million casualties on the Western Front, on the Eastern Front the Russians alone had incurred as many as 1 million casualties in the Brusilov offensive (a summer offensive conducted on a long front from modern Poland's eastern border to western Ukraine), which had diverted around seven German divisions away from the Western Front battles and brought Romania into the war on the Allied side.

All this slaughter was followed by the coldest winter in Europe for many years. The ground froze. Blankets froze. Waterbottles froze. Dixies of warm food and hot tea were despatched to the frontline, but by the time the carriers had skittered hundreds of yards over slippery duckboards and icy puddles to the soldiers huddled in the forward trenches, the sustenance was often cold. It would be a grim Christmas.

Edie had wondered where she would spend Christmas. Initially it seemed they might be taking patients to England:

We hope now by Christmas we shall be there. I shall write to
Uncle Harry & Uncle Will, but probably we shall be in London
before they get my letters. Sister Swannell did a Bunny Hug &
Turkey Trot round the deck, when she heard what was likely
to happen to us … I suppose you are all looking forward [to]
Christmas, how hot it must be. I wonder where I shall spend
or have my Christmas dinner. I wonder if it will be in Suffolk.
(8 December 1916)

Those hopes were soon dashed: 'I sometimes wonder if we shall ever see England', Edie wrote soon afterwards (14 December 1916).

The *Essequibo* instead bore them to Alexandria, where the nurses stayed first at their old stamping ground, 17BGH. The authorities reminded service personnel of their no-fraternisation obligations. Each year nurses and servicemen – soldiers, doctors and orderlies – pragmatically gave the required undertakings then promptly applied common sense and fraternised like mad:

[T]he Doctors & Chaplains gave us an evening. It was most
enjoyable. Coffee cakes & sweets were served during the
entertainment, & at half past 10 we had supper. Claret cups,
wines & liqueurs were provided (on my word of honour I didn't
touch any, no champagne was there). The Alex string band
played most delicious dance music all the time. Lots of the
patients were having a quiet dance outside of course. They should
have been in bed at that hour, but they all declared they enjoyed
it as much as we did …

I didn't tell you about the rules & restrictions we had to read
& sign … Sisters & VADs are requested not to have dinner,
afternoon tea, ride, drive, smoke, talk, walk, or be seen with
anyone in Khaki except near relations (I wonder how many near
relations I could squeeze out) or anyone else for that matter.

England at last

> Since these rules have been out Sisters have asked the MOs [medical officers] & Chaplains to the evening on New Year's Eve & in return Matron has given an 'At home'. The doctors have given us an evening too. So what is the good of rules, I should like to know. (17 December 1916)

The *Essequibo* nurses spent Christmas at 21st British General Hospital, which was established in the Ras-el-Tin barracks near the Ras-el-Tin Palace close to Alexandria's port:

> Our quarters are very like stables. A huge room is divided up by means of wooden partitions which are whitewashed. The floor is cemented. The windows or apertures have no glass panes but wooden shutters. But at any rate everything is very clean, airy, & roomy. We are on the sea front & I felt the sea breezes on my face all night. Most of my belongings are on the Essequibo. I only brought a suitcase with me. (28 December 1916)

On Christmas Day, Edie opened a gift from her Sydney friend Sister Athol. It contained a small civil service cake, some nuts, muscatels, meat paste and a tin of milk and coffee, and an Australian Red Cross parcel from Miss Lily Buckley of Manly, containing soap, tooth powder, bath powder, tooth brush, handkerchiefs, writing paper and envelopes, and a tin of chocolates.

Edie's Christmas parcel from Sans Souci did not arrive until January. It contained a bottle of perfume (cracked when the tin was dented), gloves, handkerchiefs and nuts (all stained by the perfume) and her mother's cake and sauce. 'We shall cut the cake on the ship. It will be lovely when we cut it to taste Mum's cooking again. Food here is pretty good but not well cooked. We always feel the food here might not always be as clean as might be. The Arab cooks are not too particular' (12 January 1917).

In Alexandria time hung on their hands very heavily, for they didn't know what was to become of them.

> Our Christmas was a very quiet one. On Boxing Day Matron sent for us to her office when she told us that we were to leave the ship & take up duty in the 21st General ... So yesterday we commenced duty in hospital once again. We are not wanted here for there is no work for us to do. I am on duty in the ward writing this. We do not know why we were sent off the ship. Though we think it is to keep us out of mischief. For it is not to be expected to coop up a number of young men & women & not expect us to talk to each other. For it is hard to keep out of their way. Not that there is anyone on board we could likely fall in love with. The majority of them (men) are much younger than I am [although] only a few of them are married. (28 December 1916)

At this time, Edie and Swannell were asked to sign on 'for duration' with an extra £20 a year. This would have put them on a similar standing to their friends in the AANS, but it was never about the money for Edie. Rather, one uncertainty particularly bothered her: when would she be allowed to go home to Australia?

> Matron gave us the paper to read, it implies that we sign on for any time they may require us. I don't think I could possibly do that. I don't mind so much for duration, but I shall be very disgusted if I couldn't be free to return when peace is proclaimed. Wouldn't you? I have decided to leave things as they are. (12 January 1917)

After a month they were back at sea. Ten days later the *Essequibo* was steaming past the 'Gib' and the coasts of Spain and Portugal into the Bay of Biscay. Despite rough weather, Edie was not seasick. She was also delighted that sixty Australian sisters were on board:

England at last

'[S]ome of them are good sailors so they volunteered to do duty for those who were sick. They seem a nice lot of girls, & a good looking lot into the bargain. I have spoken to a good many of them, many of them know nurses I know … We have had many long conversations' (22 January 1917).

Moored in the darkness off the Isle of Wight, the *Essequibo* hunched her bow into the wind. Edie was so close to her original destination she could almost touch it. She was nearly two years late, and old England's welcome was distinctly frosty:

> Oh dear! It is so cold the temp is 29° [Fahrenheit]. I never experienced such cold before. I went up on deck & went for a promenade walk, my hands & face felt as if they had been flayed with tiny whips, the wind was so sharp & keen. At 8pm we passed St Catherines revolving light & at 9pm we anchored somewhere near the Isle of Wight. We cannot discern a thing, & can only hear the whistling wind. Tomorrow we go up Southampton water. I want to see the scenery but I'm afraid I shall be too busy, for we disembark as soon as we anchor.
>
> I must close now, & will write at the end of the week again & tell you all that I have seen …
>
> Much love from
> Edie in England (at last) (25 January 1917)

Keen as she was to see her father's family, Edie had only a few days' leave in Southampton.

> The weather is frightfully cold. I saw icicles for the first time. All the water lying about is frozen, we even saw some kids skating this afternoon. They say it is too cold to snow. I felt as if I had nothing on me the first night here, I couldn't sleep for the cold.

Do you know we sampled Mum's cake last night, it is beautiful. Mum didn't think when she made it that I would eat it in England. We are keeping the sauce till we go back to the East, that is Mediterranean, for picnics. (28 January 1917)

She and Sister Swannell made the most of their opportunity to go sightseeing. They went to Netley Abbey, the remains of a medieval monastery, on the Sunday. 'The walk was very pretty, every scrap of water was ice & children sliding everywhere', she wrote. 'The Abbey was in ruins dating back beyond the Tudors. We couldn't get in.' The next day they went to Tudor House, which, since Tudor times, had been variously the home of wealthy influential Southampton denizens or merchant premises. It had opened as Southampton's first museum in 1912. '[It was] the stopping place for Phillip II of Spain when he came to England to marry Queen Mary. It is said he was so well entertained by the Southampton people, that he forgot Queen Mary' (2 February 1917).

Tuesday was a free afternoon spent wandering Southampton before they sailed for France:

> Southampton looks more warlike than any other place I've seen. Tommies returning after leave, others coming on leave. Hospital ships, troop ships everywhere, ambulance trains & waggons. Such horses, beautiful beasts, really the English look after their animals. They were fat big beasts I should think they would be used for heavy guns. The legs of the horses are of thick hair, so as to protect them in the mud of France.
>
> We passed many Australians, they were in a shed. Swannell & I insisted in going amongst them, to see if any amongst them we knew. But we didn't see any we knew. I thought of Joe Dodd.

England at last

Matron took us to the common to see some skating … [I] was very amused to watch a girl learn to skate, I so wanted to skate myself. I should like to learn …

Wednesday morning we sailed out of Southampton. The trip across was calm but oh! So cold. We sighted land at 4pm. It was very pretty. The rocks on the shore covered with snow. It snowed on board but very powdery snow. At any rate we got enough in our hands to pelt each other with it. Swannell got caught in the eye. I on my forehead. I didn't think snow could make you feel it when thrown at you.

This morning I wanted to clean my teeth. The water was a lump of ice. The water in the washstand wouldn't budge it was frozen stiff. So I took the water out of my hot water bag to wash in then I melted some ice on the top of my radiator. When I did get some water I couldn't hold the glass. I cleaned my teeth with trouble, but it showed me that my teeth were in perfect order to stand it. (2 February 1917)

The *Essequibo* loaded nearly 500 patients at Le Havre, then sailed for Dublin. Edie hoped for views of Devon, but only caught glimpses of the English coast: 'We passed the Lizard at 2pm. I must have been too busy to see Eddystone when we passed it. The Lizard is pretty. Don't think I look out of the port all day. But my head often bobs up to look out, when doing my dressings' (4 February 1917).

Dublin was cold but the welcome was warm, from a people Edie readily judged as 'an impulsive impracticable people, charming and hospitable'.

We had a glorious time in Dublin. After we had disembarked in the muddling Irish way a gentleman came to Matron asking how many of us [were] on staff, as he was sending cars for us to see Dublin. Well at 3.30pm we got into the cars with all the clothes on we could get, & all the rugs we could collect … We went all over the city passing all places of interest. We went through Phoenix Park, 7 miles across. This was absolutely beautiful, the snow lightly covered everything making it look like lace work. The sun was shining on it. Swannell & I just gazed on it … We were then taken for afternoon tea at the Irish war hospital supply depot …

There were a great number of women working making up all kinds of materials necessary in hospitals, & also many comforts for the tommies. It was an eye opener to me. We had tea in the kitchen, all the girls were having tea too, they waited on us & swarmed round us like bees round a honeypot. Their hospitality is charming. They asked us millions of questions & thought we were great heroes, nothing was too much trouble to them to show us anything. They seemed most anxious that we should know the Irish women were loyal & were doing something in the great war … The way they received us … you would have thought for the moment that we were the highest of the land.

We went down Sackville street & saw the ruins caused by the rebellion. This seems to be a thorn in their side, & [they] look upon it in a shameful [sic] way, for it really is …

Really the Irish do some funny things. As we moored into the wharf, we heard someone on shore shouting out to move the ship back, so as to be in the right position for the gangway. I looked to see the gangway, & couldn't help laughing, for it wouldn't take two men to push it along! (6 February 1917)

England at last

In the morning on 6 February 1917 the *Essequibo* sailed for Liverpool, mooring at midnight on the 7th in the foggy River Mersey at the Brocklebank Dock, so familiar to Edie's father, Charles, in his seafaring youth. Edie now had ten days while the ship was refitted, to get to know, as an adult, the English family whose letters had helped sustain her this far.

26

BACK TO THE OLD PLACE

Edie had written to her uncles and aunts before she left Alexandria, and a swathe of invitations greeted her. She wired Aunt Alice from Liverpool and they met in Birmingham at 5 pm on 8 February 1917. Alice was now about 48 years old and, since childhood, Edie had only seen her aunt in photographs:

> I would not have known her, for I had in my mind a photo of her we have at home, but it is quite different to what she is like now. Her face is round & her complexion is a pretty pink & white ... Her face & figure [are] young & it seems such a pity that [her hair] is so white. (17 February 1917)

Alice was employed in Sutton Coldfield as a live-in secretary to a very wealthy man: 'I think he is a magistrate ... Mr Glover & his daughter treated me as if I was a lady of high birth. I was given I suppose the guest room, which was warmed by a fire, at which Auntie & I sat till after midnight talking' (17 February 1917).

They visited Mildred Crocker Brown, now working in a British hospital. 'It is so far away from Birmingham & then again so far away from London, that she gets very few visitors. She said I was the 3rd visitor in six months, so [the] poor girl is feeling very lonely' (17 February 1917). Crocker Brown wrote in her diary, 'Awfully pleased Blake & her Aunt came out to see me. Blake ... does not look nearly so well or fat'.[1] Neither knew that Crocker Brown's isolation was nearly over; in barely a fortnight she would be in France.

Back to the old place

On the Saturday Edie went to London and met her uncle Will at Euston Station:

> I pictured in my mind standing on the station like a package waiting to be called for. But before the train stopped I saw a man peering into the carriages as they passed, who resembled Dad closely. I nodded & he raised his hat & followed the carriages till they stopped. It was Uncle Will. He is exactly like Dad. We had dinner then Uncle took me all round London. I couldn't tell you all the places he showed me & as he talked & walked beside me, it seemed as if I was talking to Dad. (17 February 1917)

Uncle Will was a keen substitute host for Uncle Harry, who had been taking care of Edie's mail and finances in London but was ill. For five years, Will had been the chief electrical engineer of Willesdon Borough District Council. According to his siblings, it was an important position: Will had told them so. Aware of his reputation for self-promotion, Edie had reported from Egypt on his first letter:

> [He] hopes that I shall be able to extend my travels to London & will be only too pleased to take me in his car not only over London, but over the surrounding country ... He says he is too much of a fossil to go to war, & he himself says he is not quick enough to get out of the bullet's way so thinks it is better to stop at home & make cars for the front. He thinks they will be more serviceable than he is. He belongs to the Engineering Volunteer Corps of London & goes to military training three times a week & at weekends makes lathes etc for munitions, but cannot give up all his time to war work because he has public duties to perform ... The tone of the letter is a wee bit of the 'I am', I think you suspect that of him. (1 August 1915)

There was no doubt, though, that Uncle Will was generous. He had written to Edie very often and he now took her to stay with him and Auntie Beth in Cricklewood, squiring her around London to see the changing of the guard at Buckingham Palace, St James' garden, the Marble Arch, then Uncle Harry and Auntie Fanny in Stamford Hill.

Uncle Harry was suffering another bout of bronchitis, which had been so bad a year before that the doctor had said his lungs were 'almost gone': 'He must be consumptive', Edie had speculated. 'If that is the case, his time is very short' (19 December 1915). Harry's compromised lungs had defied her dire prognostications, but he was now very thin with a hacking cough. 'He was downstairs for the first time [in] a week. Auntie looks [the] same as I remember her only she is quite white & she has false teeth' (17 February 1917).

Harry was considered the intellectual of the Blake siblings. He and his son Charlie were schoolmasters and his daughter Lily, another teacher, had married Arthur Pace, schoolmaster at a Poor Law School, in June 1916. Edie had privately queried whether Lily's 'get[ting] married in these troublous times of war was an expensive luxury' (27 August 1916) but the Londoners had refused to be bowed. '[Lily was] married in pale blue with a trimming of pale pink tiny roses ... She had nearly 100 presents, she sent me a list, type written. She (Lily) gave her husband a mahogany writing chest. His present for her was a gold wristlet watch' (17 September 1916).

When Edie visited, only her cousins Louie (Louise) and Arthur were home:

> Cousin Louie was there she looks somewhat like Queenie. Louie is fairly tall. Arthur is 13 years old & stands about 5 foot 10. I took a fancy to him. Uncle Harry is going to put him to engineering ...
>
> On Tuesday Uncle [Will] & I caught the 10 am train for Woodbridge. Uncle wouldn't hear of me going by myself.

Back to the old place

All the way down Uncle pointed out places of interest & Uncle is himself most interesting to talk to, I found the journey all too short. We ordered a vehicle [to take] us to Dallinghoo.
(17 February 1917)

Edie's grandparents now resided with Aunt Tilda in Dallinghoo, a village 12 miles north-east of Ipswich. It was set among fields, nestling in the elbow where two muddy lanes met. They lived in the Old Hall, a handsome home with a steep red-tiled roof. It lay adjacent to the red-brick schoolhouse where Matilda once taught, and only a short walk to the 14th-century St Mary's Church of England where Tilda played the organ every Sunday. 'We found Grandfather & Grandmother very well indeed ... Grandfather has plenty of wit, & kept us in fits of laughter all the time' (17 February 1917).

Andrew was now nearly ninety years old. His life's circle had been drawn within a few miles from where he was born in Pettistree, and he was good-natured and resolutely optimistic. Seven when his father died, Andrew was apprenticed at fourteen to John Motum at the Works, a combined smithy, carpentry and wheelwright's premises in Dallinghoo, and later at Ransomes agricultural machinery-makers and engineers in Ipswich, coming home on weekends to sing and play his violin in church. Upon completing his apprenticeship he was employed at the Works, which he purchased when Motum retired in 1857.[2]

The Works lay half a mile from the village, close enough in its busy heyday to hear, over the clang of hammer and anvil and rasp of wood-saw, the rectory bell that rang thrice a day to mark school hours and time for men in the fields to knock off.[3]

Edie found the Works, which she had seen as a child, 'the same as my memory serves, but much smaller everything seems'. They turned off the lane into a muddy yard. Uncle Will led a brief tour. To the left was the carpentry shop, benches laden and walls hung with saws, planes, lathes, rulers, chisels and such. To the right was the wheelwright's. There was the bow-saw used to cut out the six 'fellies' (fellows) that would form the wheel rim, and the adze to shape the inner part.[4] In the smithy, where countless horseshoes, plough counters, harrows, door-hinges, wheel rims and parts had been fashioned,[5] the massive bellows lay poised, but the forges were cold and silent. In front of them was the 16th-century thatched cottage *Robin's Nest*, where Uncle Frank and his family lived. Andrew was still known to potter around his old premises, but the Works, where once Andrew had employed up to forty men,[6] was now rundown and in a state of disrepair:

> Everything is in a tumble-down condition, the lawn, well you couldn't call it a lawn, it was overrun with fowls, rats & rabbits & weeds, the vegetable garden is not a garden at all. It made one feel depressed to see the dilapidation & ruin of it all. Uncle Will asked me what I thought. I said I was disappointed. He said he would like a bomb to fall through. We went into the house, & [were] met by Frank's ... (17 February 1917)

They had probably been met by Frank's wife or son, but for the second time a page of Edie's letter is missing. Perhaps Charles or Kate confiscated it before their daughters could read it. Frank's marriage was unhappy at this time and Edie's next observations – possibly informed by Uncle Will's 'most interesting' talk on the train to Suffolk – might have been deemed too personal or uncomplimentary to be retained for posterity.

Edie rejoined the *Essequibo* at Liverpool: 'We are not going into the danger zone at all. I can't tell you where we are going. But we are going to a new place altogether where it is very cold & in 10 days I shall write to you' (17 February 1917).

27

'A PLEASANT VOYAGE'

Edie's next letter was written as HMHS *Essequibo* bucked and tossed its way to Halifax, Nova Scotia, bringing home wounded Canadian patients:

> We are on the Atlantic rolling for all we are worth. We are a good deal out of our course sailing almost as far south as the Azores, in order, I hear, to get the best weather as this is the wrong time of the year to go to Canada ... How glad I shall be to land ... [L]ast night it was frightfully rough, things went flying all over the place, a fair amount of stuff was broken. (25 February 1917)

To add insult to injury, once the *Essequibo* reached Halifax, they were not allowed to disembark. 'The Canadians were not ready for their people much to the disgust of the men, who played up top ropes & in reality took charge of the ship' (11 March 1917).

For four days the ship lay in the harbour, full of frustrated patients and staff impatient to be off the ship.[1]

> The [men] are grumbling very much about it & say that they have been forgotten or not wanted ... It seems to me to lack management. Fancy not be[ing] able to take off their own cases. Fancy too not having hospital ships like Australians have. How they run down their own sisters. In all if our own boys ran down us, as these men run down their own, I wouldn't own them. The people seem to have provocation, but wouldn't you

think they would be loyal & say nothing. We are taking back 90 Canadian sisters to England. The boys this morning asked me if the concert party, which is to be given on board this afternoon, contained many ladies. When I told them that if they stayed on board, there would be 90 of their own sisters, they immediately answered that they had enough of them. This harbour of Halifax is rather pretty. Every where is snow, & great slabs of ice floating about the water. We can see skating near the shore. We are all dying to get ashore. We may get rid of our patients tomorrow, then I shall be able to post this. We shall have to change our money into dollars, I wonder why all the world can't have the same coinage. I have all kinds of moneys now. Egyptian Greek & French also Indian, now I'll add the mighty dollar. (3 March 1917)

On the third day at anchor a snowstorm provided a distraction:

> The snow on the deck was 9 inches deep. So Swannell & I went up & tried to make snowballs, but couldn't, we found out the snow was partly freezed [sic] & not damp enough to cling. So we amused ourselves with pelting each other with it. Some of my patients had a game too. The snow did not melt on us but just froze, our hair was stiff with ice, round our necks & sleeves was all ice & Oh! How [our] hand[s] tingled with the cold, they were absolutely painful till we got warm with the fight. We thoroughly enjoyed ourselves. (11 March 1917)

At last they unloaded their patients and had one day free to explore Halifax. An anvil-shaped peninsula on Canada's far eastern shores, Nova Scotia abounded with natural beauty – hills, forests, thousands of lakes and miles of winding Atlantic coast. However, Halifax was a port town made for business, not pleasure. The waterfront bustled with sea and rail traffic, and its buildings were two- or three-storey utilitarian wooden structures. It was mild in summer, but Edie found the spring thaw had not yet arrived:

> [W]e went into town, the snow was feet thick & in the streets it was banked up, so high you could hardly see the street on the other side. We saw a few motors but nearly all sleighs. The horses wear bells because the sleigh on the snow is almost noiseless. We found everything extremely expensive & here again we had trouble with money for we had to deal with dollars & cents.
>
> In the afternoon we were taken for a sleigh drive by the ladies of Halifax. We were not suitably dressed for sleighing. I couldn't feel my ears or fingers & when feeling came back my ears ached frightfully. One of the ladies assured me my ears were alright as they were red. When they become white, then they are frostbitten. After seeing the sights of the city we were taken to government house, where the governor & his wife & daughter entertained us at afternoon tea. They were interested in Swannell & I as we were Australians …
>
> On Wednesday we embarked 60 Canadian sisters & sailed that night. (11 March 1917)

The return journey was smoother, but marked by an extraordinary incident:

> You will be very surprised to know that our ship was held up by a German submarine yesterday.
>
> About 3.30 [pm] some of the sisters said that there was a submarine not very far from us – I didn't take any notice. Then we heard shots three in succession. Then we began to wonder, the engineers had their orders to stand by in the engine room. I did

not realise what danger we were in, till I saw the 'sub' come near us. I knew then that we would have to get into small boats probably if they gave us the time, before 'spitting at us' as Dad says. But I didn't feel very upset as we were only 40 miles from land.

The sub came nearer & nearer & then circled round us, we had stopped & a small boat lowered with the chief officer & several sailors went to the sub. We anxiously waited for its return. The sub wanted to know what we were carrying & if we had sighted some ship they wanted to catch, also if we had sent a wireless concerning the sub. The sub then steamed away, putting up the flags reading 'A pleasant voyage'. We answered with flags 'Thank you'.

Now don't you think we have had an experience. The Essequibo seems to have a charm, we ride through everything without trouble. (16 March 1917)

Edie's confidence that if anything went wrong good sense and courage would carry the day was reinforced. There was a postscript:

I suppose you have heard the Hospital Ship 'Asturias' was torpedoed in the Channel. It seems she was sailing in the forbidden zone & that was why the Germans struck her. Do not be afraid, we shall never go where we shouldn't. The submarine that held us up was caught the next day – the Captain of the trawler who caught her met one of our medical officers. It seems that the trawler sent a lucky shot through the sub's conning tower thus disabled her & [she] was unable to submerge. The trawler sent for help. The sub put up a fight, but had to surrender. The Captain of the sub said he had held up a hospital ship off the Irish coast letting her go with the signals of 'a pleasant voyage'. Then we knew she had been caught. (30 March 1917)

'A pleasant voyage'

The *Essequibo* was lucky to have run into a submarine whose captain respected the London Declaration's ideals of hailing ships before firing upon them. This manoeuvre was fraught with danger for submarines, which were particularly vulnerable to attack when they surfaced. It was less risky for a submarine to fire without warning, and extremely rare for a German U-boat to act as this one had. Most U-boat commanders had interpreted their February 1915 orders as to simply destroy hostile merchant ships, although Germany temporarily abandoned this tactic the following September in an effort to appease America.[2] The Americans were outraged at the May 1915 torpedoing of the passenger liner *Lusitania* by a U-boat, which killed some 1200 civilians, including 128 Americans.[3]

On 1 February 1917, Germany, increasingly desperate to break the naval blockade and impede Britain's sea traffic, made 'unrestricted submarine warfare' formal policy. They would fire first, no questions asked. The gloves were off in the war at sea. This even applied to hospital ships in the Mediterranean and a defined 'forbidden zone' covering the English Channel and the North Sea – encompassing every port from Land's End to Yorkshire – within which hospital ships were fair game.[4] This made the actions of the submarine that hailed the *Essequibo* while Edie was on board just a month later quite remarkable.

Germany's justification for this escalation was that 'enemy Governments, especially the British', were using their hospital ships illegally, to carry military personnel and armaments.[5] The crew of HMHS *Essequibo* had satisfied the submarine that they carried no contraband. Within the forbidden zone, they would not have had that chance, as was the case when HMHS *Asturias* was torpedoed without warning off Devon five days after the *Essequibo*'s encounter; over thirty people were killed. Little more than a week later, HMHS *Gloucester Castle* was attacked by a U-boat off the Isle of Wight, but all 400 cot cases were safely transferred to destroyers and only three lives were lost.[6]

At Liverpool, Evelyn Swannell would leave the ship. A poor sailor at the best of times, she had been incapacitated on the rough Atlantic crossings and Matron Ingham and the RAMC OC agreed that 'this disability will continue except under the most favourable conditions'.[7]

> Swannell has been too sick to stand it so is to be put off in England into a hospital. I have asked too to come off, as it is nearly six months since I came on the sea. I hope I shall be able to get off for it is a good opportunity to get to England or France ... Auntie Beth, Uncle Will's wife, is anxious that I should come to a London Hospital. I hope I do, failing France. I should like to be on land when the push comes in the Western front. (25 February 1917)

As soon as she had boarded the *Essequibo* Edie had flagged that she wanted no more than the requisite six months' service there. On the return from Halifax she asked the matron to try to get her off the ship with Sister Swannell. '[But Matron] says that she doesn't know that it can be done. My six months are up in April, so I don't think I am asking for anything out of the way' (11 March 1917).

When they docked in Liverpool on 16 March 1917, Edie went to Uncle Will's house, leaving Swannell behind on the *Essequibo* awaiting orders from the War Office. Edie had less than three weeks left before completing both her six months' duty on the ship, and her twelve-month QAIMNSR contract. Even if Matron Ingham had some sympathy for Edie's position, the *Essequibo* was only in port for five days – hardly sufficient to wade through the necessary channels. However, the Australians weren't to be deterred by red tape. They would go straight to the top. Edie decided to seek her orders direct from the QAIMNS's matron-in-chief, Miss Ethel Becher: '[T]he day before [I was] to rejoin the ship Swannell wired me & I met her at Euston & we went to the War Office together' (30 March 1917).

'A pleasant voyage'

What must Edie and Swannell have thought as they stepped inside the polished halls of the War Office in Whitehall, the army's cool administrative heart? What must the matron-in-chief have thought when she was informed that two Australian nurses wanted to see her without so much as an appointment?

> We saw Miss Beecher [sic], the Matron-in-Chief. She was in a fearful temper & consequently was dreadfully rude. When I stated my request asking if I could leave the ship as my time was up & go with Swannell, she snapped my head off, & asked me if I would like her to arrange my private affairs for me. (30 March 1917)

Miss Becher was in charge of thousands of moving parts. Every day she bore ultimate responsibility for ensuring that the nurses of the British Empire were efficiently and effectively deployed to hundreds of permanent and temporary hospitals strewn across numerous battlefronts. Her temper was doubtless also frayed by additional work and concern for her dependable second-in-command, matron-in-chief of the British Expeditionary Force in France, Maud McCarthy, who had been ill for a fortnight with acute appendicitis.

McCarthy was Sydney-born and -raised, although she had trained in London, served in the Boer War and been with the QAIMNS since its inception. The two women had long enjoyed an excellent working relationship. Becher had been poised for retirement and an orderly handover to McCarthy when the war started but she acceded to the War Office's request that she postpone her retirement. McCarthy's war diary revealed the myriad matters of which she was apprised daily and managed with steady competence, underscoring the length and breadth of the responsibilities of the matrons-in-chief – matters such as the number of sick sisters and reinforcements, sisters returned from leave, resignations, transfers, sisters who were gravely ill or had died and numerous miscellaneous items.⁸ McCarthy's illness was so severe that she would be off duty until August 1917, increasing the strain on Miss Becher.⁹

What Edie regarded as the strength of her case – that she would soon finish her six months on the ship – was also its weakness. Her request was, in the scheme of things, trivial. Her timing, in trying to get off the ship the day before it was due to depart, was abysmal. Her ignorance, of how these things ought to be done and the demands on Miss Becher, was monumental. A moment's reflection would surely have revealed that the outcome of ambushing the head of the nursing service was unlikely to end well; but it is also an inkling of Edie and Evelyn Swannell's friendship. They tried, then philosophically accepted what they couldn't change: 'Getting nothing from this quarter Swannell & I had to part, & I came back to Liverpool & she went to Scotland' (30 March 1917).

For the first time since they met at Albury railway station in April 1915, Edie was without Swannell, marooned in the British system without the comfort of a compatriot. For the second time the idea of transferring to the Australians presented itself:

> Swannell brought my mail down for me from Liverpool. There were 12 altogether & Dad's packet of photos, 2 letters from Grace. One letter was from Sister Dickson who was at the Coast with me, she is now secretary for Miss Conyers, Matron-in-Chief of the Australians. Sister Dickson asked me to come & see her at Miss Conyers' office in Westminster. Of course it was too late but I wrote to Dickson, & I shall go & see her when I go back, & also see Miss Conyers & see if I can't get a transfer to the Australian hospitals. (30 March 1917)

28

SOMEWHERE ON THE ATLANTIC OCEAN

HMHS *Essequibo* returned to Halifax. The ship docked on Saturday, 31 March 1917 and disembarked the same day. Edie viewed the town with jaded eyes:

> I do not like Halifax. The last time we were here it was covered with snow & this covered a multitude of sins. The snow was still there but frozen, in great blocks, but blackened with soot & dirt which gave the roads an extremely dirty & neglect[ed] look. The houses are mostly wooden, & the wood seems to be arranged like shingles on a roof of a house ... Most of the houses looked dirty & badly wanted paint & most of them that had been painted were dull red. This does not give a nice idea of the place does it? I wouldn't like to live here, though the people seem very hospitable. (8 April 1917)

Edie later noted the 'awful tragedy at Halifax' (13 December 1917) that occurred on 6 December 1917, one week after she had been in port there. A Norwegian vessel collided with a French cargo ship laden with wartime explosives in the harbour, setting off a tremendous blast that flattened buildings and started fires, destroying the Richmond district. Some 2000 people were killed and 9000 injured.

In Halifax a dispute arose between Major Home, the *Essequibo*'s OC Troops, and Lieutenant Colonel Lindsay, the port's senior embarkation officer. There had already been friction when unloading the patients. Home complained in the ship's war diary: 'The disembarking officer had no medical knowledge and no idea of carrying patients, nor ... how to put them off the stretcher in the hospital train'. Home organised the unloading: 'mental cases' (those suffering 'shell shock' – a condition now known as 'post traumatic stress'), followed by walking cases, cot cases, officers, tuberculosis, then amputations. But 'the want of a competent officer in charge who would say what they wanted done ... caused immense delay and so put us on to feeding the patients'.[1]

The new issue related to what the ship could carry on the return journey. Home was concerned by Lindsay's request that they take back 'a good deal of Red Cross stores' as sought by the Canadians, because the Hague Convention on Hospital Ships of 1904 stated that hospital ships were protected as long as they were not used for any military purpose. It was the discovery of additional stores that had seen the *Kyarra*, then marked as a hospital ship, unload offending material in Melbourne in late 1914. Major Home was precise, officious, and perhaps all the more sensitive because he had just joined HMHS *Essequibo* after surviving a narrow scrape when HMHS *Glenart Castle* was mined. The *Essequibo*'s captain agreed with Home that what the ship carried must comply with Admiralty orders and told Lindsay accordingly.[2]

The question of what people, stores and equipment hospital ships could legitimately carry was even more important since Germany's declaration of unrestricted naval warfare, which it blamed on Britain's misuse of its hospital ships. This claim was partly self-serving, to justify tactics that might provide an advantage in the war at sea, which was now really starting to bite in Britain and Germany, as imports were restricted and stores were diverted to support their armies.

> Uncle Will says he doesn't think he will be able to get petrol for his car, so doesn't think he will get a licence for the car if he

can't get petrol. So when I come back to London next time, he says he will hire a car & take me through Epping Forrest [sic] or anywhere I would like to go. Uncle is very good, but I feel an expense [as] everything is frightfully dear. Potatoes & sugar are almost unobtainable. People stand in queues waiting to get a pound & fares are up 80%. (30 March 1917)

Copious correspondence had been exchanged between the War Office and the Admiralty since the war started as to what the hospital ships could carry without breaching the Hague Convention. The Admiralty's priority was the safety of its ships and passengers and to therefore avoid giving the Germans a pretext to attack hospital ships. The War Office favoured interpretations expedient for the army and the overall war effort. The more conservative the interpretation of what a hospital ship could carry, the more space would have to be found elsewhere. The Admiralty Weekly Orders of 4 February 1916 listed what definitely could not be carried on hospital ships, such as arms and stores for the troops and the weapons of dead men; and what probably ought not be carried, including batmen accompanying their sick or wounded officers (although the War Office fought long and hard for this). Nor should hospital ships carry ciphers or codes: apart from the doubtful legality, they could fall into enemy hands.[3]

In the latter half of 1916, the transport of medical personnel became a vexed issue. Were khaki-clad RAMC reinforcements on British hospital ships validly aboard if not attending the needs of the ship's patients, but were instead bound for the battlefield to care for patients there? To the Germans (as well as crew of some French vessels), the RAMC looked like troops bound for the front.[4] The War Office was eager to continue the convenient practice and argued that, as the doctors and orderlies were provided solely for the care and comfort of the sick and wounded (albeit not on the particular ship), this complied with international law. The Admiralty took the view that if the extra men looked like troops, it endangered the hospital ships carrying them and the practice must therefore cease. HMHS *Britannic*, carrying hundreds of reinforcements like this, was sunk in the midst of this debate. The Germans later claimed that the large number of men on deck in khaki uniforms justified the sinking.[5]

Still the War Office continued to fight for the expedience of sending RAMC reinforcements on hospital ships, but the Foreign Office agreed with the Admiralty,[6] so the case went to the War Committee for final judgment. By the time the committee agreed in February 1917 that it was 'better not to give the Germans a pretext for taking action',[7] the declaration of unrestricted naval warfare had been made, citing Britain's use of hospital ships to carry troops as 'the worst breach' of the Hague Convention. The real reason lay elsewhere. The German chief of the naval staff, Admiral von Holtzendorff, had pushed for unrestricted submarine warfare, suggesting that sinking 600 000 tons of merchant shipping per month was possible – and five months of this would force Britain to sue for peace by August. It was worth the risk of war with America.

After the declaration, U-boats attacked like dogs let off the leash. Merchantmen, neutrals and passenger liners were ambushed indiscriminately, mostly without warning.[8] The death toll was awful, and shipbuilders could not keep up; in April alone over 869 000 tons of Allied shipping was sent to the bottom of the sea[9]: over 550 000 tons of this was British merchant and fishing vessels carrying over 1100 crew.[10] Britain faced its 'gravest peril'.[11] American public opinion, already tipping after the *Lusitania* was attacked, plunged in favour of the Allies. This was a major factor in the United States' declaration of war against Germany on 6 April 1917.

On the open ocean, the convoy system provided a measure of protection. Groups of merchant ships were accompanied by warships as a deterrent, which ultimately proved effective. They usually followed a carefully choreographed zig-zag course to help avoid any torpedoes fired from a submarine. A number of different anti-submarine weapons were used from the warships in a convoy, the most effective one being the depth charge.

The convoy system was also employed in the more confined waters of the English Channel and the Mediterranean. Close watch was maintained for submarines at all times, both from the ship and by the Royal Naval Air Service (RNAS), which conducted reconnaissance flights looking for U-boats, and had a measure of success in bombing them from the air. Nevertheless, the unrestricted submarine warfare fought by the Germans took an enormous toll on Allied shipping, and there was much concern in Britain for hospital ships in the Channel and the Mediterranean, where the Germans refused to recognise them. In May 1917 all nursing sisters were ordered off Imperial hospital ships. Those operating in the English Channel had their distinctive markings removed as it was feared these merely made them easier targets. They would instead be painted grey and operate as ambulance transports.[12]

It was initially suggested that, in the Mediterranean, hospital ships carrying patients must be escorted for their safety, even though this would forfeit their protection under the Hague Convention,[13] while those without patients should remove their distinctive markings and be defensively armed.[14] This was postponed as negotiations commenced for each hospital ship in the Mediterranean to carry a neutral Spanish commissioner to verify that it was 'not improperly used'.[15] Once this arrangement commenced a few months later, nurses were allowed back on the ships.

The *Essequibo* returned to England without incident. Edie wrote home from 'somewhere on the Atlantic Ocean':

> The sea is gloriously beautiful just now, the sun is shining & dancing on the water. It isn't cold either. I am sitting on deck writing without coat or sweater. (8 April 1917)

[I have] taken to knitting. I find it a soothing occupation. I don't knit socks well but I can knit & read at the same time. I have started a pair of khaki socks which I think I shall send to France … Fancy in a few days it will be two years since I left Sydney. How time flies, I wonder how long it will be till I get back.
(30 March 1917)

Although the end of her contract was coming up, Edie was determined to keep serving. She tossed around options, though little was in her control:

[W]hen we left Liverpool everybody had the idea we were going to the East … I shall have another try to get off the ship when I get to London … If I get back to the East, it may be that I shalln't get back to England again …

Much love to you all … From Edie – who is in the pink of health. (8 April 1917)

The *Essequibo* docked in Liverpool on the evening of 15 April 1917, and the nurses disembarked the next morning with orders to proceed to Dover. At long last Edie was going to France! She took only a few essentials, leaving the rest of her luggage packed and ready to be forwarded on. Some she had stowed before the last voyage: 'I thought I should leave some clothes behind me so packed a suitcase & sent it to the station to wait for me in case we were torpedoed, I had no wish to arrive in England with only the clothes I stood in' (21 April 1917).

Watching the green fields as her train rattled through Kent, Edie was thrilled. Back to real war work, close to her friends … But the exhilaration was shortlived:

Somewhere on the Atlantic Ocean

When I got to Dover I had orders to go back to Liverpool to get my luggage. I felt horribly disappointed. I could have wept. I did so want to go to France …

I had to rush to get the train back to London. The officers saw me running so held up the train … I arrived in London 8.30 pm. You know Dad I'm getting very clever. I have had no difficulty as yet in getting about London, all you have to do is ask a policeman. They really are a philanthropic community. I got back to Cricklewood without mishap & much to the surprise of Auntie & Uncle who had been discussing the possibility of a good crossing to Calais. The following morning I went to Liverpool. Oh! how tired I was of the journey. I got into Liverpool 5.30 pm. (21 April 1917)

Edie had to return to the *Essequibo* to receive her new orders. She collected her luggage and caught a cab. 'My suitcase was rather heavy to carry and it is four miles to the dock and [I] wasn't sure of the dock the ship would be in', she wrote. On arriving, she thought the ship had gone, but

> The ship instead of being white is now black. I told the cabby it couldn't possibly be the Essequibo as she was a hospital ship … The Essequibo is now a troop ship … Now I must tell you why we are sent off the ships. There has been many ships torpedoed, & the [hospital] ships being without guns go down without the pleasure of putting up a fight. So all women are being taken off the ships. They are painted like troopers, that is dark grey like the war ships. They are to carry guns, I have been told the size but I'm not sure, 4.6 inch I think. They are to carry wounded back to England & troops from England if necessary. (Don't know if this would pass the censor) …

> I found the ship desolate. It was Saturday afternoon. I had to report to the OC & the orderly who was on the gangway couldn't find him so in the end I found the acting OC (Officer Commanding). Now my orders are to return to London & wait for orders with the possibility of going to Salonika. This is indeed a blow. (21 April 1917)

Exhausted and put out, Edie passed a restless night in Liverpool.

> I secured a bed for the night & went to bed tired out, though I had been sitting in a train for hours. I dreamt all night of horrible difficulties in train travelling, unable to lock suitcases, seeing trains going out that I should have been on etc etc.

> In the morning I rose & went to breakfast & found out that the train went 10 minutes earlier than I thought. In the hotel restaurant being a woman I had to beg for my breakfast – men always get first served & women have to wait. I was on pins & needles for time was flying, oh! How slow they were, when breakfast came it proved to be too big for me, two large eggs & three rashers of bacon. I also found out that I should have ordered breakfast the night before ... I got my ticket, of course I'm not travelling [at] my own expense, I had a warrant which properly filled it. I told the man at the ticket office that it was most important that I should go to London on the 8.40 am so with difficulty he let me fill it in. I saw my luggage into the Euston luggage van, got into a first class carriage. I sat down, the whistle blew, the train went off, I had only got it by the skin of my teeth. (21 April 1917)

Edie had started this letter on the fast train from Liverpool to London, feeling disgruntled:

Somewhere on the Atlantic Ocean

I have just found out that my pen is dry … my letter will have a queer look. [In pencil:] But my lish [sic] these are trying times, & I've been grousing for all I'm worth, I have no right to, so many hospital ships have gone down, we have been held up by a submarine & have been let off, so I should be very thankful. I do hate travelling on trains by myself looking after luggage & thinking of the £.S.d all the time. Men & porters standing round doing things for you with the only thought of tips. They seem so contemptible to me, but I can't do without them so I must tip them, or miss trains & get bad tempered. I would sooner do a day's hard work in the wards than travel on trains in wartime. On ship we were spoilt, the orderlies do everything for us, without thought of payment. (21 April 1917)

She finished the letter in Cricklewood. There she also wrote to the matron-in-chief, asking if she might have home or French duty because her time of service was up. Uncle Will helped her write the letter, because he was anxious for her to remain away from the Mediterranean theatre:

I told [Miss Becher] that I thought of resigning, but before doing so I would ask for home duty & then I would sign for another 12 months …

If she doesn't grant my request, I feel like resigning. I feel more like facing a torpedo than facing that hot bed of dysentery & malaria in Salonika.[16] I have no wish for my health to be ruined. Egypt did not agree with me. My good constitution & reserve of strength served me well. There is plenty of work in England & France. This is selfish of me I suppose. But I think I have done my share in the East & I don't think it unreasonable to ask for home or French duty. (21 April 1917)

Within days Edie had a reply from the War Office: 'It contained a form for me to sign on another 12 months, also a note to say that my request was granted & I would be posted for "Home duty"' (28 April 1917). There was no need to pursue the notion of joining the AANS: she had what she wanted, and a week to explore greater London before she had to leave for her new position.

Most of London's museums and galleries had been closed since early 1916: priceless artworks and antiquities were covered in sandbags and hoardings or moved into tunnels beneath the city to protect them from air raids. Only the Victoria and Albert Museum and the National Gallery remained open, but Edie made the most of her time.

> On arriving in Stamford Hill found everybody well. Uncle Harry is much better ... Auntie Fanny & I went to the theatre in Leicester Square Wyndham's called 'London Pride'. It is the first theatre I've been to since I left Sydney. I thoroughly enjoyed it, though it is wartime the theatre was packed ...
>
> On the Thursday I left Stamford Hill & went into Liverpool St Station to meet Sister Swannell ... we went in an electric tube to Tottenham Court Rd & Oxford Street. Do you know the places? We did a little shopping & had lunch. Afterwards we went to Westminster Abbey [then] passed Trafalgar Square to the National Art Gallery ... The best pictures here are taken away, not because of zepps in this place but because of the suffragettes before the war. I was disappointed in the Gallery. There is not such a great variety, the building is something like the Sydney one but ours is bigger & superior I think ... the best monuments & sculpture of the Abbey [are] banked up with sandbags ...
> Of course we have nothing like the Abbey. That stands by itself. (28 April 1917)

Somewhere on the Atlantic Ocean

[On Sunday] afternoon a car came, one Uncle [Will] hired ... A little two seater. So Auntie & I went. We went round Kew Gardens into Richmond Park & Kingston. We caught a glimpse of the Thames every now & again. We passed Hampton Court & followed the river some distance & passed a house where the Magna Carta was signed. We went on to Windsor. The Castle was opened to visitors. Auntie & I went in the grounds, one embankment was covered with daffodils growing wild. We went into the Chapel, but as service was going on we couldn't explore properly. From the terrace we could see the Thames. After afternoon tea we passed on to Eton through Beaconsfield then on to Harrow & back to Cricklewood. Do you know the road Dad? or could you follow. The weather was perfect as if made for us. The country lanes are really beautiful. One lane was all rhododendrons. I thoroughly enjoyed the trip. We started off at 2.30 & returned at 8.30pm.

On the following morning I got my orders to go to Belmont War Hospital. Uncle looked up on the map to find out where it was, it was only 12 miles from London in Surrey. So the next morning I started off for my new diggings. (5 May 1917)

29

I'M NOT GOING TO NURSE ANY GERMANS

On May Day 1917 a woman waited on the Sutton railway station platform. She was short and slight, wearing a grey dress and cape. A straw boater encircled with red, white and blue ribbons was fixed above the dark bun resting on the nape of her neck. The nurse had alighted from the London train, and the railway guard correctly surmised where she was headed: '[T]he guard came up to me & asked if I were going to Belmont Hospital as a new hospital for prisoners was being opened. I declared I wasn't going to nurse any German prisoners. My feelings went down to zero when I found out only one hospital is in the locality' (5 May 1917)

Poor Edie. Miss Becher had given her home duty all right. It was especially galling to know that, had she listened to Sister Dickson, she could have signed up with the Australians. Then she could have been in France nursing soldiers from her own country. Now she was nursing the enemy! She had gambled and lost. But Edie was nothing if not resilient. And pragmatic. More than a little curious, she caught her connection to Belmont.

As the train crawled to a halt, a vast Victorian ediface with towers and dormer windows hove into view, sprawled above a slope adjacent to the railway line. A porter took her luggage and she gained her first glimpse of the village that would become so familiar.

Across the road lay a row of bay-windowed red-brick terraces. The high street swung uphill to the right, crowned by the recently completed St John's Church of England and lined with business awnings: a bootmaker, draper, hardware and ironmonger's. There was also a new high school for girls and junior boys where pupils would be prepared for Oxford and Cambridge Local Examinations.[1] Off the high street, King's Road and Belmont Road ran parallel to the train tracks. They were crowded with rows of identical brown terraces, built to house the families of employees of Banstead Asylum on the far side of the tracks. At the end of these roads, only a few hundred yards from the railway station, a barbed wire fence marked the grounds of the former Fulham Workhouse, a complex that comprised a similar area and population to the rest of the village combined.

The workhouse had been constructed in the early 1850s with high aspirations 'for the maintenance, education, and industrial training of the pauper children',[2] but, from the early twentieth century, became briefly a mental asylum then, until a few weeks earlier, the Fulham Workhouse and Infirmary for the physically and mentally ill and 'habitual paupers'.[3] Now its transformation into a military hospital was in full swing:

> I found the place topsy-turvey … full of workmen. Painters plumbers & cleaners etc. I also found out that I was the first arrival – standing in the hall were several medical officers, one of them I nursed on board ship. I didn't feel quite so lonely. Another officer hearing my name, asked me if I were Irish, his face fell when he found out I didn't come [from] County Galway, as all the Blakes come from there.
>
> This hospital is the Fulham Workhouse – it is a fearfully rambling place, I am always lost. The place is to hold 1200 patients. We have no patients in as yet, everything is in preparation. (5 May 1917)

This wasn't the only workhouse in Britain to be taken over for military purposes or to be converted into a POW hospital. The facilities were ideal. At Belmont, two large blocks would contain 48 wards. A third accommodated the staff, orderlies and nurses. There were already sufficient bathroom, kitchen and dining spaces, plus a bakery and barbershop. An operating theatre, X-ray room, pharmacy, laboratory and disinfection room were installed.[4]

The workhouse was largely self-sufficient, with extensive vegetable gardens, a chicken run, pig pens, pastureland for the milking herd and neat rows of fruit trees on the slope down to the railway line. On the far side of the tracks, Brighton Road bustled with traffic.

> Around the workhouse is the home farm. So far we are eating the produce, such as vegetables, milk, eggs etc. We are more fortunate than others. I got a letter from Queen today saying that you have tons & tons of tomatoes. I wish we had them here. Some people are pessimistic enough to think that in 2 months' time we will understand what hunger means … I suppose you hear a good deal about the food question. I suppose it does one good to eat less, but I never really feel satisfied. Never before have I been tempted to buy cakes or sweets. Though I can't understand why they are being sold as they are.
>
> All this week we have been preparing for patients but we do not work after afternoon tea, so we go for walks. Sutton is not very far from us. It is only 20 minutes walk on the Brighton Road. It is [a] very pretty walk …
>
> I am sitting beside a fire here, it is bitingly cold, though May. Almost as cold as Halifax. Have just heard about the boys on the Ballarat.[5] I wish something could be done about this submarine warfare … surely something will be done [about] this menace.

I'm not going to nurse any Germans

Much love from
Edie
PS Everybody tells me how well & brown I look. (5 May 1917)

The first patients arrived a day after Edie and three other nurses reported for duty:

Last time I wrote we had no patients. They arrived on Wednesday last ... We are equipping a temporary operating theatre & I am to run it until some sister comes to relieve. We are very short handed. I will be glad when some new sisters come ...

The Huns have not given much trouble, they cannot. But Oh Dear! The people in authority do. We have very little furniture. What we were to get was stopped, but the prisoners came, with not even enough guard to look after them. You would have smiled if you had of seen me with the officer in charge telling me that the prisoners were not to [be] left without a sister or orderly with them. I did not realise fully what it all meant. With the usual British management I found the sergeants had taken all my orderlies, the other sister had gone for supper. Then I realised what the Colonel meant. For I found myself on guard, with 63 German prisoners! If they only had known it. Fancy me trying to stop one let alone 63, if he wanted to escape. I was quite an hour alone. But the Huns didn't know & I don't think they will try to escape, unless someone helped them from outside. (12 May 1917)

30

OUR FEELINGS ARE
VERY MIXED HERE

Edie was determined to dislike her German patients. She had heard the stories: women raped and children murdered in Belgium. Passenger ships torpedoed. Zeppelins bombing civilians. Yet she had to admit that the men in front of her were not monsters:

> I do not like them. But somehow when I am dressing their wounds I forget their nationality until I ask a question & find I can't understand them. A few speak pigeon [sic] English. Some of them are handsome smart men & very English looking … some of them are brutal looking, the German type are flat faced & pale & fair. The head is flat at the back & very high on the top. (12 May 1917)

She soon began to identify differences:

> Lately we have been getting in Prussians. A month back we got a lot of Bavarians, I think they are better than the Prussians. The few Bavarians we have are not so 'German looking' as the Prussians. If I can say so, the Prussians are square-headed (bullet-like) [with] sallow complexions & look generally unhealthy. The Bavarians & Saxons are more English looking. Their heads are not square & their complexions are much clearer. (24 August 1917)

Our feelings are very mixed here

Even before she saw them for herself, Edie had known that the Germans were not the apish brutes depicted in posters or the 'devils' derided in the corridors of 17BGH (17 October 1917). But how different were they to the British, or to each other? During the war anthropologists of both sides photographed, poked, prodded and measured their captive research subjects every which way; here, ostensibly to classify ethnic variances between men from Saxony, Bavaria and Prussia, rather than in any phrenological search for criminal or warlike tendencies.[1] At Belmont POW Hospital prisoners' skulls were measured by a professor of anatomy from the University of London.[2] Edie might have been aware that something was happening; although she added, 'of course these [are my] own observations' (24 August 1917).

Despite protesting that she did not like them, Edie was interested in the Germans. She took photos of the hospital and grounds and the guard taking out a gang of men to work in the grounds. She also interacted with them:

> While going round my patients, one showed me his iron cross. It is shaped like this & about that size [she sketched a little cross], very little iron in it & the silver is poor looking, on one side has 1813 on it, on the other 1914. I don't know why 1813 is on it. On the ring at the top [a] black & white ribbon [is attached]. While in the trenches they wear only a black & white ribbon. This man gave me a piece of the ribbon, as a souvenir. (9 June 1917)

The relationship between patients and staff was hostage to the ebb and flow of war news. Every air raid on England and attack on the Western Front raised conflicting emotions in Edie:

> I don't think anybody resented nursing huns [more] than we did when we first came here. But poor beggars, when you see them

downhearted when they get their home letters (for they are not as cheery as our boys) & they sometimes drop a few tears, we can't help feeling the kindred spirit that makes us wondrous kind, & yet when you hear of the raids in London & loss of non-combatant life you feel you could screw all their necks, & we know that the Germans would poison the air we breathe only they would have to breathe it themselves. Our feelings are very mixed here. (27 June 1917)

The battle of Messines began in Belgium on 7 June 1917, a month after Belmont POW Hospital opened. Nineteen enormous mines had been placed during two years of covert tunnelling, undermining German positions along the Messines Ridge to the south of Ypres.[3] The battle was launched at 3.10 am with the detonation of these enormous mines; the earth erupted with a fiery roar along the front, sending tons of soil, steel and human debris high into the black sky. British, Australian and New Zealand infantry continued the attack, following an artillery barrage across no man's land to take all of their objectives within a few hours.

Within days British newspaper headlines hailed 'Haig's Brilliant Victory – Messines-Wytschaete Ridge Blown-Up and Captured – Biggest Explosion in History of Warfare'.[4] Prime Minister Lloyd George was reportedly listening at his home at Walton-on-Hill near Belmont: 'I believe he was up at 3 in the morning to hear the explosion of Messines Ridge, & he heard it distinctly' (14 July 1917). Edie reported gleefully that they received a wounded officer:

[He] was captured during the bombardment of Messines. Of course, these [prisoners] know nothing of what is going on until another batch of men come in. This officer informed the others what happened at Messines. You should have seen their faces. They were as long as a fiddle, & they wouldn't smile for sour apples. We felt rather pleased we had said nothing about it to them. (23 June 1917)

Her ambivalence was complicated by the attitude of the guards and orderlies, whose unequivocal contempt for the prisoners was exacerbated by the attitude of the Belmont locals, many of whom hated the Germans and resented anyone who treated them well. Even if the sisters' relations with the patients were cordial, Edie knew that this must be hidden from public scrutiny inside and outside the hospital walls.

> Did I tell you about the German doctor who was to be repatriated? Well it seems that the German government will not give up ours unless they have double the number of theirs in return. So the doctor couldn't go back to Germany, much to his disgust. But before he left, he asked if I would come & say goodbye as he wished to thank me for kindness. Of course I didn't go. But afterwards I went into the village to post a letter & on my return passed the prisoners on their way to the train. The doctor saw me & saluted. You should have seen the look of disgust on the guards' faces, of an officer daring to salute. For the guard think we are too good to the huns. So I told the men they were not to recognise us in the grounds that it wasn't correct. So one said in German to another (one sister understood) 'we may love enemies, but in England we mustn't show it'. The people or some of the people of Sutton despise us because we have to nurse these people. They seem to think we volunteered to do it. I do hope we shalln't be left here. The first loophole I see of getting out of here I shall certainly try for it. (23 June 1917)

Curiously, she described one incident as a 'joke':

I must tell you something that happened today. It is worth putting in Punch or John Bull. One of the maids couldn't eat her dinner because the meat was too tough. So she went outside to put it into the bucket, where there was a party of German prisoners working. One of them came near her & she gave him the meat, as he had gone to search the pig bucket before, & she being a tender-hearted soul couldn't bear to think of a human being searching a pig bucket for food. Someone reported her to the Colonel, & so poor creature she had to appear before him today we haven't heard the result yet. Don't you think that a joke. (27 June 1917)

It is unclear whether Edie thought the joke was on the desperate prisoner, that the treatment of the kindly nurse was unfair, or that the war was eroding their humanity in all sorts of ways. Regardless, she hated it when the prisoners complained about their food because in her view it was the Germans' fault they were fighting and supplies were short: 'When on duty & the men tell me they are hungry I always feel angry with them' (27 June 1917).

Although she would rather nurse easygoing Tommies than officers, she preferred the German officers to their rank and file, saying, 'I have officers to look after, they all rank Lieutenants … Their manners are good, & [they] are extremely polite' (12 May 1917). She later observed,

I find also that the higher the rank the better the man. The officers (some of them) & the Sergeant Majors are far superior to the rank & file. The former pick up the English language readily, so that we can converse a little, they make funny mistakes of course, so do we. I made a funny mistake the other day, which caused a great deal of amusement. After I had finished some of the S/Majors dressings, one of them got hold of a piece of wool & a bandage & made it into a doll, & rocked it in his arms the same as a little girl would do. The German for doll is 'Puppe' taken from the French, but I got mixed up with 'Pupshun' (phonetic spelling) of course there was a roar of laughter. I afterwards found out that 'Pupshun' means a sweetheart.

They use the word 'Becomin'' (phonetic spelling) which means 'to have or get' so one man asked me, 'to become a pill', another to 'become a weak pillow', meaning that they would like a pill or a soft pillow. (24 August 1917)

Just at present I am reading Carlyle's 'Hero & Hero Worship'. It is most interesting. You will be surprised to know that one of the German Officers lent it me, he couldn't manage it. He asked me if I could get him 'Westward Ho' out of the library as they are studying that book in German schools at present. But instead I got 'Hereward the Wake'. He is getting on with it very slowly. Imagine, these men could speak but very little English when they came & [are] now trying to read Carlyle & Dickens. But I think they find it harder than they care to let me know. They enjoyed 'Daddy Long Legs' … & 'Ships that pass in the night' – these I can understand but 'Carlyle' is a different matter.
(7 October 1917)

When surrounded by British at 17BGH, Edie could hardly have felt more Australian. Now, beside Germans, she identified as a 'Britisher': 'I have been reading a book called "The Retreat from Mons". I am sending it home by this mail. You must read it. It makes one feel proud to be a Britisher' (11 September 1917).

As a 'Britisher', she valued loyalty and stoicism. She wrote that while she found the patients polite and helpful, 'They are sneaks though & will not uphold each other at all, as Britishers will' (24 August 1917). And although she pitied the Germans if they were hungry or in pain, she despised them should they complain of it.

> We are very busy just at present, convoys coming in straight from France. Each sister has now 50 acute cases each & it is no joke. I am on night duty & I have 100 patients. I have a patient with tetanus or lockjaw. I don't think he is going to live. I nursed a lot of tetanus in Egypt when we first went there, but this case is different to any I've seen. His jaw is stiff & there is some rigidity of the muscles at the back of the neck. He is suffering very much from abdominal pain. The muscles of [the] abdomen [are] hard as a board, & he has every now & again spasms which affect the abdomen. He has had a quarter [of a grain] of morphia so is quiet at present. These German[s] sleep excellently, no matter how severe the wound. They shed tears very easily. They will tell me they have pain (schmerzen) & before I have time to get a hot water bag or anything to relieve them, they are asleep, so much for their pain, don't you think? (28 July 1917)

Yet her patients may have suffered more than usual, for they seemed to have received minimal care en route to England: 'I am now waiting for a convoy, it is coming at 11 pm. Such an hour to bring in patients & they are usually so badly wounded & their dressing[s] have often [been] left without dressing for two or three days' (18 August 1917).

Despite the Germans' various states of physical impairment, Edie commented that 'the people here are afraid of the prisoners escaping during a raid so there is always extra guard on duty' (16 June 1917). Being prepared to die fighting for your country was respectable, a quality that had been admired in the Ottomans, who at Gallipoli 'had displayed an admirable manliness' so doing.[5] Whatever the actual circumstances of their capture, prisoners often wrestled with shame and guilt, feeling that they were perceived to have surrendered. Some sought redemption via escape attempts, disobedience and nationalistic displays at POW camps. Prisoners and captors eyed each other with suspicion, and even a hospital like

Belmont was encircled by barbed wire.[6] Although she was trained to tend bodily wounds and naturally felt 'the kindred spirit that makes us wondrous kind', Edie recognised that her patients suffered in ways that none but those who had had a similar experience could truly understand:

> Strange to say, the orderlies here who have been to the front & know what it is to be in the trenches, are much better to the huns than those who have been conscripted, & as yet never seen fighting, or the hardships of a campaign. The officers I have met lately, who have been to the front, all say 'Be kind to the poor beggars. They know what it is to be in the trenches'. (27 June 1917)

31

THESE MEN HAVE TO WORK

The hospital was rapidly expanding: 'Two days ago we had a convoy from France. There were eleven ambulances all in a row' (2 June 1917).

The prisoners with lighter wounds were put to work and, despite her antipathy towards them, Edie could not fail to notice their work ethic.

> There is a large farm connected with the hospital [in] which these men have to work.
>
> If the prisoners are taken out in the evening to work (it is light here till 9.30pm, the sun is now shining brightly though it is nearly 8 o'clock) they get a basin of soup. This evening they didn't go out to work so didn't get any supper. They were very indignant when I told them 'no work no tucker' (I had an interpreter). Then I added that these Germans had the cheek of 'old nick'. They roared laughing when interpreted. For all that they are easier to manage than the British Tommy who isn't fond of work. I have more trouble with the orderlies than the patients. (2 June 1917)

Up to 9 million soldiers were captured by both sides during the war. Most were taken on the mobile Eastern Front. On the relatively static Western Front,[1] the British took over 325000 Germans prisoner, of whom more than 130000 spent time in the 500 or so camps around the United Kingdom.[2]

At the commencement of hostilities, Britain had established

its Prisoners of War Information Bureau in compliance with the Geneva and Hague conventions.[3] The bureau gathered each prisoner's name, regimental number, age, place of origin, rank, unit, wounds, and date and place of capture. Weekly updates were provided to enemy governments of where the prisoners were interned, and of transfers, parole, exchanges, escapes, hospital admissions and deaths. The bureau also listed and stored prisoners' personal effects, letters and valuables. Any cash was held and receipted by their camp commandant.[4]

International law recognised that prisoners could be forced to work for the captor nation.[5] Australian soldiers received a list entitled 'The Soldier's Don'ts of International Law' that included:

DON'T become a prisoner of war if you can help it ... But if caught:

DON'T resist your guard.

DON'T refuse to work; you have no right to jib at any work except such is connected with the fighting actually in progress ...

DON'T fail to escape if you get a chance.[6]

Nearly 90 per cent of Allied prisoners held in Germany were put to work. Britain also used German prisoners for labouring on the Western Front, but was slower to do so on the home front, mainly because the trade unions opposed it, fearing cheap POW labour would detrimentally affect civilian employment and rates of pay.[7] By 1917, though, the shortage of manpower in Great Britain was so great that prisoner labour was not merely convenient; it was necessary, and being used throughout Britain. They were paid a nominal amount for their work and could use the income to purchase extras such as cigarettes and food at the camp canteen.

Delegations from neutral countries inspected POW camps in all belligerent nations. Captain Schwyzer and Dr Vischer from the Swiss Red Cross systematically inspected British POW camps and hospitals to report on the conditions under which the prisoners were held. Were the rooms draughty? Warm enough? With adequate bedding? Hot and cold water? Sufficient food? They recorded and followed up on prisoners' complaints and the nature of any forced labour. For example, at Port Clarence POW Camp in Middlesborough, the men made roads and quarried, receiving 1–1.5 pence per hour for around forty-four hours' work per week. In Scotland, at Rosyth, Inverkeithing, the prisoners made bricks: one gang dug the clay, another operated the presses, another the kilns. In one Northamptonshire camp, prisoners laboured in an ironstone quarry. The inspectors commented, 'Many of them are slightly disabled and not fit for a full day's labour ... The work is rather hard for this special lot of prisoners, and we wish that stronger men could be sent here'.[8]

There was no expectation that officers would work, and they passed their time in sport and leisure activities. At Colsterdale Officers Camp in Yorkshire, POW officers enjoyed flushing lavatories, an extensive library and a piano. The officers paid orderlies 2 pence per hour to provide services that drew on their civilian professions as cooks, waiters, barbers, tailors, shoemakers and cabinet makers. The inspectors said the German senior officers 'deserve credit for the manner in which they dispel discontent by interesting the men in sport and other occupations.' Schwyzer and Vischer adjudged Colsterdale the 'best officers' camp in the country'.[9]

Although they were not put to work, British officers in Germany did not receive such privileged treatment. Evidence of this came in a letter to Uncle Harry. Edie's cousin Charlie had enlisted in 1914 aged twenty-one and had been in the trenches since mid-1915. When he went to officers' training camp in St Omer, Edie wrote, 'Uncle Harry & Aunt Fanny are not very pleased about it. They think he, as an officer, would be potted quicker than as a Tommy' (31 December 1915).

Their concern was well founded. The young scions of Britain's social and political elite trooped out of the halls of Oxford and Cambridge to enlist, full of lofty ideals and a sense of duty that encouraged them to set an example for their men. It was often the role of a junior officer to peer over the top of a trench or lead a scouting party to assess a situation for higher command. Officers were targeted by the enemy, and junior officers were often the first to hop the bags, and among the first to be cut down. By the end of the war, almost 12 per cent of Britain's Tommies were dead, but 17 per cent of its officers.[10]

At 4 am on 16 December 1916 Charlie's luck ran out. He and another officer were captured in no man's land while leading a party to inspect an abandoned German trench. The five men crept up to the wire, hesitating as flares cast flickering shadows. Suddenly a volley of revolver fire resounded from the 'disused' trench. Charlie flung himself to the ground, crawling out of the way as bombs followed the shots. He lost sight of his men but glimpsed 'at least fifteen' Germans as he attempted to shoot. His revolver misfired and he was captured.[11]

In the days afterwards senior officers wrote to Uncle Harry. One said,

> We have no means of telling whether he was hit or taken
> prisoner and all we know is that he is still missing. I have given
> you now all the information we have ourselves and it only
> remains for me to tell you how very much I regret the loss of one
> of my most promising officers and to offer you my condolences.[12]

A letter from Charlie himself, received a month after he disappeared, relieved Uncle Harry and Aunt Fanny's anxiety. Harry's response masked the turmoil they must have endured:

22 January 1917

My Dear Charlie,

We were indeed pleased to see your handwriting once more. We have been wondering about you every day. It is five weeks since we heard you were missing and believed to be a prisoner. We were of course awfully disappointed at not seeing you at Xmas time, but your disappointment must have been dreadful. We felt however that whatever your lot you would make the best of it ... We had a quiet Christmas time – I started school on the 8th – Mr Sanderson had been transferred and I had his class to take ... Harry is quite well & so is Arthur ... All send love and every good wish. We are just feeling thankful. We are sending off a parcel tonight.

Yours ever, Dad

Charlie's officers' camp was in Clausthal, at the base of the Harz mountains in central Germany. Their privations were outlined in a letter to Uncle Harry from an officer who had been imprisoned with Charlie and probably achieved early release, as repatriations and prisoner swaps were increasingly agreed in 1917 and 1918.[13]

Hotel Royal, Scheveningen, Holland.

Dear Mr Blake,

Your son whom I had the pleasure to meet at Clausthal, desired me to assure you of his health and to give some idea of things in general in Germany. I left him fit and in good spirits ...

These men have to work

I saw pictures of English camps such as Donnington Hall, the other day. I wonder if people at home for a moment imagine we have such housing or treatment in Germany, or the games. No, one is rigidly confined to the most cramped areas where high boards obscure all view, though in this respect Clausthal is the exception. Boxing is not allowed, baths but twice a week, no lights in one's rooms except from 9.30–10, and the garden, the only recreation ground, remains frequently closed for weeks on any attempt to escape, despite the fact of it being enclosed by double lines of high wire and watched all round by sentries. Thus one is deprived of exercise, and one walk a week was the maximum I ever knew. When I add that with the exception of a very short period of a few days we had no fuel whatever, living in huts in the most severe weather, with snow to the level of the windowsills, you will understand how little our chivalry is responded to. One lives on relations strained continually to breaking point.

However, all this is petty spite, and of these annoyances we are completely indifferent, and the only way is to ignore their arrogance.

The Non Com's and their men, poor fellows, have lost a very large number of their roll in Germany, the salt mines and the relays labour gangs are about the cruellest form of tyranny imaginable, and it is a shame but now at last people will know. Literally thousands of Russians and Romanians have been starved to death. I've seen them, and they will almost bark for a crust of bread. We understand their shortage but our grouse is against the labour they are forced to do upon those dreadfully inadequate rations and they are driven at the point of the bayonet if they are sick.

> I only mention these things because they are what all the world should [know] that we may realize the hand that would oppress us. 'Might however unjust is right' in Germany and until the people have the sense to act together we must consider them all as one, and destroy them till they weaken. I am sure this is a Medea's cauldron and we shall see good come out of chaos but I always think it is a bit hard their lesson has to be taught at such a price.
>
> Clausthal will be rather nice in summer in spite of the Commandant for the views are pretty and it is hot enough there and your son has his books which he loves to study.
>
> If there is anything I can inform you further upon or anything I could do for your son, I shall be only too pleased.
>
> Yours sincerely —[14]

Although she recognised the dejection of the German POWs, Edie saw that they were comfortable. Particularly, of course, the officers. So she had limited sympathy for her cousin's predicament: Charlie was unwounded, out of harm's way and undoubtedly enjoying all the perks of the officer class: 'He must be a wee bit of a snob. They have to send him over boots very often, he can't get his boots soled there let alone get a new pair, and as you can imagine playing tennis, football, cricket must run away with a good deal of shoe leather' (11 November 1917).

Charlie's boots had been the subject of ongoing correspondence because a pair his parents sent went astray. His fellow inmate told Uncle Harry,

I may say that parcels do not always arrive, and very often they are rifled, or someone takes his good percentage. Things like boots should never be labelled as such, but rather as turnips, or what is just as effective is to send them one at a time or two of the same foot, if sending two pairs at a time.[15]

32

THE FOOD QUESTION IS A SERIOUS ONE NOW

Aunt Fanny fretted that her captive son did not have enough to eat, and they sent him regular food parcels. Edie observed,

> Uncle Harry must find it difficult. Charlie in Germany requires so much food, & only food of the best, as he is interned with officers who get better parcels than he. I really think he doesn't know what a drain he is to Uncle. Uncle says he costs over £5.0.0 a month ... [Cousin] Harry of course also wants parcels, he is more of a worry I think as he is near the firing line. (11 November 1917)

Meanwhile, at Belmont, the hospital's main concern was to get the men healthy enough to move on to a POW camp, but sufficient nutrition came at a cost. Prisoners were expensive to house, clothe and feed, and Britain and Germany were both starting to struggle to feed their own citizens and armies, let alone their prisoners: 'I suppose you have read about the two Australians who escaped from captivity in German hands. It seems dreadful they haven't enough to eat. The doctor of my ward came along with a paper giving account of how they were treated' (2 June 1917).[1]

The newspaper's report was based on a despatch from Charles Bean concerning two Australians captured during the first battle of Bullecourt in April 1917. The escapees complained that they were fed one slice of bread, some fermented mangolds (a type of field beet)

The food question is a serious one now

and two cups of coffee per day.² Undoubtedly ignorant of conditions in Germany, where people died of starvation and malnourishment in the 'turnip winter' of 1916–17 (induced not only by poor domestic cereal and potato harvests in 1916 and restricted imports due to the British naval blockade, but by the management of, and costs of the war to, the Central Powers' economies), Edie continued in high dudgeon:

> I feel like starving them (the prisoners) for the day. One who speaks English a bit asked the orderly what Doctor & I were discussing in the paper. So I went up to him & told him in the simplest language I could think of. He only laughed & said he didn't believe. It wouldn't be ladylike to use my hands on him, but I felt like it. It isn't economy to neglect these men. Give them the treatment that will fit them for internment camp is the simplest way & easiest for us nurses, besides it takes less material for dressings.
>
> They don't really get enough to eat, but then the food question is a serious one now. Germany means to starve us out. So I don't think they should have all they want. There is some talk of sending them to the colonies. If they did it would relieve us as regards food. (2 June 1917)

Edie knew the Belmont patients were not being fed enough. Their bread ration at this time was 4 ounces (about three modest slices) of bread two days per week and 5 ounces on the other days. When Captain Schwyzer inspected the hospital in July, the shortcoming had been corrected to the 9 ounces of bread per day prescribed by the War Office for non-working POWs. Schwyzer had no other criticism of Belmont's accommodation, kitchen or cleanliness, and found that the surgical treatment was 'kind and efficient'.³

Dr Vischer made a follow-up visit to Belmont in October.

Although the number of patients had almost trebled, from 342 to 1069, the hospital diet was now comparable with that of other POW hospitals and camps.[4] The officers now had a room for reading, writing and recreation, and the garden area had been extended and was open all day. The alterations 'add greatly to the comfort of the prisoners and are much appreciated by them'.[5]

Before the war, Britain's agricultural industry was in recession due to cheaper imports. As conflict loomed in 1914, government research revealed that the nation could be fed more efficiently on cereals and vegetables than on meat, eggs and dairy products.[6] Pastureland was given over to crop farming. The harvests of 1914 and 1915 were healthy, allowing Britain to pursue a 'business as usual' policy and refrain from controlling food supply or prices.

In 1916 the desire for free trade could no longer prevail. This was not going to be a short war. The army was hungry, and, after conscription started in March 1916, growing. Supplies of flour were thinning due to a poor harvest in the United States and the U-boat campaign. In April 1916 Britain had on hand a mere six weeks' supply of grain.[7] Public appeals were made for households to voluntarily restrict their consumption of bread, meat and sugar. The recommended weekly maximum for bread products was 4 pounds: equivalent to the War Office prescription for prisoners.[8] Prices went up and there were complaints of profiteering and hoarding.

The government had to act, and in December 1916 established a Ministry of Food Control to oversee war agricultural committees that dictated how land should be used. Ploughing Orders were issued and even golf courses and cricket fields were converted for cropping. Food exports were prohibited. A Wheat Commission purchased cereals, rationed grain for animals (feeding pigeons and stray animals was outlawed) and regulated ingredients commercial bakeries could use.[9] Edie was not fond of 'War Bread' that was plumped out with barley, oats and rye flour and, later, with soya and potato flour, complaining, 'The bread is very dark almost brown & if stale it tastes like so much chaff' (5 August 1917).[10]

In rural areas, children were taken out of school to help on the farms due to labour shortages. In urban areas, it was harder for people to supplement their diets with home-grown produce. Uncle Harry lost an unfortunate staffer who ate rhubarb leaves, not knowing they contained toxic amounts of oxalic acid when eaten in quantity. Edie wrote, 'I suppose you hear all about the difficulty of food, & people are trying all kinds of things. We have little bread & several meatless days a week, no butter but margarine, very little sugar'. And yet, she added, 'no one looks starved' (9 June 1917).

Edie was right. Although malnutrition increased among some urban poor,[11] others actually became healthier as more vegetables and unrefined grains entered their diets.[12]

> Living is dearer in England than elsewhere & food is scarce & we get barely enough to eat, so we have occasionally to go out & get a few things. We supply our own morning tea milk & biscuits, bread & butter is out of the question & very often sugar. But a grocer here took pity on us & gave us a 1lb the other day. So of course this left me a bit short: 15/- in pay doesn't go very far ... [However] I am in the pink of health ... I think in ordinary times we really eat too much. Though I'm thinner I never felt better. I very seldom have a headache & I read & sew a good deal. The air of Surrey is very bracing. (27 June 1917)

The harvest of 1916 had been poor, and Britons viewed the signs for this year's crops pessimistically. Edie's sweet tooth suffered; luxury items were not for those on a nurse's salary.

> The money here slips through one's fingers. Our tea & sugar allowance isn't enough, so we have to buy it ... I bought some tea

3/- lb yesterday, we often have to buy butter & biscuits & things like that. The smallest tin of biscuits costs 2/- a tin … Tomatoes you would smile … you could hold three comfortably in your hand. I can't say I like berries very much. All that I have had are sour & there is no sugar to eat with them. The strawberries weren't too bad. But the currants were decidedly sour. The red gooseberries are sweeter than the white. Apples are not in yet. (5 August 1917)

I couldn't help smiling to myself, when I read [Queen] had been to La Perouse [and] had 6 pieces of toast. That would be a crime here. Everywhere you go, you read 'Eat less bread'. As for sugar I cannot drink my tea without it, consequently I have far less tea now than ever I did in my life. (11 September 1917)

When compulsory rationing was finally introduced, it was not due to a failed harvest, which turned out to be good. The first item to be so rationed, from January 1918, was sugar.[13]

33

MURDER IN MY HEART

When Edie arrived at Belmont, she noted, 'The zepps trouble is practically over' (5 May 1917). Germany had commenced air attacks on the island nation on the night of 19 January 1915. Zeppelins attacked Norfolk. Specific locations in London – the docks and to the east of the city – were bombed shortly afterwards, but although London was an obvious target, the Kaiser only reluctantly approved unrestricted raids on the city. This was done the following July on the proviso that historic buildings be spared, because of concern for his relatives in Buckingham Palace.[1]

The airships couldn't fly in bad weather and were at the mercy of high winds that blew them off course. Gravesend was bombed in mistake for Harwich, over 60 miles away, on 4 June 1915. Pilots navigated by sight, identifying landmarks from which they could take a compass bearing, or following main roads or a river like the Thames, which was as difficult at night for the airship crews as it was for the fighter pilots who hunted them. By the time fighters scrambled after a 'Zepp' that had been caught in the beams of coastal searchlights, there was no certainty they would find it, for Zeppelins mostly flew too high for them and were adept at hiding above the clouds. After an often fruitless pursuit the hunters then risked crashing into a treetop or hedgerow, as landing strips were ill lit and few and far between.

Zeppelins captured the public imagination – and inspired fear. People never knew when they might look up and see the silvery, cigar-shaped outline of a deadly balloon, two football fields long, gliding among the clouds on a moonlit night.

> Lily says that zeppelins have been over Stamford Hill, so the house has been insured & they have respirators & dressing gowns & shoes ready to slip into if a bomb was dropped … if a bomb happened to hit their house, there would be no time to slip into these things, I should imagine. But perhaps the respirators would be useful if poisonous gases were emitted. (9 July 1915)

Airship pilots ostensibly aimed for strategic targets such as gas works, fuel tanks and military barracks; but given the imprecise nature of dropping bombs from Zeppelins, civilians were too often the unwitting victims, earning German airmen the name of 'baby killers'. Zeppelins killed fewer than 500 people in 1915 and 1916 but had a disproportionate effect on public morale. Those who had once felt safe tucked up under their blankets now went to bed uneasy at the prospect of those cumbersome terrorists slipping through the night and shattering their dreams. Typical of the British attitude was this June 1915 article:

> There was a time when people in this country described the Zeppelin as a gas-bag in a double sense. It was too cumbrous, offered too big a target, and was so much dependent upon the elements. They have recently had cause to revise their opinions. Without accepting the view, that it is the fearful menace the enemy would like us to believe, it is clear that it is a dangerous instrument of German frightfulness, which can sally forth like a thief in the night and murder women and children in sleeping cities … the mischief they accomplish may have no military value, but it will please the Huns who delight in murdering non-combatants, inhuman scoundrels who shell poor fishermen for fun after torpedoing their ships.[2]

Zeppelin-type airships had been patented in Germany in 1895, and were so successful that any rigid airship became known as a Zeppelin. The first cross-Channel flight took place in 1909, and they were flown commercially the following year. Anticipating attacks might one day come from the sky, Britain experimented with how to bring them down long before war was declared, but had largely dismissed them as 'gas-bags'.

Early defensive measures taken against Zeppelin attack during the war, however, suggested that anti-aircraft fire was too low, and fighter aeroplanes would struggle to apply the early technique of dropping bombs on the airships, as the latter could simply drop ballast and rise out of range. As the Zeppelins kept coming, Britain improved its aircraft, airstrips, ammunition and firing techniques. Key to their defeat was the introduction of explosive and incendiary ammunition, which could ignite the airships' hydrogen to devastating effect. On the night of 2 September 1916, during the largest airship raid of the war, William Leefe Robinson became the first pilot to destroy a Zeppelin over Britain, using new incendiary ammunition in concentrated Lewis Gun fire. SL.11 exploded into flames and plummeted into the Hertfordshire earth. Robinson was awarded a Victoria Cross.

While only nine raids reached Britain in the last two years of the war, the airships were used in supply and transport, and were particularly valuable as a reconnaissance tool, especially over the North Sea, and were in widespread use by the German Navy. Therefore the Germans persisted with the dirigibles despite their increasing vulnerability and extraordinary construction cost. Each balloon required the intestines of a quarter of a million cows to fashion the leak-proof hydrogen chambers, and the nation that Allied soldiers nicknamed 'the sausage eaters' was forced to ban sausage production.

Long after Zeppelins ceased to represent the chief air threat to them, Britons nervously scoured the sky on still nights: 'The moon is on the full now. Beautiful still nights, but this time no air raids. Last week the zepps came, but evidently lost their way & were found wandering over France ... It is too cold now for the bounders' (28 October 1917).

In the summer of 1917 new raiders invaded English airspace. The heavy bombers had arrived. They conducted two night raids in late May and early June over London, Sheerness in Kent and Shoeburyness in Essex, before launching the first daylight air raid against Britain.

On Wednesday, 13 June 1917, London's citizens went about their daily business. Late morning, a dull droning could be heard. As it grew louder, people went to their windows and out into the streets, peering into the sky. They could see what looked like a flock of black birds, but this quickly materialised into something far more sinister: 'Gothas' – huge bi-planes sweeping in from the south-east. Crowds gathered, mouths agape.

People did not run because they did not realise the danger they were in. Some thought the aircraft were friendly, because it was daylight, and the Germans had only ever attacked at night. Until now. At 11.25 am, the Gothas' bellies split open, and bombs rained down on the East End. It was the dawn of a new era.

Airfields around London and Kent sprang to life. Ninety-four little RNAS and Royal Flying Corps (RFC) aeroplanes – Sopwith Pups, Camels and Triplanes; Bristol Fighters and Scouts; BE12s – took to the skies, ready to challenge eighteen raiders that were each some three times their size. They were too late. The Gothas returned unharmed, leaving shocked Londoners to contemplate the carnage. One hundred and sixty-two were killed, many of them children at a primary school in Poplars. It proved to be the worst single air raid on Britain in the war.[3]

Murder in my heart

Today I went to London & met Auntie Alice ...

You have heard of the dreadful air raids we have been having lately. We went through the Strand into Fleet St & Holborn, but couldn't see any evidence of the raid on Wednesday. Shoreditch I believe suffered severely, nearly 100 people killed. Yesterday news came that another raid was coming. I listened all night, heard some guns but there was some gun practice. There is no mention in the paper this morning of an air raid or the stopping of one. Here we had all extra guard on duty. (16 June 1917)

Surrey was near London and the routes the Gothas took to bomb the capital. Belmont was close enough to hear the anti-aircraft guns and saw its fair share of aircraft, but these were mostly British training flights and, far from feeling threatened, Edie enjoyed the aeronautical antics. 'This morning we walked ... There were several aeroplanes about, they seemed to be having a sham fight, they were chasing each other, looping the loop, turning upside down, sideways & all-ways' (1 July 1917). In fact, she reassured her family, 'I don't think that the Germans will bomb a German Hospital. So far I am fairly secure' (23 June 1917).

On 7 July 1917 Gothas attacked London again. Edie saw it unfold:

This morning a Scotch sister & I went to Croydon just to see what it is like. We went into a shop & on coming out we saw lots of people looking up & when I got out we saw a horde of German aeroplanes, between 30 & 40 it looked. They were like black specks in the sky. They were making for London. On our journey back to Belmont we heard that many bombs had fallen & that the P.Office was in flames, part of Piccadilly & the Strand.

We knew many people must be killed & Oh Dear! & to think I have to nurse these people. I never before felt it, but if I had been near them at that moment I would have killed them, for I had murder in my heart. But Dear me! There I am on duty forgotten all about the bitter feeling I had towards the[m]. We are waiting now for news of damage done for more raiders came over than was ever sent before. I wonder how many came down in flames. (7 July 1917)

Twenty-two Gothas made it to the city. More than 100 British fighter planes attacked them on the return journey. The Gothas spat back, bullets ripping through wings and fuselage. Two RFC aircraft crashed, killing their crews. One Gotha was brought down into the sea. Alarmingly, around one-quarter of the 250 casualties were caused by falling debris from anti-aircraft fire.[4] The next morning Edie heard all about the raid: 'It seems that 100 bombs were dropped, about 37 people killed & 141 injured. The London people are very anxious for reprisals' (8 July 1917).

This raid was particularly upsetting to Londoners. The authorities could be forgiven for being unprepared against the first attack, but surely they should have been protected from a second! In East London a crowd of angry men and women surged through the streets ransacking the homes and businesses of people thought to be German and smashing and looting shops bearing Germanic names.[5] In one of the affected areas, a tradesman said, 'You can well understand these people. This morning, when the raid was on, there were nearly a dozen women running up and down outside here holding their children in their hands, shouting, "they killed his daddy, and now they want him!"'[6] Questions were asked in Parliament about the 'failure of our aerial defences to guard London'. Lloyd George responded that '[t]he attack, in fact, had not been made with impunity ... no measures that we could take would give complete immunity. The nearest approach to immunity [lies] in making their visits so costly that they would not become worth the Germans' while'.[7]

Although the armies on the battlefield needed as much air support as it was possible to give, a squadron was temporarily brought back from France to help defend London from the Gothas. Within days of the raid, the War Cabinet agreed to form a committee to consider Britain's air defence and organisation, which led to the formation of the Royal Air Force in 1918.[8] Approval was given for twenty balloon barrages to help protect London.[9] The first was operational in October 1917. Three giant balloons were tethered 7500 feet high, dangling between them aprons of 1000-feet-long steel wires like something dreamt up by HG Wells.[10] Edie found it 'frightening' (7 October 1917).

34

'BABY KILLERS'

The anger the raids stirred in Edie's heart was short-lived. She did not blame her patients. She took a forthright, practical approach and soon found that many were intelligent and good-humoured and as keen to practise their English as she was to try some German. Some were good company and she could not help but like them:

> I am sending you some photographs I have taken of prisoners. You will think they are like Huns & baby killers. In the large group (these are all officers) they are the younger & nicer men & seem anxious to give a good impression & to behave as English gentlemen, but their manner is a wee bit exaggerated. The tall man standing on the extreme right is a doctor. He helped me a lot in dressings & was very thoughtful. The nicest man of the lot is the third last standing wearing glasses, he is a Bavarian law student. We call him the censor, nothing passes his eyes. He is the senior & is responsible for the discipline of the ward. The two boys [with] their eyes bandaged are 20 yrs old. The end one speaks English almost perfectly. The second boy with his eye bandaged is called or rather his name is Leis pronounced Lice. One day one of them came & asked me what we called animals on the head so I said 'lice'. They teased the life out of Leis. They had heard me say 'what an awful name'.
>
> The other group are anything of the nicest though they are polite. These are very German looking don't you think?

'Baby killers'

> The other day I went into the Sgt Majors room. A visitor (German) had given them some flowers. They are learning English these men. One handed me a flower saying 'you are a flower'. I told him it wasn't right to say such things, he couldn't understand but kept saying 'you are a flower'. After a lot of talking I mentioned the word 'compliment'. He then said he didn't mean a compliment he wanted me to have a flower. He got mixed up with his verbs & used the word 'are' instead of 'have'. They all asked then if it was customary for English Gentlemen to pay compliments to ladies by calling them flowers. One is a Bavarian and said that they were in the habit of saying 'titmouse'. Fancy being called a titmouse. (7 July 1917)

The people at Belmont became accustomed to the sounds of war:

> Today we went for a walk & while we were out we heard the anti-aircraft guns. We met a man who had just seen the special constable hustling everybody to take shelter, so we learnt that there was an air raid on. But the sound of the guns did not seem to be coming from the direction of London. We think it must be from the East Coast again. We often hear guns at night … Sometimes we hear a noise & every window in the building will rattle, there will not be a breath of air moving. (22 July 1917)

On this occasion, the Gothas had made a deadly hit-and-run attack on Felixstowe and nearby Harwich. Three weeks later they swooped again at Southend and Shoeburyness, killing over thirty. Edie heard about it that night: 'There has been an air raid at 6 pm but we don't yet know where. I do hope little damage has been done'. She added without rancour, 'We have an airman in now, he is a pilot. He isn't a bad sort of chap, his plane was brought down over our lines. He laughingly calls himself the "Baby Killer". He told me this evening he likes babies in a distance only' (12 August 1917).

When the raiders next ventured over the Channel, on 22 August 1917, London was again assumed to be in their sights. Edie was visiting the city.

> Sister Beresford, her brother & I went to Guildhall ... to see the pictures. We had been through three of the galleries when the first warning came of an air raid, but we went on looking at the pictures, till we got the second warning. We were then told to go to the Guildhall Crypt. Oh Dear! How I wanted to stay in the street, I walked slowly from the gallery, & it seemed queer to see the people all trying to find shelter. Cheapside was crowded before, & [now] the streets were almost deserted. The paper said the next day the Crypt sheltered 2000 people. It was crowded, & how oppressive it became. We were in there an hour when we were told that all was clear ... The raid stopped us from going to St Paul's. (26 August 1917)

The Gothas were making for targets around the mouth of the Thames, and Dover and Margate. They had a torrid time of it themselves. Of fifteen that embarked for England, five turned back with engine trouble, two were shot down by fighters, and a third was shelled down by a coastal gun battery. The remainder limped home, only to be attacked by British fighter squadrons based on the continent as they flew back over the Belgian coast. This was the last daylight air raid over Britain.[1]

As the RNAS and RFC honed their techniques against daylight forays, the Gothas recommenced night raids. At the end of September they struck London on six nights out of eight in what proved to be the most intense phase of aerial bombing over England in the war. Edie was on leave at Cricklewood:

> On Thursday last I went to Uncle Will's ... It was such a beautiful night – just a night for an air raid. Uncle had to go to a

meeting. Auntie & I went out to see what the sky was like, both of us agreed that it wouldn't prove a good night for gothas, as there were too many clouds. Oh dear! How nervous Auntie was. If she saw clouds in the sky she imagined it for there wasn't one to be seen, the moon was shining as beautifully as the moon can shine, but Auntie seemed comforted. I went back to Victoria Station, on the top of a 'bus, people kept scanning the skies to see if anything could be seen, but nary a thing. The next morning we learnt that the Germans were stopped in Flanders. The cartoon that evening was like this [Edie drew the moon smiling over what were 'supposed to be tombstones', and included the caption 'the end of a perfect day'] – underneath were the lines:

Fifteen little gothers
All in a line,
The RNAS [Royal Naval Air Service] spotted them
& then there were 'nein'.

'Nein' is the German word for 'none'. I thought I could make the cartoon look better. In the left hand corner represents the moon laughing. When our orderlies saw this, they were down like a shot to show the three German airmen we have in. They only laughed. I cannot understand why they are airmen, for they are fearfully chicken-hearted, for last night during the raid they had their heads under the bedclothes. (30 September 1917)

Edie was back at work when several Gothas and new R-type Staaken 'Giant' bombers attacked. The nurses watched a thrilling show:

Last night proved a big air raid & we saw everything distinctly from our bedroom windows. Early in the evening we drove them off, but they came back at nine o'clock. We saw the rockets go up & we heard the hooters. We could see our airmen go up in clusters. They have a light near the propellers. They looked like a lot of fireflies darting here & there. There seemed hundreds of them. If we could have only seen the 'planes what a battle it would have been. We could see a flash of light & then an explosion. Our anti-aircraft guns were booming & booming in succession. The Gothas did not get into London. They were in Kent & Essex. The night or sky was wonderfully clear & still, except for the guns. With the rockets, the flashes of light, & darting lights of our 'planes made a really wonderful display of fireworks. I wouldn't have missed the sight for anything. The only thing that was wanted was the location of the enemy craft. For the quickness of the darting lights of our machines showed how the enemy was being chased. The darting lights appeared all over the sky. I wish I could write better. This seems a very poor description of things. (30 September 1917)

In one busy week, nearly 100 bombers terrorised the south, while Zeppelins assaulted the north. More than 200 people were killed and nearly 400 injured in that intense September.[2] These numbers paled in comparison to the hell on earth in France, but the trauma lingered. And relativities aside, the danger to their homes and families was real:

> Everybody complains much of nerves several days after the raid, more than they do at the time. The people of London are getting very 'panicky'. Though the papers say they are not.
>
> I am not at all surprised at that. It is not the bombs that frighten so much, as our guns. The Barrage is frightening & the shrapnel rattle[s] down on the houses like hail. It is our guns' shrapnel that causes the casualties. People will run out into the streets. During a raid people crowd into the tubes that the air becomes so foul that it is not breathable. Several persons have been

'Baby killers'

crushed to death ... I believe that during a raid the rattle of the Guns & shrapnel, the bombs, the women & children screaming, the dogs barking, the fire engines racing through the streets, the continual hooting, causes a fearful pandemonium. We here in Belmont only hear the guns bombs & hooters & that is bad enough. No wonder Londoners want reprisals & now they are to get them. I think it will be easier for our men to bomb German towns than it is for Germans to bomb London. We are superior airmen at the front, perhaps we shall make a better attempt to frighten & subdue the Germans, than they did us. (7 October 1917)

35
IT IS DELIGHTFUL WALKING HERE

As spring turned into summer, rambles in the rolling countryside of Surrey had become Edie's favourite pastime. Epsom Downs was less than 3 miles away. The air was light and clear. From the Downs, she could see over woods and thickets to where the very top of the dome of St Paul's peeped through.

Among the nurses who reported to Matron Fairchild that first day at Belmont POW Hospital was Rebecca Rose (Rose) Beresford.[1] Seven years older than Edie, she was about to turn thirty-nine. She had commenced training in Taunton in 1907, a year before Edie started at the Coast Hospital, and embarked on a midwifery course in July 1914 but soon found herself tending wounded soldiers in the 110-bed Hôpital Temporaire d'Arc-en-Barrois. The hospital was founded in a chateau in north-eastern France by four English sisters with the support of the British Red Cross. The sisters' connections saw a procession of writers, poets and artists volunteer their services alongside a core staff of qualified surgeons and nurses.

Over many long walks in the countryside, Edie and Rose Beresford became close friends:

> I am enclosing a snap of myself as you will see. I had been out over the Downs & I had been getting some Harebells, some Scalia & meadow sweet, & it looked so pretty in my vase that I would experiment in photography at taking flowers. Sister Beresford my friend here helped me, but she insisted that I should be in it. (7 October 1917)

It is delightful walking here

It was no doubt under Beresford's influence that Edie was soon reading *Gallipoli* by John Masefield. The future poet laureate had volunteered as an orderly for a few months at Arc-en-Barrois during Beresford's time there. Edie wrote that the book 'would make your heart ache, & yet it makes one feel proud' (9 June 1917). She mailed it home to Sans Souci.

This was the England Edie had looked forward to. The land of Shakespeare and poets; of green fields, leafy woods and wildflowers; the rose-coloured England that lived in the remembered history of so many Australians, in her father's reminiscences, and in the fragments of her childhood memories:

> A couple of days ago I went for a walk with another sister across the Downs. The breeze was in our faces. We walked on & on not intending to go very far, when we found ourselves at Burgh Heath, a place about 4 miles from here, we walked 8 miles that morning. It is delightful walking here, it is much prettier than in Sydney except of course in the mountains. The road[s] are very smooth, often with high shady trees. The scent of the country does you good. Everywhere they are bringing in the hay. Poppies are still blooming everywhere which gives a very nice touch of colour … On our way back, we noticed an aeroplane hovering very low. He took a sweep upwards, & then came straight down head-first as if falling & at a tremendous rate. Our hearts were in our mouths, then he made a small circle upwards flying upside down. (14 July 1917)

Edie was slim, fit and tanned as ever as she and her colleagues walked many miles in Surrey's gentle countryside and soft weather:

> The air is beautiful here in the morning … The sister who was with me took a snap of me so I'm sending you one. In my dress I have some lilies of the valley & some bluebells in my hand. It

isn't the best picture of me but I wanted you to see me in the fields. (16 June 1917)

[A]nother sister & I walked to Chipstead woods & got lost. The bluebells, daisies, buttercups, violets, hawthorne were all in bloom. The bluebells or some call them wild hyacinths, were so thick that you couldn't help treading on them, & in parts when the sun was shining on them they looked like a blue mist. (1 July 1917)

This morning Sister Beresford ... & I went across the Epsom Downs again ... We walked on & on till we got to Banstead village, & then we had tea at a funny little country inn,[2] with a funny little garden, the little cosy nooks in unexpected places. (28 July 1917)

Later, 'Sister Beresford & I ... walked from [Leatherhead] to Box Hill', a famous beauty spot strewn with box and yew trees that commanded views south over the Weald. In their ankle-length dresses and sensible leather shoes they slogged their way up:

The path ... goes straight up & is of slippery clay soil. It was hard work, but it was worth it ... we had a glorious view of the surrounding country. The sunset was glorious & lasted for such a long time ... [The] leaves are all on the turn, & there were shades of red gold & brown... A gust of wind comes & the leaves fall about like snow ... We found a tea garden & had some tea & then tried to come back. Oh it would have been much easier if I had sat on an iron tray & slid down. (28 October 1917)

Belmont was only 10 miles from Sydenham, where Rose Beresford's widowed mother, brother and sister lived. They happily included Edie in their circle:

> Sister Beresford & I … got up at 4 o'clock & … went for a long walk across the Downs. The air was perfect & very clear, a sign of rain here, I believe, I never grow tired of looking at the green fields. The wheat has been cut & it is now in sheaves … [We] had some afternoon tea on the Downs with Sister's brother & sister. (18 August 1917)

In August, usually England's hottest month, it rained, and the Germans ribbed the staff mercilessly:

> All this week it has been raining! raining! & raining. The Germans keep pointing to the weather saying 'English weather English summertime'. They had a point of course. It is cold too. On Saturday I had to go to London. It rained the whole of the time. This weekend brings in Bank holiday. As I got on to Victoria Station we could see loads & loads of baggage & people sitting on it all waiting for trains to Brighton, Bournemouth, & other seaside places. There were long queues of people waiting at the ticket offices. They did look so miserable with the rain pelting, anything [other] than trippers. (5 August 1917)

The nurses rambled for miles during the long summer twilights, then Edie wrote her letters, read and sewed during the quiet hours as the patients slept.

> I am so tired tonight, for I'm still on night duty, we went for a walk & had some coffee at a 'so-called' hotel, at any rate it was very nice, two of us parted company from the rest & Beresford & I went further on of course got lost. We found ourselves at Epsom & then at Ewell, we were miles out of our way, but I thoroughly enjoyed it. I think we must have passed through an estate. We were passing down a lovely avenue & near a large castle-like building flying the Stars & Stripes perhaps some

American magnate bought the estate. How lovely it is to go to bed, when you are sleepy. Queen knows that feeling now, I dare say. (12 August 1917)

36

FAMILY FOOTSTEPS

In March 1916 Edie had been informed that then-nineteen-year-old Queenie was determined to follow her into nursing:

> I didn't think Queen would apply for the Coast. If she has set her mind to nursing hope she will get in, though she is rather young yet. Hope she has made up her mind for hard work. It would be strange if I came back to the Coast & found Queen there, especially if I had to run her round. Can't imagine her scrubbing up dirty people & scrubbing lockers etc etc!!! At any rate all will go well with her there I hope. (26 March 1916)

In due course the news arrived that Queenie had ranked at the bottom of the waiting list for nursing places. In the meantime she began work at Greycliffe, a stately home in Vaucluse that had been converted into a children's hospital.

Edie commenced writing separately to her, offering advice and encouragement when she was weary or dispirited, because Queenie liked to get letters all to herself.

Dear Queenie

I have just heard that you are a 'pro' at Greycliffe under Sister Marriot. How vividly my pro days are all coming back to me. How do you like it? I suppose by this time you have got used to your 'choker'. I wonder if you have the same hours as we had at the Coast …

> I hope the 'new pro' goes to bed without aching feet, as I used to do. I wonder if she has to use Meth Spirits. I know you will love the babies. It would be lovely to have a baby to nurse now. Only men we see.

> Much love & Good luck from Edie (18 November 1916)

Edie encouraged her sister not to be afraid of the hard work: 'if I can get through you can' (14 December 1916). Queen was eventually offered a place at the Coast and commenced her training in June 1917. Edie suggested she look in a tin trunk that she had left there:

> My name is on the top of it ... I have most of my nursing books with me, though Furneaux's Physiology was amongst the books I sent home before I left. Queen could find that. It is much better for Queen to have her own books, first to study from & then to use them as reference. I wouldn't be without mine. (26 August 1917)

Edie delighted in talking shop with her younger sister and sharing advances in treatment that came as the war progressed.

> Well you have got in a good deal in your first year, such as urine testing, giving of antitoxin etc. But I smiled when I read that you had applied a foment of Hypochlorous acid. We haven't used Hypochlorous acid since 1915. It is all Eusol now. Eusol contains Chlorinate of lime & Boric acid half & half I believe. The word Eusol is made up of the following words Edinburgh University's Solution of Lime. We used it for dirty wounds but when they are clean we often use saline sol. Have you heard of Dakins treatment?[1] We use it a good deal at Belmont, sometimes with success. Thanks so much for the snaps, you are getting very fat Queen. Hospital life can't disagree with you. (13 November 1917)

At Belmont, Edie hung up photos of home. She pinned a photo of her family to her cubicle curtain, and, after numerous reminders, she finally received from her father two snaps of the house at Sans Souci: 'The first I got framed in a little black narrow frame ... There is a Tasmanian girl here, I found her standing in front of it one day & she said, how that makes you feel homesick to see a bungalow again. I have never seen one here' (11 September 1917).

The faces of her family were the last thing Edie saw when she retired and the first thing she saw when she woke up. They were 10 000 miles away but never wavered in their support. Just as she wrote regularly, they did too, and their letters travelled with her, packed within reach in her trunk. She never doubted that she was in their thoughts. Even when the letters didn't come, Edie knew it was not because they hadn't been written, but because the postal system was slow or the mail steamers were at the bottom of the sea.

Belmont allowed Edie more time with her Blake relatives. The family members had an unshakeable trust in each other and believed in familial duty. Although Aunt Tilda had the daily care of Edie's grandparents Andrew and Matilda, the siblings shared the cost of their upkeep. Edie told her father, 'Uncle Harry is writing to you & also sending you a balance sheet, as to how the old people are being financed. Uncle Jim is [the] only one in arrears' (14 October 1917).

Charles had absolute faith that his brothers and sisters would take care of his daughter, and they did not let him down. They had consistently written to her and advised her. They rallied, too, when his namesake, Edie's young cousin Charlie, was imprisoned at Clausthal. When news of his capture came through in January 1917, his aunts and uncles wrote to him to distract him and keep up his spirits. Aunt Alice joked self-deprecatingly from Sutton Coldfield, '[W]e all felt very sad about you ... My hair ... seems to be getting very thin, so I may have to get a red wig like Queen Elizabeth, so when you come home I shall have become rejuvenated'.[2] Uncle Frank wrote jovially from *Robin's Nest*, 'We are all so glad to hear that you are safe so far after your trying experience … The "old people" still knock about … Grannie's memory is often a blank but the governor keeps extremely fit considering'.[3] Young Charlie would see out the war safely as a prisoner, returning to England in December 1918.

In September, Edie and Aunt Alice visited Suffolk together. Their train 'arrived at Woodbridge at 7 pm. So Auntie Alice & I had a very pleasant [4-mile] walk to Dallinghoo. The evening was beautiful & the sunset was gorgeous & we occasionally picked a few blackberries, till it was too dark to see' (22 September 1917).

Old Andrew had celebrated his ninetieth birthday in August, and they 'found Auntie Tilda, Grandfather & Grandmother very well. Indeed the old people looked in the pink of health' (22 September 1917). The next day Uncle Frank came by on his motorbike and 'took me in his trailer all over the place' – whizzing from Woodbridge to Melton to Ufford then back to Dallinghoo. 'It was most enjoyable … Today is my [32nd] birthday & Auntie Tilda sent me a sweet little silver pencil & Auntie Alice is sending me a suitcase' (22 September 1917).

Edie sent on recent photos of her family in Sydney to her relations at Dallinghoo, but, she wrote, 'When Grandfather saw the photo with you all on the garden seat, he wouldn't have it was Dad … his memory is very short' (14 October 1917). It was surely unsurprising that the old man was confused by the image. After all, it was a picture of a son he had not seen in the flesh for twenty-five years.

Soon the first baby of the next generation arrived: 'Lily's baby was born. It is a son. Charles Arthur. We do not seem to get away from our family names. They seem all Charles Arthurs & Harry's' (21 October 1917).

37

FOR WEAL OR WOE

There was much Edie enjoyed about Belmont. She loved the picturesque countryside and the proximity to London and her extended family. However, she remained determined to get to France and be as close to the action as her friends were. Mildred Crocker Brown had been there since February 1917, and Evelyn Swannell since the following August.

> Yesterday Swannell wired to me asking me to come & see her [at the Croydon War Hospital], as she was leaving for France today. I went, & while I was waiting, I looked amongst the letters on the rack, when I came across a name I knew. An old Coast nurse, she was my pro for a while in my ward at the Coast. The girl herself appeared. It was very nice to see some Coasters again. The Australians have taken over the hospital Swannell was in. Swannell did her best to get me transferred, but Miss Becher wouldn't grant [it]. I wonder if ever I shall get to France. (18 August 1917)

As delightful as she found Surrey in the warmer months, Edie was not looking forward to a winter in Belmont. 'We have quite 10 minutes walk from our quarters to meals, all in the rain & in winter time it will be in the snow' (12 August 1917). The weather soon began to turn:

The days are drawing in now, & will be getting colder & colder. The hips & haws are in abundance, also the mountain ash berry, & there are lots of other berries of which I don't know the name. They tell me that the abundance of berries signifies a hard winter. (9 September 1917)

The food question is going to be a hard one to crack this winter. People have to stand in queues for sugar, butter, bacon & tea. Tea is almost impossible to get these days. But there has been no mention of bread this time. Potatoes are plentiful. I suppose the frost will soon nip all the vegetables. (28 October 1917)

By October 1917, even as the Allies were making little headway on the Western Front, there were ominous portents elsewhere. Russia was riven by internal strife. The tsar had been forced to abdicate in March 1917 and was subsequently exiled to Siberia; the country was now but weeks from civil war. Meanwhile, there was trouble on the Italian front. In 1915, the Triple Entente had persuaded Italy to abandon its alliance with Germany and Austria-Hungary and join them with the promise of tracts of Austrian territory when they won the war. Fighting on their border with Austria-Hungary, by late 1917 the Italians were in trouble. Struggling supply lines had cruelled their efforts in the mountainous country and German troops, freed from the Russian front following the failed Kerensky offensive in July 1917, reinforced the Austro-Hungarians. On 24 October 1917 the Germans and Austro-Hungarians launched the battle of Caporetto, resulting in the collapse of the Italian Second Army. British and French troops were sent to reinforce the Italian front, and although they played little role in stopping the Central Powers at the Piave River, they were a valuable commodity to be sent away from the Western Front. As 1917 wore on, it became increasingly clear that victory in the war could only come on the Western Front.

For weal or woe

> Today the news has been very depressing, some 65,000 prisoners taken from the Italian front. There must be some gross neglect somewhere there, & you know a great number of our gunners are there too. The papers are read here by the prisoners. I often ask what the news is. I'm very often told that there is no news, but today they tell me of the 65,000. Russia seems in a sad way & now the Italians are not coming up to the scratch. One German admitted that there was very little credit in beating the Russians & that the English were a foe worth fighting. (28 October 1917)

Edie's thoughts increasingly turned to getting out of Belmont. Ultimately, it was not the state of the war, dislike of the prisoners, weather, food or England itself driving her desire. Her main grievances were with the hospital. She had, from the first, felt like she was serving with the 'B' team: perhaps the RAMC was disinclined to waste the cream of their men on a POW hospital? She appeared to judge that, unlike Egypt, shortcomings here were less due to the haste with which the hospital was conceived than to the want of care, competence and common sense in those in charge.

Many of the orderlies and guards had been classified as unfit for active service (no doubt the case for many hospitals in Britain, as so many new hospitals and staff were needed), but it was not being surrounded by such men that concerned Edie so much as their attitude. Many were conscripts whom she thought lazy, unmotivated and uncommitted to their tasks and to the war effort. For over two years she had seen soldiers fight and die for a cause she believed in, and now she was surrounded by men she considered to be shirkers.

> These conscript men are not the flower of England. The men who were at Gallipoli were the men. It is a pity our best men should go first. The men in Egypt would tell you, they didn't think it honest to stand & look on. They were the men to nurse.

It was a pleasure. These conscripts think they are 'hardly done by'. (2 June 1917)

Urgently needing more men for its army, in January 1916 the British government had passed legislation allowing it to conscript single men and childless widowers aged between 18 and 41 for active service. In May 1916 this was extended to married men, despite anti-conscription demonstrations in Trafalgar Square the month before. The medically unfit, clergymen, teachers and certain industrial workers were exempted, as were conscientious objectors: men exempted or seeking exemption on religious, pacifist or political grounds. Some of the orderlies were among Britain's 16 000 conscientious objectors. Edie was clear about what she thought of them.

> [One] afternoon [I] went [with] Sister Beresford to
> Merthesden a very pretty place some 10 miles from here & we
> spent a very pleasant afternoon with Beresford's Aunt & Uncle.
>
> While we were there another visitor came. In the course of
> conversation we told the visitor where we were working. He
> hoped we had pleasant company so Beresford told him that we
> were surrounded by lunatic asylums, Conscientious Objectors
> & Huns. We also told him lots of other things concerning
> these people. When it was time to go, this particular gentleman
> expressed his sorrow & wished he had been an earlier visitor
> & would talk to us about these Huns. I could see Mrs Parkes
> (Beresford's Aunt) was just enjoying herself, she looked full of
> mischief. When we got outside she told us that we had been
> talking to a pro-German & consequently a Conscientious
> Objector. I hope he enjoyed our society. If I should meet him
> again he shall know what I think of Conscientious Objectors.
> (21 October 1917)

Mrs Parkes' visitor may have been 'pro-German' – or so characterised for objecting on other grounds. Edie and Rose Beresford would have debated him whatever his justification. Their distaste was almost universal in Britain. The conscription debate was also highly emotional in Australia. Prime Minister Billy Hughes was in England when Britain introduced conscription. Having originally rejected the notion, by the summer of 1916 he believed it was necessary as Australia's voluntary enlistments slowed and the AIF incurred significant casualties on the Somme. Twice Hughes put conscription to the Australian people. Twice they narrowly voted against it. Every man who served for Australia did so by choice – even if some arms were twisted by a little emotional blackmail. Of nations involved in the First World War, only Australia, South Africa and India never introduced conscription.[1]

Hughes first put conscription to a referendum in October 1916. He tried again in December 1917, following a year in which the AIF suffered its highest losses of the war, including almost 77 000 casualties on the Western Front: nearly double the 40 000 of 1916.

The single question on whether or not to introduce conscription went to the heart of Australians' views of citizenship and duty, the exercise of power and Australia's place in the world. As a result, the Australian conscription debates were complex, bitter and divisive, splitting the population roughly along political, class and sectarian lines. Political and social conservatives, including Protestant church leaders, saw the war as necessary to defend the British Empire and, now, to support the volunteers already fighting. Catholics, largely of Irish descent, were suspected of anti-Empire sentiment; Daniel Mannix, elevated to archbishop of Melbourne in 1917, spoke against conscription during both campaigns.

The labour movement also opposed conscription, arguing it was an opportunity for wealthy capitalists to profit via wartime production and by putting the working classes in the trenches and replacing them with cheaper immigrant labour. The Industrial Workers of the World was a movement of mostly unskilled workers, founded in America, that advocated acts of sabotage against industrial targets. Members of the movement spoke against conscription on Sundays in Sydney's Domain in the lead-up to the 1916 referendum and were subsequently charged with treason and crimes related to arson and conspiracy: it was alleged that they had 'preached the doctrine of sabotage'.[2] Edie had struggled to comprehend the details of what was happening at home:

> Oh! I forgot to mention that the paper cuttings Dad sent are quite alright. I have only read three of them. They take some taking in. I didn't know that so much damage was premeditated. Swannell & I didn't know what the I.W.W. meant but one of Swannell's letters, she was told that the letters meant 'I won't work'. A very appropriate name for them. We can only imagine what sabotage means. (12 January 1917)

At Belmont, Edie watched with barely concealed disdain as 'avoiders' served the enemy, rather than fighting beside their fellow Britons. The prisoners looked good in contrast. They, at least, had fought for their cause and were by and large considered a better class of men.

> How I wish this cruel war was over & could get back to the Coast, & have 'pros' for a change instead of orderlies. These men are the limit & they make me feel ashamed of them, for the Huns help me far more than the orderlies & are far more thoughtful. There is no need to know the language, they anticipate your wants … If I could understand them perhaps, I should hear some language that isn't good when a man calls in pain, in the middle of the night. (24 August 1917)

Edie's attitude towards the patients waxed and waned. When tired and frustrated, she was quick to complain about them too:

> There isn't much news to tell you this time. We are very busy, very badly wounded men. These huns cannot stand pain. They cry very easily. Sometimes there is nothing else to be heard but groans & moans. It seems fatal to give them morphia for they think they should have it, even if they don't sleep for an hour. I do dislike nursing these men. I hated the idea of nursing them when I came here first, but now I dislike them themselves … We are so full up of patients that we cannot take any more convoys for a week. Thank Heaven. (1 September 1917)

Although she lashed out at the prisoners in her letters, the primary source of her frustration was the hospital administration. Belmont's poorly trained orderlies made a sad contrast to the efficient men of 17BGH, and the hospital hierarchy lacked the understanding and motivation to ensure that they were capable of adequately assisting the nurses. It was left to the sisters to direct men who were not merely unskilled, but evidently lacking in intelligence and the desire to learn, especially from women.

> I haven't very much news to tell you. We are very busy & very worried by the incapabilities & unwillingness of the orderlies. Oh! They would drive us mad. Matron asked for 6 extra sisters, but 50 raw orderlies came instead. But that only increases the amount of work. It takes a very very long time to lick these men into shape. It tells on our tempers, least it does mine. It isn't right that a woman should be over men. The latter resents it, & it makes things worse. Nursing is hard & disagreeable at times, & these men are lazy, or if not lazy they are stupid & very often untruthful. (9 September 1917)

Edie was no shrinking violet and had no doubt about the intellectual and leadership capacities of women: for nearly a decade she had been a capable working woman surrounded and directed by others of her ilk. Nevertheless, she seemed to believe that men and women had their places, and in being forced to 'lick untrained men into shape' women were having to upset the natural order in a man's world.

In some ways, the issues at Belmont echoed those that had afflicted the Australian Army nurses in the earliest days in Cairo, except there the experienced Australian matrons had stood their ground. Here, the nurses' problems were compounded by their matron. After the excellent leadership and support provided by Miss Watson at the Coast and the matrons in Egypt, Edie was very unhappy with Matron Edith Fairchild, and did not hold back:

> Our Matron it seems helps us only on the surface & is not our friend behind our backs. She has as much backbone as a jellyfish. If anything happens we mustn't have a voice in the matter, we must always sing dumb & put up with anything. We have fought for our allowance of food which did not please the Matron or the quarter master, who we thought was pocketing the money which should have been spent on us. I was not always agitator, but the New Zealanders were. After all our agitating things are much better & happier. But there is always a feeling that we are standing over a mine which will burst any moment. We have or most of us have asked for a transfer. (3 November 1917)

Matron Fairchild was still learning the ropes. Now in her late forties, she had been a member of the QAIMNS since 1904 and had been promoted to sister two years later, a rank she had maintained for the next decade in England, in South Africa, and in France since the war began. In April 1917 she was promoted to acting matron and spent a month at Dartford War Hospital for 'instruction purposes' before taking up her present post.[3]

For weal or woe

At Belmont, she was thrown in the deep end. Her first appointment as matron was not to an established hospital with a well-oiled team, but to a new hospital with staff who had never worked together before, untrained orderlies, unimpressive doctors, and patients whom everybody resented to a greater or lesser degree. It was up to the matron to ensure her girls were properly fed, quartered and assisted by the orderlies: preferably promptly and respectfully. In Edie's opinion, Miss Fairchild did not stand up for them.

Edie also knew what proper medical standards were, and even if the patients were Germans, it was a matter of professional pride to meet those standards. In her view, Belmont's medical hierarchy failed to insist upon this. To add to her woes, the mail was unreliable and the war did not seem to be going well. She poured her heart out to her youngest sister, who could now understand what working in a hospital should be.

> Well Queen I do get very 'homesick'. I thought as time goes on one's feelings would get a bit blunted. But it doesn't make any difference. I'm here amongst strangers, I haven't seen anyone I know for quite a long time. It doesn't seem as if war will end soon. In fact I feel rather pessimistic. What a lot poor England has to put up with. I wonder what will happen to Russia she seems now to be on the verge of civil war. The Germans will take possession in no time. What a terribly corrupt country Russia must be. She has been but very little use to us in fact a hindrance …
>
> You don't know how I'm looking forward to coming back to the Coast with its 'pros'. I never want to work with orderlies again. I've come to the conclusion, that women are more conscientious than men. We have a very sorry lot here, not only with orderlies but with the Doctors too. Then the German Prisoners, do not make things better. We seem to have very small & weedy

specimens of humanity around us. All the orderlies are not fit for the front. Some of them seem to be of the lowest class of men. Few of them are possessed of any intelligence at all. The doctors are all old dugouts who haven't seen the inside of a hospital for many a long day. The patients are badly wounded, small pasty-faced men, I should imagine the lower classes of the Germans. One Sister said yesterday 'Oh for the sight of a decent man.' Our training goes for nothing here. Asepsis & antisepsis are unknown in these walls. Do you wonder at me wanting to get back? (11 September 1917)

Deep dissatisfaction was taking its toll. Edie wanted out: 'My six months here is nearing to a close. I wonder if my request for a transfer to another hospital will be accepted, or I wonder if Miss Becher will grant my request to send [me] to France' (14 October 1917).

Two weeks later, Edie had her answer:

I have one big piece of news. Matron came to me yesterday and asked me if I would go on a hospital ship, as there seems very little likelihood of me going to France. I said I would go, rather than stay here. The Germans are not the only reason I want to go. The Matron is not all she should be. Though I [am] sorry to go so far from London … But I have only signed up for 12 months. My time will be up April 4th so at that time I will ask Miss Becher if I may go to France & join Sister Swannell. I'm not very anxious to go on board ship.
(1 November 1917)

But she was so desperate to get away from Belmont that she would do almost anything.

For weal or woe

I'm going on the sea once more. It is not exactly my wish. For I would sooner be near London & near my uncles ... [but] life isn't exactly the happiest here ...

I ask[ed] for France but I've got [a] hospital ship instead, & I am taking it, though I need not. As I have asked for the transfer, I will not turn back. I never dreamt of a ship. I thought that if I couldn't get France I would get somewhere else in England.

Whether for weal or woe I'm going to join the Glenart Castle at Liverpool Nov 12th. (3 November 1917)

38

HMHS *GLENART CASTLE*

Edie travelled by rail to Liverpool on 12 November 1917, where she settled in the North Western Hotel. Worn down by the POW hospital and farewelling Sister Beresford, missing home and family and facing another six months at sea, she was despondent. 'Though we [have] been here several times I have never seen Liverpool. I can't say that I like it. It is sordid' (13 November 1917). Her mood improved when she visited the sister of a young soldier who used to help in the ward at the 17BGH:

> He was with us about 6 months. Then he went to France & was on the Somme … in one of his letters he asked me to go & see his sister in Liverpool, if ever I was near there. So … I called on his sister. Such a welcome she gave me … I felt very homesick … she, Miss Christophers, made me so welcome, that I lost my homesickness. (21 November 1917)

At 9 am on 15 November 1917, Edie, along with other medical staff and two army chaplains, joined HMHS *Glenart Castle*.

> This ship is not like the 'Essequibo'. Not nearly as good. She is also much smaller, carrying only 450 patients. But she is very steady & very seaworthy. Our cabins are not like the cabins on the 'Esse'. They are much smaller & contain two bunks, but as I'm having one to myself, I make the upper bunk into a shelf. (21 November 1917)

HMHS *Glenart Castle*

Many of the medical staff and crew were joining the ship for the first time, including its captain. Nevertheless, Lieutenant-Commander Bernard Burt had spent most of his fifty-three years at sea and knew the waters around southern England like the back of his hand. By the time he took command of the *Glenart Castle*, Burt was a well-respected twenty-five-year veteran of the Union Line who had been mentioned in despatches for his work landing troops at Gallipoli in April 1915 as master of the SS *Galeka*.[1] Sporting a neatly trimmed white beard, he looked the very essence of a sea captain.

HMHS *Glenart Castle* had been a Union Castle steamship, built in Belfast in 1900 and christened *Galician*. She had already had a lively war. At the outset of hostilities, on 5 August 1914, she was steaming west of the Canary Islands when a large ship flying the German flag bore down on her. The *Liverpool Daily Post* reported,

> [The ship] signalled the *Galician* to stop at once and to cease using its wireless. The wireless operator, nevertheless, sent out the SOS, and was spelling out the ship's name – G a l – when the German vessel signalled: 'Stop your wireless. We blow up the bridge if another letter leaves.' The *Galician* was ordered to follow her captor … and they steamed at full speed to the south. Meantime German officers had boarded the *Galician* and made a thorough search of her papers. Everything was done with extreme politeness, and a receipt was given for the ship's papers, but two Army officer passengers were taken to the German ship as prisoners. In the evening the *Galician* was ordered to proceed at full speed southward [with the] message: 'On account of your women and children I will not sink your ship. You are released. Bon voyage!'[2]

In late October 1914, renamed the less Germanic '*Glenart Castle*', she was refitted as a hospital ship.

On 1 March 1917, eight months before Edie joined her, the

Glenart Castle survived a much closer call. After taking on over 500 patients,[3] more than 300 of whom were cot cases, at Le Havre, she departed for Southampton. The number of patients on board exceeded the ship's limit. Major Home, RAMC OC, had agreed to take them after consulting the ship's captain, Captain Day, and establishing that there were sufficient lifebelts, boat accommodation and food for the additional walking patients. After 4 pm dinner the walking cases were shown their lifeboat stations.

By 11.40 pm the *Glenart Castle* was slicing through a smooth sea just miles from her destination when there was a flash and explosion that sent a column of water and black smoke spewing up from the rear starboard. The ship shuddered but remained on an even keel as the port engine raced heavily. All electric lights went out, and the wireless went down. An SOS was blown on the whistle. The engineers stopped the engines and, using hand torches in the blackness of the ship's bowels, found water rushing into the boiler room. The watertight doors leading into the engine room had been warped and could not be closed completely. Upon hearing that Number 4 hold was also flooding, Captain Day ordered the ship to be evacuated.[4]

Major Home was responsible for ensuring medical personnel were aware of the 'Instructions for When an Emergency Arises'. When the ship was carrying patients, the instructions stated that all hands must sleep in their clothes and orderlies must sleep in the wards. Lifebelts for the staff were placed near the doors, or beside the rope ladders that lay at each lifeboat station.[5]

The nurses' lifeboat stations were on the promenade deck. In an emergency, the instructions directed them to take a lifebelt and packet of dressings and go to their boats immediately. The orderlies were to go to their wards, assist patients out and close watertight doors, then wait for the ward medical officer's orders to proceed to their own boats. Medical officers were to come up once their wards were empty.[6] The instructions added,

SILENCE IS OF THE UTMOST IMPORTANCE; no word to be heard except from an officer or NCO [non-commissioned officer]; thus will confusion be prevented, which means more people getting away …

Every endeavour should be made by all hands to be as warmly clothed as possible, woollen clothing greatly reduces the initial shock of immersion and buoys one up for a time.[7]

It was evident that, although the ship was gradually settling lower by the stern, there was no cause for panic. Patients and medical staff donned their life jackets as they assembled at their boat stations. As the nurses came up, the men already gathered on the deck cleared a path so the women could be handed first into a lifeboat. The worst cot cases were carried down ladders on the shoulders of orderlies.[8]

Naval patrols heard the explosion and fog sirens. Within half an hour they found lifeboats bobbing in the calm waters around the disabled ship and commenced taking her passengers on board.[9] By 12.50 am, all patients were off the ship. The remainder of the medical staff soon followed except for Major Home and two sergeants, who collected government money, the nominal rolls, and precious letters from the post box, before evacuating at 2.30 am. The *Glenart Castle* continued to take on water but tugs pumped continuously as they dragged her landwards. The crippled ship was towed into Portsmouth the same morning, and was in dry dock for repairs until November 1917. All of her 115 crew, 68 medical staff and 525 patients were safe.

Experts at the subsequent Court of Enquiry concluded it was most likely HMHS *Glenart Castle* had hit a mine. The enquiry recommended that watertight doors be kept closed when going to sea, only to be opened if necessary. Major Home suggested several improvements to the enquiry. More torches. Cots to carry and lower patients onto the appropriate boat deck. Warm suits for patients in bed as these were more convenient than blankets. Extra lifebelts and blankets to be kept on deck. Boxes of dressings to be kept in the lifeboats. And, he added, grips to hold the boats to the rail would be 'very helpful'.[10]

As a consequence of this incident, on 20 March 1917 Major Home took charge as OC Troops on HMHS *Essequibo*, in time for Edie's last voyage on her to Halifax. Now, on the afternoon of 15 November 1917, HMHS *Glenart Castle* took on Canadian patients and Edie was again bound for Halifax. It was an unwelcome return to the sea as they ran into rough weather and most staff and patients fell ill, although Edie soon regained her sea legs.[11] 'I thought I had got used to the sea but I was as seasick as if I had never been on the sea before but that only lasted about 5 days, & now I'm as good a seaman as anybody' (21 November 1917).

39

A VERY BOISTEROUS CRADLE

The conditions for the repaired HMHS *Glenart Castle*'s first voyage were turbulent almost all of the eleven days to Halifax. They arrived on the afternoon of 26 November 1917. En route, the new OC Troops, Lieutenant Colonel Furness, reported problems with the electric lighting. The green hospital ship lights failed twice, and all lights were shut out as it was considered safer to travel in complete darkness than be a target for submarines.[1] The problem was soon rectified.

After four wet, cold, foggy days in Halifax, she steamed back into the jaws of a storm. Gale-force winds and high seas carried away 'several green lights' and caused 'much seasickness'. The weather did not calm sufficiently for fire and boat drills to be conducted until a full week after they left port.[2] The sea was finally calm enough for Edie to pick up her pen:

9th December 1917   At Sea

My Dear Mum Dad Grace & Queen

Do you know the difficulties of writing when it is to be censored. Do what I will I cannot write easily, so I think this letter will be scrappy. Please don't blame me, & don't think I'm sick or anything so disagreeable if my letters are not satisfactory.

I do not know when we are to be in Port, but as it is Sunday one has the inclination to write, though I've nothing to write about.

It is very pleasant today at sea, & when the weather is like it is today, I enjoy being at sea. The sky & sea are blue & the breeze is fresh, one can't help feeling well, but the weather hasn't been like this all the time. We have been rocked rather severely in the 'cradle of the deep' too severely for sleep, pack myself in my bunk as I would I couldn't sleep.

One afternoon I was sitting in the sisters' lounge, which is situated on the boat deck, & we can see into the dining saloon through an oval aperture. When the boat took an extra roll I slipped off the couch onto the floor & slid three times across the room before I could catch hold of something to steady myself. Sliding along the floor doesn't hurt, but I couldn't help seeing the funny side of things when both the Padres and several of the stewards were chasing teapots & hot water jugs and some of the usual things for afternoon tea, all over the saloon. They sat down and slid for the required article. Walking on deck was like a cat walking on hot bricks.

I have told you I think of some of the difficulties of washing clothes on board the 'Essequibo', but here we haven't the conveniences at all. The ironing is done with a flat iron which is heated in the galley & there is some distance to walk between the galley & the place for ironing. During the rough weather something went wrong with the laundry boiler, so tomorrow I must tackle my frocks.

Would you believe it, but I have [been] trying to knit lace, if I succeed I shall adorn a piece of linen for a table centre for Mum. I know Mum likes knitted lace. At any rate if the lace isn't a success, the table centre will be alright. I hope to have it ready for Mum's birthday. I am now finishing a slip bodice which I shall send for Grace for her birthday. I've got another one for

A very boisterous cradle

Queen but it isn't yet finished. I have a fair amount of sewing to do but [it is] like me, as you will say, many things started or commenced as is more correct to say & nothing is finished, but I like to change my work occasionally.

One day while walking on the deck, my cap fell overboard. Matron had given us one each, the wind lifted mine & away it went into the sea, so now I'm struggling to make one for myself of red Berlin wool which I happen to have. I hope it will be wearable as I have to launder my ward caps & have to take care of them, so they don't get very raggy-looking from the salt breeze.

Our cabins are situated in a very awkward position, very near a staircase, & to run to the bathroom with one's hair all over one's head isn't pretty so I've made myself a boudoir cap. When I left Sydney I had some cream coloured net, some pieces of lace & some narrow ribbon, so I've put them all together, & the result I think is very pretty. I daresay you would smile if you saw me in mine.

We haven't the slightest idea where we are going after our next port & so all sorts of surmises are made. I'm getting very homesick. I wish we could take some Australians through the Panama Canal. But what's the use of wishing.

The *Glenart Castle* anchored at Gibraltar during the evening of 10 December 1917 and the following morning Captain Burt and Lieutenant Colonel Furness went ashore 'to receive orders & to be introduced to the Spanish Commissioner'.[3]

For some months, to guard against U-boat attacks, Allied hospital ships on the Mediterranean had carried a delegate from neutral Spain who could verify to Germany that the ships were used for proper purposes under the Hague Convention. In October 1917, the Spanish Embassy in Berlin had reassured Britain that Germany had reiterated its earlier declarations and marked hospital ships would be respected in the Atlantic Ocean and the North Sea. It was, therefore, unnecessary to carry a neutral delegate on board in those areas. However, no agreements had been made for Allied hospital ships in the forbidden zone that included the English Channel and part of the North Sea, so there they remained vulnerable to the U-boats.[4]

The delegate who joined the *Glenart Castle* at Gibraltar and was described by Furness in the ship's war diary as 'the Spanish Commissioner' did not speak English. But, Furness wrote, 'Fortunately one of my staff, Captain Young, speaks Spanish fluently, so we were able to make him feel quite at home'.[5] Edie observed the Spaniard warily:

> We have a Spanish Naval Officer on board to ensure our safety. I could only think of him as a German spy, but the poor old thing looks as harmless as a child & looks very delicate. He cannot speak English, but several of our doctors speak fluent French & one speaks Spanish. The Don's wife is an American & she speaks French fluently. (13 December 1917)

If the commissioner wished to go ashore, he could only do so if a Spanish officer could be found to relieve him to ensure a continuous neutral presence on board, so that the necessary certification could be given to the Germans in due course.[6]

After Halifax, Edie had at first thought they were going to Bombay, but instead they steamed for Malta. Edie sewed and read:

> There is a fairly good library on board ... I am reading a book called 'The lost land of King Arthur' by Walters & then I shall try & read Tennyson's 'Idylls of a King' ... I have been

recommended to read a biography of Cecil Rhodes. I also want to read some of Thackeray's too. If I [can] possibly manage it I want to get Mr Gerard's book 'My four years in Germany'. When I have read it I shall send it on to Dad. He would enjoy it. (13 December 1917)

A former justice of the Supreme Court of New York, James Gerard wrote about his time as US ambassador to Germany from 1913 to 1917. He forcefully endorsed America's decision to enter the war, arguing that a German autocracy would force every nation under its dominion. Gerard also claimed that there was greater danger of the Allies starving than the Germans, who he said were putting old men, boys, women and 2 million POWs to cultivating all available land in Germany: thus, even if the people suffered, the war would not end because Germany was starving.[7]

Edie's recent experiences piqued her interest in the book mightily. She, of course, had her own experiences with the Germans to share:

> I'm dying to get Gerard's book ... I see one of the medical officers with it, so if I can ask him to loan it to me, I will get it.
>
> Strange to say 5 of my patients ... were prisoners for two years in Germany. They told me of their experiences. They (the huns) have certainly treated them shockingly & until England found out what treatment our men were receiving, the Germans did not make their conditions livable.
>
> I was talking to these men for ¾ hour & it would take pages to write it all. When England threatened to take reprisals on prisoners in England, then Germany had to relax her treatment. It is we who feed our prisoners in Germany, & we also feed theirs in England. It seems to me that we bring their prisoners to

Switzerland before they bring ours out of Germany, so most of the expense is borne by us. Their conversation was interesting to me knowing how we treat theirs. (21 November 1917)

Edie's lively intellect and keen interest in world affairs brewed opinions that did not lend themselves to small talk or batting eyelashes. On the *Malwa* she had held 'casting sheep's eyes' at the soldiers in contempt. In Cairo, social awkwardness had defeated her when she was approached by a medical officer who was going to be married: '[F]or the life of me, I could not congratulate him or wish him happiness. Perhaps it was rude of me. I haven't a glib tongue, or perhaps it would be embarrassing to him, if I spoke about it, in front of other people who are writing in the room' (26 April 1916).

On the other hand, she enjoyed the company of men when she was having a proper conversation with them. She therefore found it aggravating that, rather than letting common sense and the maturity of her thirty-something nurses rule, Matron Beaufoy insisted they maintain a chaste distance from the men of the RAMC:

> The restrictions on this ship get on one's nerves. We always seem to be watched. It is considered a sin to talk to the 'monsters in blue' as one of the sisters put it. The other day Matron came & told us that we were not to walk after dinner on one part of the deck because the orderlies were always there. So I asked Matron if I would hurt them, [as] the restrictions were not [what] I was accustomed to. It is rather amusing as well as insulting, because none of us are young or prepossessing & all the doctors are old fogies. It is so amusing to see the OC & the Matron spending a great [deal] of their time walking the deck together, what is sauce for the gander is also sauce for the goose I understand.
>
> The Mediterranean is proving a very boisterous cradle tonight. I can hardly write. It is so difficult to write just at present, the

A very boisterous cradle

Matron has invited the OC & another doctor into our Sanctum. There is no room in my cabin to write, so I had to come up here, & these people are talking utter rot. I do like a man to talk as if women possessed brains. These bits of small talk worry me.
(13 December 1917)

The matron, Katy Beaufoy, was a week short of her forty-eighth birthday. Intelligent and intrepid, she had commenced training at twenty-three and within a decade was labouring over the sick and wounded in the Boer War. A return to private practices in Wimpole and Sloane streets had not been enough for her; she had joined the QAIMNS Reserve in 1908 and was posted to Rome. Her war service followed a similar route to Edie's: she was an experienced matron who had served in that capacity in Alexandria and on HMHS *Dover Castle*.[8] But Miss Beaufoy was a stickler for the no-fraternisation rules, which didn't suit Edie: 'Like all Australians [I] cannot bear unnecessary restrictions. I'm afraid I break rules very often. But everybody expects Australians to do that' (11 November 1917). She was getting fed up with things generally and was glad to be left alone to write her letter:

Oh dear I wish this dreadful war was over, I'm getting tired of all this. I want to come back to normal life again ...

Thank heaven all the people have gone downstairs to play cards. I have learnt to play Whist & Bridge, but I don't think I shall ever be a good player. I shall never have the craze for gambling, I don't think. (13 December 1917)

It took six days for HMHS *Glenart Castle* to make the run from Gibraltar to Malta, and for the next two months she plied the wintry Mediterranean, steaming from Malta to Salonika, Salonika to Malta, Malta to Stavros to Salonika to Malta, and the same again. Christmas

Day passed on a return leg from Salonika to Malta with a full load of patients, including 'thirty mental cases' for whom Furness had to make 'the necessary structural alterations'[9] (likely partitioning off an isolation ward with padded walls[10]) and place extra guards. They saw in New Year's Day 1918 ploughing through cold seas to Stavros. The ship encountered no mines, no U-boats – nothing untoward except snowstorms, fog and a 'visit by [an] enemy aeroplane' while docked in Salonika.[11] Even strong headwinds, heavy seas and seasickness were better than the mosquitos, malaria, and now the snow, on the Salonika front.[12] Edie's time off the ship entrenched her dislike of the town: she sent a postcard of the white tower of Salonika, saying 'Oh! The mud of this place is awful' (22 December 1917).

Only Malta offered relief. While they were anchored at Valletta, there was some free time. Senior officers lunched with the governor at the palace and took His Excellency and other dignitaries over the ship's hospital.[13] Edie enjoyed herself:

> Two of the ship's officers took two of us for a long (Carrozzie) drive. (A Carrozzie is a queer-looking vehicle belonging to the Island. I wonder if I could sketch one [she drew a tiny sketch] I can't sketch one, I don't think I can give you any idea. But please understand that the animal is a horse but [in my sketch] it looks more like a woolly lamb.) The weather is delightful. I wonder what it will be like after we pass the 'Gib'. (26 January 1918)

On the afternoon they sailed, 28 January 1918, a captain from the Black Watch, 'evading mental attendants in [the] ward & knocking down the man on guard [at the] entrance of the ward, rushed on deck & threw himself overboard. The alarm was at once given, vessel stopped, three life-buoys thrown overboard, ship's boat manned & lowered, and a thorough search made for three-quarters of an hour'.[14] The poor man was not found.

A very boisterous cradle

At Gibraltar, Lieutenant Colonel Furness accompanied the Spanish commissioner to the offices of the Admiralty to report his observations of HMHS *Glenart Castle*. 'He expressed himself quite satisfied with the treatment he had received on board, also that the ship had only been used for carrying sick & wounded, and that no war material had been embarked. He also gave a certificate to that effect to the Admiral. Raised anchor and left Gibraltar at 3.30 pm.'[15]

More rough seas and seasickness attended the return to England. The ship diverted briefly from her course after a lifeboat was spotted some miles away. It was found 'in good condition but empty, and without oars. We also saw wreckage floating around. There was nothing by means of which we could identify it'.[16] Two more sick men died at sea. The *Glenart Castle* arrived at Avonmouth, Bristol, on 6 February 1918, where patients, nurses and some RAMC disembarked while the ship crossed to Newport, Wales, to be refitted.[17]

Edie had almost three weeks' leave before she rejoined the ship.

40
TAKING LEAVE

Edie spent her holiday with family and friends. She was always welcomed with open arms in Cricklewood and Stamford Hill, and London also presented the opportunity to meet up with old Coasters. Mildred Crocker Brown was back in England. After plans to travel with Edie fell through, she had spent Christmas in London then toured Scotland with two AANS colleagues who had been in France with her. They saw in Hogmanay, Edinburgh, where Crocker Brown wrote in her diary, 'Another year ended & still this rotten war going on & our grand lads being slaughtered in thousands. When will it all finish?' Upon returning to London, Crocker Brown reported to Horseferry Road and was posted to 3 Australian Auxiliary Hospital at Dartford. The wonderful conditions had amazed her:

> Imagine our shock when we found all quarters, wards, Mess Room etc etc were under one roof & so no need to get wet feet. Also greater surprise to find that we each had a tiny room to ourselves, a 'real' bed & sheets, a wardrobe & chest of drawers. Gas laid on in every room & heating pipes running right through each ward, quarters etc. But what I liked best of all was the gorgeous baths with any amount of hot water laid on at any old hour.[1]

On Saturday 16 February 1918, Crocker Brown and some hospital colleagues met Edie in the city. That afternoon the little gaggle of Australians attended a concert at the Royal Albert Hall headlined

Taking leave

by the famous English contralto Clara Butt. Crocker Brown '[h]ad a very enjoyable time. It was good to see Blake once more after such a long time. She looked well but thinner'.[2]

A few days later Edie lunched with Crocker Brown and Clarice Dickson at the Army & Navy Stores. They must have had a good gossip, for Sister Dickson knew where most AANS nurses were, and Crocker Brown had seen a passing parade of sisters and men when she was in France.

Only Dorothy Cawood was missing from their coterie. In January 1918 she had moved with the 38th Stationary Hospital from Calais to Genoa, having served with distinction in France. Their friend had not only recently been mentioned in despatches; she had been awarded a Military Medal for 'coolness and devotion to duty' during an air raid on 2ACCS in July 1917.[3] Crocker Brown had been posted to the station only weeks later and narrowly avoided being shelled herself; and, like Edie, she had watched the sky with awe: '[R]ed Bosche planes soon came back & we heard the anti-aircraft shooting with a vengeance … numerous searchlights [were] concentrated on this huge "Gotha" plane making it look like a great diamond butterfly ever so high up'.[4]

Needless to say, the old Coasters enjoyed their reunion 'very much'.[5] Afterwards, Crocker Brown wrote, 'Blake & I went to the matinee of "Dear Brutus"', a play by JM Barrie, '& had a good old laugh. Had afternoon tea & then parted at [the] corner of Oxford St & Tottenham Court Road. Blake was bright & cheery about sailing again'.[6]

Three days later, Crocker Brown 'sent Blake a telegram saying Goodbye & Good luck' as Edie went to Wales to join her ship.[7]

On Monday 25 February 1918, HMHS *Glenart Castle* lay in Newport harbour, refitted and shipshape. Her mooring ropes creaked as she rocked gently beside the wharf. The docks swarmed with people barking orders, pushing trolleys, scurrying up and down gangways and in and out of the holds, loading supplies and tying things down in readiness for the voyage. The coaling was completed, and the engineers prepared to coax her engines into life. Kitchenhands stowed foodstuffs and commenced preparations for the evening meal. A dozen of the ship's crew were aged seventeen or younger. Fifteen-year-old Wilfred 'Jack' Wyatt was taut with anticipation for his first voyage.[8] Another unnamed crewman no doubt felt the tug of parting from his bride of four days.[9]

On the bridge, a familiar white-bearded figure observed proceedings then returned to the chart room. During the break, Captain Bernard Burt had gone home to his wife of twenty-eight years, Mary Jane, with whom he had a son, also named Bernard. Now it was the job of Captain Burt, with his senior officers, to review the confidential route orders that told him they were bound for Brest in Brittany, with special notes concerning the route, lights, flags and signalling the ship was to use. Indications were for fair weather.

As OC Troops, it was Lieutenant Colonel Furness' role to oversee embarkation requirements for medical personnel. Among other things, this meant ensuring that there were adequate stocks of medical equipment, linen, stationery, official forms, pyjamas for cot cases and home pattern uniforms for all patients. It also meant making certain that wards, dining rooms, latrines and staff cabins were clean and tidy; that all medical apparatus was clean and in working order; and that the orderlies were properly instructed as to how to maintain and operate the equipment. His remit even extended to food supplies: these must be adequate in quality and quantity, including sufficient stores to meet each RAMC's entitlement to 1 pint of beer per day.[10]

Of course, some responsibility for readying the ship for patients devolved to Matron Katy Beaufoy and her seven nursing sisters. After stowing their luggage in their cabins, they would have inspected their wards, made beds and checked stocks of clothing, linen, dressings, bandages and medications, and ensured that every patient would have a hot water bottle and lifebelt.

By now Edie knew the ship's routines and rhythms. But this voyage promised to be different because her friend had joined her on board. Rose Beresford had written to Matron Fairchild on 1 February 1918 seeking a transfer to HMHS *Glenart Castle*: 'I hear there is a vacancy and as my friend Miss Blake is at present on the staff of this ship, it would be a great pleasure to both of us to work together'.[11] Her request was approved the next day.

Beresford was not the only nurse new to the *Glenart Castle*. Sisters Edgar and MacKinnon were both late additions to the ship's complement. Born in Glasgow and raised in South Africa where her father was a civil engineer, Elizabeth Edgar had joined the QAIMNS in 1916 and been attached to the South African Military Hospital in Richmond.[12] Her request for a transfer to the Home Establishments was agreed but fell through; two weeks later she was off to Newport.

Mary MacKinnon was a 'Terrier' from the sister organisation the Territorial Forces Nursing Service. She was the eldest of eight and grew up in a house overflowing with siblings and cousins in Arisaig, a village on the west coast of Scotland near the place from which Bonnie Prince Charlie had fled for France. Initially posted to HMHS *Dunluce Castle*, she received orders at the last minute to join the *Glenart Castle*.[13]

Along with Matron Beaufoy and Edie, Sister Kendall, Sister Evans and Staff Nurse Henry had joined in Liverpool the previous November. Essex-born Charlotte Henry and her four unmarried sisters had anglicised their surname from 'Heinrich' as anti-German feelings ran high, even though she, Gertrude and Harriet were serving nurses.[14] Rose Kendall[15] from Birmingham and Londoner Jane (Jennie) Evans[16] had transferred to the ship together from Wharncliffe War Hospital in Sheffield. They were a pair, as Edie and Evelyn Swannell had been, and Edie and Rose Beresford had become.

The ship left harbour at 6 pm. As the night wore on, all bar those on duty took to their berths. Below decks, men worked in shifts. A layer of black dust coated the trimmers who constantly toiled between the coal bunkers and the engine room, bringing up loads of fuel for the fires. Firemen shovelled coal into the fireboxes that heated the boilers, their faces shiny and skin slick with sweat in the hellish heat. Greasers lubricated crankshafts, jacking gear and crosshead bearings to keep the pistons pumping, and engineers oversaw the smooth operation of the two clanking, hissing, thumping steam engines.

Above decks were crew responsible for navigating the ship safely through the night. The captain's quarters were near the bridge so that Burt could be quickly at hand if he was required, but for now the second officer, also known as the officer of the watch, was in charge on the bridge, with a quartermaster at the wheel, assisted by the bosun's mate. A wireless operator remained alert, for there was always plenty of traffic in the Bristol Channel, including U-boats on the prowl.

Hospital ships now generally avoided the short runs across the English Channel between Portsmouth, Southhampton and Le Havre. The *Glenart Castle*'s route would take her around Land's End to Brest, outside the forbidden zone. Despite this, U-boats posed a threat: to guard against the mines they laid, the ship's 'otters' were out[17] – paravanes on wires that extended from the sides of the vessel, fitted with cutters designed to sever a mine's moorings so that it floated harmlessly to the surface, where it could be destroyed.[18]

The crew must have been aware of other risks. Like the *Glenart Castle*, the hospital ship *Rewa* had previously carried a Spanish delegate around the Mediterranean. Regardless, she had been attacked and sunk in the Bristol Channel on 4 January 1918. Germany said she hit a mine, but after examining the evidence the Admiralty had rejected this claim and complained bitterly via the Spanish ambassador about this 'fresh outrage',[19] stating that HMHS *Rewa* had been torpedoed: 'She was displaying all the lights and markings required by the Hague Convention, and she was not, and had not been, within the so-called barred zone as delimited in the statement issued by the German Government on 29th January 1917.'[20] Perhaps the protest gained the Germans' attention. Two months had passed without incident.

Edie had personally seen the distinctive markings of the *Essequibo* respected during her encounter with a submarine in the Atlantic in March 1917, and she was too pragmatic to dwell on the risks. She had earlier implored her family to take the same view: 'Please don't think of submarines, if my time to die comes well it comes, & it can't be helped, though the thought of dying is far from my thoughts – I think I shall see Australia once more' (28 January 1917).

41

WHAT THE FISHERMEN SAW

In the early hours of 26 February 1918 navigator Jack Hill stood in His Majesty's Trawler *Swansea Castle*'s cabin as the fishing trawler ploughed towards the Bristol Channel. Light from the full moon dipped and darted over the sea. The crew wore thick woollen jumpers and sou'westers buttoned high against a biting late winter's wind. When he saw the inky outline of an island materialise, Hill shouted, 'Lundy, Skipper!'

Lundy Island was the largest in the channel, narrow but 3 miles long, and 12 miles off the Devon coast. Once a base for pirates, it had few inhabitants now, but the lighthouses at its northern and southern tips were vital references for those navigating the Bristol Channel's strong tidal flows.

Skipper Joseph Rust came on deck and surveyed their position. Hill was his second hand, responsible for navigation. Rust instructed him to keep her north by east and to call if he saw anything that he should know, otherwise to wake him when the light of North Lundy Lighthouse bore east by north.[1] Rust retired below to try and catch some more sleep before dawn.

Not long after the outbreak of war in 1914, the Royal Navy had co-opted a number of fishing trawlers and their crews to act as minesweepers and anti-submarine patrols in British waters. Some fishing trawlers were converted and armed, and their crews trained in mine-laying and -sweeping.[2] It was felt that fishing crews would be much more adept at the pulleys and winches needed to remove mines, and could adapt to the task quicker than specially trained crews. Others, like the *Swansea Castle*, were fitted with a 6-pounder

What the fishermen saw

gun, patrolling for the enemy even as they put out their nets to make a living. Gleaming white yachts were painted grey and fitted with guns; they and private motor launches were added to the force dubbed the Auxiliary Patrol, keeping watch along the coast because the main way of locating a submarine was the human eye spotting a periscope.[3] Britain also deployed Q-ships: decoys designed to lure submarines to the surface. They appeared to be mere merchantmen but were heavily armed with concealed weapons; they raised the White Ensign (indicating they were Royal Navy craft) moments before they began shooting.

As the *Swansea Castle* headed towards the Bristol Channel on 26 February 1918, HMHS *Glenart Castle* headed out of it, steaming west from Newport. The Union Jack, Blue Ensign (indicating she was commanded by an officer of the Royal Naval Reserve) and Red Cross flags flapped from her mast. High in the crow's nest sixteen-year-old Harold Joachim kept look-out and every quarter-hour called 'All-l-l is well-l-l'.[4] The bridge replied, 'Aye-aye'.[5]

At 1.30 am, Joachim saw something a few miles to the south and called down to the bridge. Second Officer Ralph Woollett checked through his spyglass.[6] Small convoy, going east. 'Aye-aye.' It was His Majesty's Trawler *Okino*, armed and escorting SS *Leonards* from Milford Haven to Barry Docks in Wales. In the bright moonlight, the *Okino*'s commanding officer Charles Beaven could, in turn, clearly see the green band and red crosses on the *Glenart Castle*'s port side.[7]

In time the north light on Lundy Island became visible. Around 3 am another light showed to the south. It was another trawler. William Fletcher, the skipper of that trawler, *Dynevor Castle*, also saw the hospital ship pass, her regulation lights burning brilliantly.[8] Soon after, back on the *Glenart Castle*, Joachim signalled a light on the starboard bow.[9]

Woollett could not see anything but Joachim insisted he had seen a bright white light. Quartermaster Jacob Schiller, at the wheel, also saw the light, lying low on the water. The light briefly appeared again off to the starboard, but the men were not unduly concerned. The *Glenart Castle* was a hospital ship. They saw no need to disturb the captain. The strange light was last sighted at 3.30 am.[10] Schiller later recalled, 'After that I took no further notice'.[11] He concentrated on the task at hand, continuing their south-western course at a steady 10 knots.

Lurking near the surface was UC-56, a small mine-laying U-boat commanded by Kapitänleutnant Wilhelm Kiesewetter. In almost a year, Kiesewetter had not sunk a ship, but at official functions he assuredly heard his colleagues' stories.[12] Now he had been stalking a ship for over an hour. He later claimed that he only saw ordinary navigation lights, nothing that marked her as a hospital ship, but fancied that she rode low in the water and must be carrying a heavy cargo.[13] He made his decision and gave the order to get ready to fire.

When the *Swansea Castle* was some 10 miles west of Lundy Island, Hill raised his spyglass. As he looked to starboard, he saw a hospital ship with a band of green lights shining around her saloon. Her red side and masthead lights were on, together with another red beacon that he supposed was the Red Cross light. The ship was heading west, into their path. Minutes passed and Hill saw the hospital ship drawing off into the distance portside. Suddenly, all her lights went out. Hill 'remarked to [his] mate at the wheel that it was funny' and 'picked up [his] glasses and looked around the horizon'.[14]

There was no sound except the splash and slap of the waves and the chug of the trawler's engine. Hill could vaguely make out the ship's profile in the moonlight. As he scanned the choppy surface he spied a strange shape to the north-east. It took a moment, but all at once he realised what it must be and shouted down, 'Submarine, Skipper!'

Joseph Rust stumbled up to the cabin. In seconds Hill told him what they had seen, but the object had disappeared. 'Over her!'

What the fishermen saw

shouted the captain. Hill left the wheel and ran aft to call all hands to man the gun, shouting, 'Submarine!'[15]

The crew took their positions, loaded gun trained in readiness, eyes straining, hearts pounding, but there was no sign of either vessel. The freshening wind from the south-west carried no distress signals. What had happened to the hospital ship?

Rust felt 'a bit dubious about her lights going out. [He] thought she had seen the submarine and wishing to avoid it, had put them out'.[16] He walked around the deck and scanned the horizon. Nothing. Someone said the hospital ship had probably got away, for she was going too fast.[17] The unspoken questions hung heavy in the air. Should they investigate further, knowing a submarine was lurking in the vicinity? Should they go looking for trouble? They were but one little craft; what could they alone do? 'Poor look-out, Skipper, she will not give us another chance', said Hill.[18]

Rust made up his mind. They would run into Lundy and raise the alarm that there was a submarine in the area. He reassured his crew, saying, 'We have done our bit for the country'.[19]

Unknown to the *Swansea Castle* crew, HMHS *Glenart Castle* had been struck by a torpedo launched from UC-56. By the time they turned the *Swansea Castle* towards Lundy, the stricken ship had slipped beneath the surface. She had been carrying 182 crew and medical personnel.[20] Some were now struggling for survival in the darkness. Many more had gone to the bottom with the vessel.

42

THE SINKING

Minutes before 4 am on 26 February 1918, HMHS *Glenart Castle* was about 10 miles west of Lundy Island. Members of the crew were preparing to change shift.

Thomas Matthews, bosun's mate, had finished his watch and was about to turn in. 'I was talking to my mate about coffee and I said that it was all ready for him', he would recall afterwards.[1] Suddenly there was an explosion that Matthews described as being like the thunderous fall of breaking glass, and the ship jolted, flinging them across the room.[2]

Captain Burt was startled out of sleep. He leapt out of bed and ran to the bridge. The men there were sure they had been hit by a torpedo. Burt rang down to the engine room. They had been struck in Number 3 hold behind the starboard engine room, tearing a gaping hole in the ship's side, ripping open the deck and smashing lifeboats. The ship plunged into darkness. Water gushed in. Burt ordered the engines to be stopped, and the hum and throb of the living ship ceased. The wireless operator tried to send an SOS, tapping urgently over and over as the ship foundered, but it was no use: the wireless transmitter had been disabled, and no distress call could be sent.[3] They were alone and could only hope that someone was watching.

Alfred Bale, a greaser, had been going on watch: '[I] had just got to the top of the ladder to the engine room when there was a loud explosion, all lights went out immediately'.[4] He fumbled his way along the starboard alleyway and climbed up to the moonlit boat deck, where men were already gathering at their assigned boats. Bale

The sinking

went to his portside station and began helping to clear his lifeboat, ready for lowering.[5]

Fireman Thomas Casey was in bed asleep when he was woken by the explosion. He groped his way in the darkness to the rear hatches but found they had been blown up, forcing him to stumble back along the corridor to find another way up to the saloon deck. As he ran to his boat station he passed Thomas Matthews. He asked Matthews, 'How is it, Tom?' and Matthews said, 'Stand by!'[6]

'He sang out asking where the sister was', Casey said later. But Casey didn't know and the bosun told him to stand by the falls and wait for orders to lower his boat.[7] As people gathered on the boat deck, Burt blew the steam whistle six times, the signal to lower the lifeboats.[8]

RAMC Lance Corporal Colin Beveridge had been thrown out of bed by the impact. He 'gave everyone a shout that something was wrong as all the lights had gone out. [I p]icked up a lifebelt and ran up on deck'.[9] As Beveridge made for his starboard lifeboat, he encountered Burt. 'Skipper ordered me back, as other boats were being smashed against the side by the heavy seas', Beveridge said.[10]

Watching the men work feverishly to lower the boats, fighting as water rushed into the *Glenart Castle*'s yawning wounds and dragged her sideways and downwards, faster and faster, Captain Burt knew she was doomed. Those who had made it to the decks or could yet make it deserved every chance to live. He gave the order to his chief officer, Samuel Hutchings, that no captain ever wanted to give.[11] Hutchings ran and called out above the sloshing waves: 'EVERY MAN FOR HIMSELF!'

As the cry went up, Burt turned to Schiller, who had remained at the bridge waiting for orders. 'Now, my lad, jump into the boat or you will get drowned.'[12] The captain then retired to the chart room. He was never seen again.[13]

Thomas Casey was waiting at his portside station. 'When the whistle blew [we] were told to lower the falls, we were to get the boat half-way down – to lower it down to the … saloon deck to take in people. [The bosun] then saw that the blocks were alright and we lowered away then. I chucked the fall clear and I went on the falls and shinned down.'[14]

Bosun Matthews was in the boat and, after Captain Burt gave him his leave, Jacob Schiller ran and just had time to jump in and shove off. They clung to the sides as the boat bucked and tossed but stayed upright, not raising an oar as they were knocked clear by a wall of wash as the ship went under only some 20 feet away.[15]

When Alfred Bale heard the chief officer's order, his boat had just been put on to the water: '[I] slid down the boat's falls with two other men but before we could cast the falls adrift the ship sank'.[16] As the *Glenart Castle* thrust downwards with the lifeboat still attached, Bale was thrown into the heaving sea.

Fourth Officer George Scarlett was starting his shift when the torpedo struck. He had run straight to the bridge and the captain ordered him 'to go and get [his] boat away at once … [It was] No 5 Lifeboat; the third boat on the starboard side. I then saw that the ship had been struck just abaft amidships on the starboard side under No 7 boat which was wrecked. The boat's crew were standing by'.[17]

Scarlett ordered his lifeboat to be cast adrift:

[It had been lowered] about 4 to 5 feet when the Chief Officer came and shouted 'Every man for himself'. The ship then took a heavy list to starboard, the water swept the boat up against the davitt heads and smashed it to pieces before we could do anything to cut it adrift. I saw the other boat crews on the starboard side trying to get theirs away but none were cleared away in time.[18]

The sinking

Scarlett saw two or three men jump overboard and as he waited for them to get clear he was swept overboard as the ship went down.

Beveridge was already climbing down a ladder when he heard the call. There was no chance to get into his starboard lifeboat. As he reached the water, 'the ship went under, drawing me with it'.[19]

The *Glenart Castle* was dragged down sternwards as water filled her holds. People screamed as they tried to jump or were washed off her decks. Caught by the suction of the sinking ship, they were battered by a whirlpool of debris as they clawed desperately for the surface.

Some seven minutes after Kiesewetter's torpedo tore into her side, the *Glenart Castle* was gone. The last belches and bubbles were forced from her carcass as she plunged down, coming to rest in a muddy cloud over 230 feet below. Some were entombed. Other bodies may have floated free in the strong currents, never to be seen again. For those on the surface, it was a race against time and the elements.

Although Bale, Scarlett and Beveridge were dragged under by the sinking ship they managed to kick free and emerged gasping for air, spluttering as waves slapped over them.

Weighed down by his uniform, Scarlett managed to get hold of a raft and crawled on to it. 'There was another raft close to me with three men on it. I saw nothing of anyone else from the ship, but could hear cries from the water for some time afterwards.'[20]

Bale saw an overturned boat with three men clinging to it: '[I] hauled myself up on the keel. Soon after I saw what I took to be a schooner coming towards us'.[21] They shouted and waved to gain the boat's attention, but soon realised their mistake:

> A minute or two after I saw it was not a schooner but a
> submarine on the surface and said to the man next to me on
> the boat 'We can expect nothing from him, it is the submarine'.

> The submarine was not more than 100 yards away then and I could distinctly see the outline of the hull and the conning tower. About ½ an hour later a raft drifted alongside and I got on board to make more room for the men on the boat.[22]

Bale held on to the boat, trying to keep the group together, but eventually had to let go: 'I did not see the men on the boat again'.[23]

Beveridge had been in the water for about half an hour struggling in the wreckage with about 20 others when he saw a vessel approaching. 'I thought at first it was a boat or something coming to rescue us.'[24] The U-boat passed within 25–30 yards of them.

> We all shouted to them to take us aboard, but they passed on and did not answer us, although some of the fellows were drowning then. The submarine was on the surface, and I plainly saw the conning tower and two men on it, but before this I saw the periscope coming towards us … One man appeared to be standing on a little platform of the conning tower, and the other inside, leaning over and looking at us.[25]

Kiesewetter's U-boat offered no assistance.

Only one lifeboat survived the night. It was crammed with nineteen crew, including Matthews, Casey and Schiller, and three RAMC officers. Many had bare feet and were wearing only the clothes they had been sleeping in.

The sea was rough and cold. As the lifeboat leaked and water washed over the gunwale, the men were forced to bail constantly. Their battle for survival intensified at daybreak as the wind freshened and the waves grew bigger. Experienced tillerman Schiller fought to keep the boat's bow facing into the wind, and the bailing grew more frantic to prevent them from being swamped.[26] They were drenched and freezing:

The sinking

The twenty-two men in the boat ... were clad only in trousers and shirts, exposed to a biting wind, and had to take every form of exercise to try and keep warm. But we suffered agonies from exposure. Our feet and legs were immersed in the water which was continually accumulating in the bottom of the boat. There were three buckets, and we took it in turn to bale in relays. We were hours without food, for the few biscuits and the little water we had taken into the boat did not go far. At ten o'clock we thought the end had come, for we knew that unless we were picked up in the next hour we should all be dead. But only a quarter of an hour after that one of the men saw a vessel on the horizon. We waved our shirts to attract their attention and shouted when they got nearer, and before long we found ourselves safely on board the French steamer Feon.[27]

The *Feon* was a former fishing trawler, crewed by just four men and a boy.[28] For the skipper, Joseph Stephant, bringing the wrecked men on board represented a challenge in itself:

It was as much as Captain (Joseph) Stephen [sic] could do to avoid his own boat being swamped, while every moment the danger of the smaller boat foundering became greater, its occupants being up to their knees in water and drenched to the skin. A line thrown across was caught by one of the men in the boat, and she was allowed to drift astern, and was gradually hauled up until she was close enough to the ketch for the men to be transferred. The little cabin of the ketch could not accommodate more than half a dozen of the strangers, and for the others a tarpaulin was stretched across a corner of the deck so as to afford some sort of shelter. Meanwhile others were busy preparing hot coffee and other food in the little hut near the wheel which the crew had labelled 'Hotel Des Poilus' [hairy hotel]. After scouring round in a vain search for other boats the Feon made for Swansea,

where I saw the vessel today, I found the deck strewn with
lifebelts which had been discarded by the *Glenart Castle* men.[29]

For others of the ship's company, the ordeal continued. Around 1 pm, the American destroyer United States Ship (USS) *Parker* located a raft about 6 miles from the southern end of Lundy Island. In it was Alfred Bale, who thought he must be the sole survivor, but, over the next two hours, the *Parker* managed to find three more rafts.[30] It was no easy feat to get the stranded men aboard. The House of Commons subsequently acknowledged the gallantry of the 'American bluejackets who jumped overboard to save life'.[31] '[T]he sea was still running high and the immersed British sailors were in submarine-infested waters, so that the destroyer was unable to stop to enable a lifeline to be thrown or a boat to be lowered.'[32]

Two crew jumped in and swam to the rafts, passing the exhausted men ropes and dragging them back one at a time to board the *Parker*. Fireman Jesse White lost his grip, washed astern in his weakened state and was severely injured by the propeller. The crew managed to get him on deck, but he died soon after.

The *Parker* brought eight survivors and White's body into Milford Haven. One man was unconscious when he was hauled from the water and passed away the next day in Pembroke Hospital, having never regained consciousness.[33] Subsequently identified as RAMC Private Samuel 'Harry' Lund, he was buried in Pembroke Dock Military Cemetery. Jesse White was buried in Southampton Old Cemetery, near where he had lived with his wife, Helena.

Naval authorities conducted an urgent Court of Enquiry into the sinking of HMHS *Glenart Castle* two days after she went down. Several survivors were interviewed, as well as men from the *Swansea Castle* and *Dynevor Castle*, as the enquiry sought to establish what had happened and the chances of finding anyone else alive. Reports were inconsistent as to the fates of any other lifeboats.

Matthews thought that seven boats had been launched,

The sinking

including his, and two floated empty off the poop deck. He did not see them after the *Glenart Castle* sank.[34]

Fireman Alfred Olden also saw lifeboats 'just when we got away – after the ship sank I saw no other boats'.[35] He had no views as to what may have happened to them, but Matthews thought they must have been sucked down by the sinking ship, whereas his, being further aft, was instead forced outwards.

Schiller said he saw portside boats floating after the ship sank – right side up, with people inside, shouting. '[T]he boats went in several directions … I think three or four boats got away.'[36]

Casey also claimed he saw three lifeboats after the sinking, but he could not say where they headed. '… I could not see them in the dark.'[37]

All agreed that the weather conditions worsened in the early morning and the waves became bigger. They also agreed that any lifeboat taken to the south of Lundy Island stood a chance. However, if the tide drew it into the fast-running White Horse race, a treacherous current north of Lundy, it would be a different story. There, said *Swansea Castle* skipper Joseph Rust, 'They were liable to be swamped'.[38] Quartermaster Schiller speculated on what may have happened to the few lifeboats he was adamant had got away: 'The sea was very rough. If they made for the shore close to Lundy, there are very sharp breakers. I am of the opinion that they have probably been wrecked on the "White Horse" Race off Lundy Island'.[39]

In the days that followed, only one more lifeboat was located, upset and damaged, 2 miles from Lundy Island. It was empty but for boots and stockings found wedged inside, indicating either that people had been in it, or had intended to get into it.[40] Given how hard twenty-two men had had to bale to save their own boat, others might have been swamped well short of the White Horse race.

One last person from the *Glenart Castle* was recovered. The body of twenty-three-year-old wireless operator Michael Sinnott, from County Wexford in Ireland, was picked up by a drifter off Trevose

Head, Cornwall, on 2 March 1918.[41] He was still wearing his lifebelt. Sinnott was not originally meant to be aboard the ship but had been drafted in as a late replacement.[42] He was buried in Penzance after a naval funeral service.[43]

Newspapers carried stories that the body of a junior officer picked up not far from where the ship sank was found to have sustained gunshot wounds, one in the neck and the other in the thigh. 'While there have been no reports that the Germans fired on the escaping crew of the hospital ship at the moment of the outrage, this discovery suggests that an attack was subsequently made on some of the boats.'[44] There was no credence to this report.

Although figures vary, the final death toll from the sinking of the *Glenart Castle* appears to have been 153 out of 182 aboard.[45] Twenty-two survived in the Swansea lifeboat, and seven on the USS *Parker*. Ninety-five of the 120 crew died, including Captain Burt, Chief Officer Samuel Hutchings, Second Officer Ralph Woollett, teen Harold Joachim on watch in the crow's nest and fifteen-year-old Jack Wyatt on his maiden voyage. Both chaplains died, along with forty-eight of the fifty-two RAMC personnel. OC Troops Lieutenant Colonel James Furness and the Spanish-speaking Captain George Young were among the dead.

The newspapers and the Admiralty were all concerned about the fate of the nine women on board: Matron Beaufoy, her seven nurses and one stewardess. Chief Cook Burton told the press that he

> saw the nine nurses [sic] on deck, but did not know what became of them ... Another survivor stated that nine of the ship's lifeboats got away altogether, but whether the nine nurses were in one of them is not known. When the vessel went down there were piercing shrieks coming from the water, but it was too dark to distinguish the forms ... Burton stated there was no time to save anything, and it was a case of getting into the boats at once or going down with the ship.[46]

The sinking

Asked by the enquiry, 'Do you think any of the nurses got away?' Bosun Thomas Matthews responded, 'I could not say, Sir – I was in the last boat'. Asked then, 'Was there any order given for the nurses to be put into the boat first?' he answered, 'There was no time to do anything. The ship sunk in seven or eight minutes and there was no time to rescue anybody'.[47]

43

THE NEWS THEY HAD DREADED

It was summer in Sydney when Charles and Catherine Blake heard the news they had dreaded, but had surely never really believed would come. Edith was missing. Such awful news could have come via a grim-faced clergyman's knock on the door of their weatherboard bungalow. Or they may have simply found out via the press: the first reports appeared in Australian newspapers within two days of the sinking.

They prayed for a miracle: that one more lifeboat or raft might wash up with their daughter safely aboard; but all such hopes were soon banished. On 4 March 1918 the Army Medical Services wrote to Charles Blake. The letter said, 'with the deepest regret ... Miss Edith Blake, Staff Nurse, Queen Alexandra's Imperial Military Nursing Service Reserve, is not in the list of saved from the Hospital Ship "Glenart Castle", and it is believed that she was drowned when that vessel was lost on the 26th February'.[1]

The news stunned her friends. Mildred Crocker Brown wrote in her diary,

Wednesday 27th Feb.

About 5pm the RC padre handed me the evening paper, casually remarking 'Another of our Hospital Ships has been torpedoed.' I was horrorstruck when I looked & found that it was the Glenart Castle that had been torpedoed & feared that all had been drowned in a cold wild wintry sea in the Bristol Channel.

The news they had dreaded

From the very first all accounts seemed very hopeless, but naturally we hoped against odds for the best news. However we had to face the very worst for all hands (except a few of the seamen) were drowned. Padres, MOs [medical officers], Matron & 7 Sisters.

Poor little Blake will be very much missed as she was a favourite with her friends. She is the first of our dear old Coast Hospital girls to give her life in her country's service. Dickson sent a cable of sympathy to her parents from all old Coasters on active service.[2]

A memorial service was held at Belmont POW Hospital. Matron Fairchild wrote to Uncle Will,

[I am] enclosing a copy of the sermon we had at the Memorial Service for Miss Blake and Miss Beresford. The latter had only left us on the Sunday before the tragedy to join the Glenart Castle and she was looking forward so much to being with your niece as they had become great friends in the time they were together here. It seems terrible to think of them going in the way they did. I wrote to Mrs Blake in Australia, giving her all the particulars I had, which of course are little or nothing. If their bodies could only have been found or even something belonging to them but there seems to be little hope of that now. If you ever hear anything in connection with them, I should be so grateful if you would let me know, as we all feel the loss so much.[3]

Captain Whitaker's eulogy mourned

the passing hence of two of our sisters, who until quite recently – only a few days ago in the case of one, were with us in life and vigour. Not only had they answered duty's call and for months had ministered to the needs of the enemy wounded, but they voluntarily offered themselves for further service in their noble profession, though in so doing they knew they ran risks of danger and death ... They were truest friends in life, loyal and devoted to each other and in death they were not divided. Those who know them best have paid spontaneous tributes to their unaffected grace and unostentatious piety and they live in hearts made better by their presence ...

The mysteries of life and death are everywhere about us, the enigmas that meet us at every turn are well nigh insoluble yet conscious of the righteousness of our cause, and the rightness of our course, we can only possess our souls in patience, and hope and pray that God Almighty may overrule the issues of this war to the lasting benefit of the nations and that the time may speedily arrive when 'Dovelike Peace shall stretch from shore to shore, And war and slaughter vex the land no more'.

The eulogy struck a chord with Charles and Kate. On the first anniversary of their daughter's death, they published a small notice in the *Sydney Morning Herald* echoing words from the eulogy:

> For her there were no flowers
> To adorn the unmarked surface of the water:
> The ocean alone decks her grave with gifts of pearls and shell
> And wreathes her brow with seaweeds rare.

It was as public a display of grief as the Blakes of Sans Souci would ever articulate.

On 10 April 1918 a memorial service was held at St Paul's Cathedral in London to commemorate nurses of the British Empire who had lost their lives in the war so far. The service booklet included a roll of honour. Little more than a month after their deaths, listed in alphabetical order on the first page under deceased QAIMNSR, were the names of Katy Beaufoy, Rebecca Rose Beresford and Edith Blake. Four places lower was Sister Butler, who had drowned off the rocks in Alexandria in 1916.[4]

Aunt Alice represented the Blake family at the service. Mildred Crocker Brown also attended:

> A number of us from here went to the Memorial Service in St Paul's to the memory of Sisters & Nurses who have fallen in this war (350 in all from the beginning til this date).[5] That huge edifice was packed with Sisters & nurses in full outdoor uniform. Every unit of the service in the British Army was represented. It was an honour to be able to attend such a service. A memorial service whose chief note was not one of sadness & sorrow, but rather of love & honour to our friends & comrades who have fallen in the service of our Empire & a note of victory on their behalf … The Last Post was sounded by the trumpets. Queen Alexandra & several Princesses & other people of note were present.[6]

In her own way, Edie had made it to St Paul's at last.

Uncle Will stepped in to handle some of the worldly matters that beset grieving families. He received sums of money due to Edie's estate and sent her effects home via the AIF at Horseferry Road. The receipt was for 'one suitcase (in crate) containing: Nurses clothing, 2 dresses, quantity books and records, quantity souvenirs, photographs, views, metal trays and fancy table cloths, trinket boxes, ornaments, brooches, necklaces, letters'.[7] The crate arrived home in Sans Souci in April 1920.[8]

Britain was outraged by the attack on the *Glenart Castle*. The bishop of London said, '[T]he cries of the drowning nurses will echo in our ears forever, and will brand us as a nation of cowards if we ever cease to strive that such appalling wickedness may be made impossible forever'.⁹ The *British Journal of Nursing* listed the names of the *Glenart Castle* nurses missing, believed drowned, saluting their courage and adding,

> In the present war [British nurses] know full well that every voyage they take on a hospital ship they are subjected to the risks of murder most foul at the hands of a barbarous foe ... [This] demands rare courage, but British nurses have not flinched. We salute with profound respect the members of the nursing staff of the *Glenart Castle*.[10]

Germany initially claimed that both the *Rewa* in January 1918, and *Glenart Castle* nearly two months later, must have hit mines. The Admiralty was satisfied by overwhelming evidence that both were torpedoed and protested via the Spanish ambassador that despite displaying prescribed lights and markings they had been sunk outside the forbidden zone, in breach of the German pledge.[11]

Despite Britain's protests, barely a fortnight after the sinking of the *Glenart Castle*, a third hospital ship, HMHS *Guildford Castle*, had a near miss on 10 March 1918 when attacked in the Bristol Channel while carrying nearly 450 patients to Avonmouth.[12] Britain again complained, but the greatest atrocity of all was to follow. On 27 June 1918 HMHS *Llandovery Castle* was torpedoed and sunk in the northern Atlantic Ocean when returning from Canada. Two hundred and thirty-four of the 258 crew and medical personnel died, many killed as the U-boat crew rammed and shot people in lifeboats and in the water, apparently to destroy evidence of the attack.

Kapitänleutnant Kiesewetter made for Zeebrugge after sinking the *Glenart Castle* and laid low. In May, UC-56 was prowling the Atlantic for victims when mechanical issues forced Kiesewetter to put into the nearest neutral port, Santander in northern Spain. Still awaiting repairs when the Armistice was declared, the submarine was promptly interned by the Spanish along with several others. The crews were placed on a Dutch steamer for repatriation to Germany. British Intelligence was aware of Kiesewetter's presence on board and, when they docked in Falmouth, Admiralty officers descended and arrested him. He was held in the Tower of London for his suspected war crime. Kiesewetter and his crew claimed not to have known the *Glenart Castle* was a hospital ship, despite evidence that she was brilliantly and appropriately lit and the submarine had tracked her for an hour before firing.

The German government protested Kiesewetter's arrest. The case was reviewed by British government lawyers who concluded that Britain was not entitled to arrest him because he held a document assuring him safe conduct for his return to Germany. After eighty days in solitary confinement, the man dubbed 'a pirate Hun of the worst description and a destroyer of hospital ships' was released.[13] British papers were appalled: 'Such folly increases the scepticism as to whether any German criminals will ever be put on trial'.[14] Although his name was published in 1920 on a 'Black List' of Germans 'whose extradition is demanded by the Entente',[15] Wilhelm Kiesewetter was never brought to trial. He served again in the Second World War as Germany's oldest U-boat commander, but HMHS *Glenart Castle* remained the only ship he ever sank.[16]

The *Rewa*, *Glenart Castle*, *Guildford Castle* and *Llandovery Castle* were all attacked in waters in which Germany had declared that hospital ships would be respected under the Hague Convention. Germany maintained that they were sunk because the submarine commanders hadn't recognised them as hospital ships due to 'circumstances of a technical nature, or difficulties of observation existing in consequence of atmospheric conditions'.[17] Britain pressed and in July 1920 Berlin sent the cases to the state attorney-general in Leipzig.[18] Only the commander responsible for the attack on the *Llandovery Castle*, Helmut Patzig, was charged with war crimes at the Leipzig War Crimes Trial of 1921. Before the matter could be settled, he left German jurisdiction. The indictment was quashed in 1931, and he was never brought to justice. Patzig too served again in the Second World War. His two subordinates were convicted at the Leipzig War Crimes Trial, but had their convictions overturned on appeal on the grounds that they were following orders.

Germany commissioned some 375 or 380 U-boats before and during the First World War. They carried out over 7600 attacks on Allied ships – half of them British – sinking almost 16 million tons of shipping (equivalent to 2200 *Glenart Castle*s).[19] Among these were eight British hospital ships, mostly sunk in waters in or near England and Ireland. Over 200 U-boats were lost – rammed, mined, sunk by gunfire, torpedoed or simply disappeared – costing nearly 4800 crewmen their lives. In an interview after the war, Kiesewetter made the exaggerated claim, 'Our U-boat losses were frightful. Between 90 and 95 per cent of our U-boat officers and men were killed. The number of U-boats was fairly well sustained, however, by new construction. But death was not all on one side, you will see'.[20]

The last letter her family received from Edie had been written 'At sea' after leaving Malta. It was dated 26 January 1918, one month to the day before she died:

My Dear Queen,

Such a big mail I got. 14 letters in all. Two were from you & 1 from Grace also 1 from Matron (Miss Watson). She has asked me to call on her sister in Sterlingshire in Scotland & when I go to Scotland as I hope I shall one day, I shall certainly go & see her. Sterling is one of the places I wish to see, it is full of historical interest. Matron was telling me how large the staff has grown.

The news they had dreaded

In your letter you spoke of ward 18. Well in my day at the Coast Ward 18 was a number of huts built some distance away from Scarlet quarters towards the reformatory. We called it the chicken run. Now somehow I think of Ward 18 as one of the wards in the new building. Where I hear the floors are polished. Yes they would be hard on the feet I should think …

Don't forget to tell me about your exam, & tell me the questions you got.

We are now ready loaded to go back to Blighty.

I notice in your letter that you write the letter 'B' so 'Bz' [exaggerated capital Bs]. Well Queen all the time I was in the German hospital I saw some of their writing. They make their 'Bs' so 'Bz'. So next time you make a 'B' like that, you will think of the enemy.

We have started on our way back to Blighty. I will write home, as soon as we get to Avonmouth, or wherever we land unless we strike a torpedo instead …

Give my love to all the girls who know me.

I hope Mum is quite alright now.

I wonder how long it will be till I come back to the Dear Old Coast.

Much love from
Edie

44

AFTER THE WAR

The war they called the Great War cut a bloody swathe through an entire generation.

Nearly 40 per cent of Australian men of military age enlisted.[1] Some were underage boys and overage men who lied in order to be accepted. More than 330 000 served overseas for Australia. Almost 216 000 casualties were incurred – killed, wounded, gassed, died of disease or accident, or POWs.[2] According to the official figures almost 62 000 of them died during or as a result of their service. The Roll of Honour for Australians during the First World War was officially collated between the dates 4 August 1914 and 31 March 1921. Nevertheless, many more died in the years that followed as a result of their war service. Per capita, Australia's losses were as high as any nation's on earth.

It is estimated that around one-third of the world's 10 million military deaths in the war were due to disease (excluding the 1918–19 influenza pandemic, which killed more people than the war). This was in contrast to previous conflicts such as the Peninsular Wars, Crimean War, American Civil War and both Boer Wars, in which deaths from disease exceeded combat deaths. It is testament not only to the scale of the industrialised conflict, but to medical advances that introduced vaccinations and the use of tetanus antitoxins, and to improved medical care.[3]

More than 1500 nurses died serving in the First World War.[4] Hundreds were nurses of the British Empire. Thirty were Australian women serving with the AANS and QAIMNSR. Most of the Australian nurses died as a result of illness and disease, including

After the war

around one-third who died in the 1918–19 influenza pandemic. Only Edith Blake was killed in action.

At the end of the First World War some 160 000 servicemen and women were repatriated to Australia according, so far as possible, to a 'first in, first out' principle, which gave those who had enlisted early priority in getting home.[5] It was an enormous task, carried out relatively swiftly and smoothly under Lieutenant General Sir John Monash, who had proved his leadership and planning skills throughout the war, no more so than his time in command of the Australian Corps on the Western Front in 1918. By the end of 1919, the bulk of the returning personnel were home,[6] including Edie's friends Evelyn Swannell, Mildred Crocker Brown (who suffered a bad dose of influenza in late 1918 as the pandemic ravaged England), Clarice Dickson, Dorothy Cawood, Eena Copeman and Elsie Graham. By all accounts they were strong, practical women, who were successful and well respected, with strong lifetime ties to returned services organisations – they never forgot 'their boys' and the camaraderie of their wartime service.

Evelyn Swannell had come home early, after her mother, Catherine, wrote asking her to return because Swannell's brother-in-law had died and her sister needed help.[7] Swannell arrived in Sydney in September 1918 to a heroine's welcome. A dinner in her honour was attended by 200 people including the mayor of Dundas and invalid soldiers.[8] For the next ten years, she put her career aside to care for her mother. After Catherine's death, Swannell took charge of the new Baby Health Centre in Albury, returning to Sydney in 1944 to become matron of the War Veteran's Home at Narrabeen until her retirement.[9] Evelyn Swannell died in 1953 aged 73.

The Coasters each initially returned to the Coast Hospital, where Queenie Blake was two years into her training. Most of those who had embarked on overseas service with Edie stayed at the Coast for several more years, moving on as their careers advanced. All of them, bar Mildred Crocker Brown, became matrons: Dickson at the

Coast, where she remained until she retired in 1936; war heroine Cawood[10] at Berry, where she was matron for nearly two decades until she retired in 1943; Copeman at 'Montrose' Maternity Hospital, then the Office of the Director-General of Public Health until she retired in 1945; and Graham for almost twenty years in Scone before she died in 1945.

Elsie Graham married in 1924 at the age of forty-three, but her husband turned out to be a rogue with a long criminal record for petty theft. The bride may have known about her new husband's chequered career, but it seems likelier she only became acquainted with his questionable character after the wedding. The match was soon over. Graham went to live with her brother and within two years had taken up her career again.

Mildred Crocker Brown's career was interrupted when she met and married Dr Gerald Archbold, who had served with the 4th Light Horse Field Ambulance in the war before obtaining his medical degree from Sydney University. They had a daughter, Margaret, and spent many years as pillars of the community in Tamworth, busy in local activities including the Returned Soldiers League, of which he was a patron, and she a founder and life member of the league's Women's Auxiliary. During the Second World War, Gerald served again as a regimental medical officer in the Middle East and New Guinea, and Mildred volunteered with the Red Cross. Dr Archbold died in October 1977 aged eighty. Mildred passed away three months later, aged eighty-eight.

More than ninety Coast Hospital nurses served overseas in the First World War, and nearly twenty doctors. Several Coast nurses were recognised for their service with the AANS. Seven, including Clarice Dickson, were awarded the Royal Red Cross for exceptional services, devotion to duty and professional competence, and several

After the war

were mentioned in despatches. Eight Australian nurses, including Dorothy Cawood, were awarded the Military Medal, the highest decoration available for their heroism in France. Only one Coast nurse did not return.

One Coast doctor was killed. On 8 October 1917, Dr Thomas Frizell was shot in the abdomen, left arm and right leg at an advanced dressing station during Passchendaele. He died of septicaemia on 2 December 1917.[11]

Several Coast doctors were wounded serving in field ambulance units at the Western Front, including Dr Thomas Furber, who, in three years on the Western Front, suffered a fractured wrist, gunshot wounds to his left leg and shell wounds to his right foot and right hand; and Dr Fletcher.

Dr Mervyn Fletcher was promoted to major in November 1916 then appointed medical officer to the 14th Battalion, which was in the thick of the action on the Western Front in 1917. Fletcher was mentioned in despatches.[12] In October 1917 he was wounded by shrapnel during Passchendaele. His war effectively finished in early October 1918 when he left for Australia on '1914 leave', a six-month leave granted to those who had enlisted in 1914 and were still on active service. In September 1919 he married Jean Middleton and they raised a family in Haberfield, where Dr Fletcher was a respected general practitioner and member of the Returned Soldiers League, heavily involved in his local church and community. He passed away in November 1954 aged almost sixty-eight.

Physical changes took place at the Coast Hospital during the war. Six new pavilions containing 300 beds were built, named after the minister for Health who approved them, Fred Flowers. The vegetable patch was extended and the bob-a-day men cleared another 10 acres for cattle, as Acting Medical Superintendent Dr Wallace sought increasing self-sufficiency for the hospital.[13] After his return Dr Millard remained Coast Hospital medical superintendent until his retirement in 1933, twenty-five years after he started there.

Alice Watson remained matron until she retired in 1926 after twenty-one years at the Coast.[14] During her time, the nursing staff increased from seventy to 227, paralleling a tripling of admissions.[15] Although she remained as socially conservative as ever, in the post-war years she relaxed certain strictures. Starched collars and caps disappeared, and uniform hems rose several inches.[16] As the roaring twenties dawned, mixed bathing in Little Bay was permitted (despite her opposition), and in 1924 her nurses even started to bob their hair – although the first to do so was severely rebuked when Matron's gaze lit upon the new 'do in the ward. Miss Watson even bought a car, although she continued to undertake her rounds by horse and cart.[17]

In 1934 the Coast Hospital was renamed Prince Henry Hospital by the minister for health as a surprise for the king's third son's visit to Australia. The prince never visited the hospital named in his honour. Dr Millard wrote that the 'change was deeply regretted …[but] protests were unavailing'.[18] With that decision the 'Coast Hospital' ceased to be.

Prince Henry Hospital continued to be a noted teaching hospital and training facility. Its surgeons performed the world's first kidney transplant in 1965. In 1988 the government decided to consolidate Prince Henry and Prince of Wales hospitals, and in 2003 Prince Henry closed its doors for the final time.

In 1925 Queenie Blake married Wilfred 'Bill' Kneeshaw, a war veteran and brother of a fellow Coaster. Her father built them a house on the Sans Souci parcel, and there they spent the rest of their married life.

After the war

Charles Blake died a few days before Christmas 1938. The fit and active eighty-year-old snapped his femur when he stepped in a hole as he dismounted a ladder after pruning a tree. In hospital he developed the blood clot that killed him.

Kate suffered a stroke in 1946. Trained nurse Queenie undertook her mother's daily care until her death a year later, aged eighty-eight. Gracie rose to head teacher of dressmaking at Darlinghurst Technical College, capping a forty-year career. At the end of her life, she developed dementia and Queen took care of her until she died of a stroke in 1959 aged seventy-one. When Bill developed stomach cancer he refused to go to hospital, because 'Queenie's a nurse, she can look after me'. She cared for him with her trademark mix of practicality, love and compassion up to his death at home in 1966.

With Queenie's death in April 1993, a month shy of her ninety-seventh birthday, the last direct link to Edie died too.

EPILOGUE

In February 2018 I travelled to England to attend a service to mark the centenary of the sinking of HMHS *Glenart Castle*.

On a windy morning under a watery winter sun, some seventy people gathered on a clifftop at Hartland Point in Devon, the closest point on the mainland to the wreck of the *Glenart Castle*. Access to the site necessitates climbing numerous steps and a short tramp over a ploughed field. Just off the South West Coast Path, nestled between gorse bushes scattered with yellow flowers, squats the memorial stone. Deborah and Sarah, the granddaughters of Edie's cousin Charlie, joined me. We had all met Edie through her letters and glimpsed our Blake forebears through her eyes.

A lone bagpiper played. Four bearers stood firm as their standards flapped in the wind. The group stood solemnly in front of the memorial as we said prayers and sang hymns. The haunting notes of the Last Post hung on the breeze then died away. In the ensuing silence I stared out at the Bristol Channel. In direct line of sight beyond the stone lay Lundy Island. The sea was like mercury, blotched with the shadows of scudding clouds. Exactly 100 years before, some men from the *Glenart Castle* were being rescued by the French. Others were still fighting to survive in these implacable waters. Edie's struggle was over.

At the end of the service, people filed forwards to lay wreaths. Several were relatives of individuals who were lost: Matron Katy Beaufoy, Lieutenant Colonel Furness and Quartermaster James Long. And the grandson of Alfred Bale, who survived.

I laid a wreath for Staff Nurse Edith Blake, one that I had brought with me, as it seemed important that I should leave a little

Epilogue

bit of Australia there for the girl from Sydney. A girl who went off on a grand adventure and 'wouldn't for all the world have missed it'.

Much love, Edie.

ACKNOWLEDGMENTS

This project has been years in the making and I have many people to thank.

To the team at NewSouth Publishing: my sincere thanks for bringing Edie's story to the world and ensuring we had a shipshape vehicle for doing so. Big thanks to Elspeth Menzies, Paul O'Beirne and Jocelyn Hungerford for their care, professionalism and attention to detail.

I want to particularly thank two people for their time and expertise: Verona Burgess, who was invaluable in helping me to refine my initial draft into a publishable state and who gave me confidence in the power of a good story; and Meleah Hampton, one of Australia's foremost First World War historians, for her incisive (and sometimes uncomfortable!) questions, and key polishes and corrections. This book is considerably better for their attention.

I am grateful to the relatives of Edie's friends and colleagues, for their assistance, patience and graciously granting me access to family papers and photos – in particular, Robert Cull, Gillian Campbell and the late Margaret Cull; Helen Bryan; Robyn Atherton, Judith Godden and Di Whelan; Hartley Cook; the Breen and Sinnott families in Ireland; and Gill Morgan.

I also thank members of the Blake family in England – Robert Blake, Jacquie Beckett, Deborah Patten and Sarah Johnson – for their help and support. Robert showed me Robin's Nest, the Works, and family 'sacred sites' around Dallinghoo. We were fortunate to meet in person and correspond as we shared our history and pieced together the background and stories of people who are distant relatives to us, but who loved and supported Edie.

Acknowledgments

I would also like to acknowledge the staff of these institutions who go about their business so professionally and helpfully: the Australian War Memorial; NSW State Archives (special mention to Rhett Lindsay); State Library of NSW; National Library, Canberra; UK National Archives; Imperial War Museum, London; and the volunteers of the Prince Henry Hospital Trained Nurses' Association Museum.

My early readers very generously provided suggestions and encouragement: Tom Vane-Tempest, Heather Sheldrick, Mike Hawley, Steve Hooke, and in particular my 'accidental' readers Jill and Bruno Yvanovich (the only people to have read the whole blowsy first draft).

Thank you too to so many people who have offered all sorts of assistance and support along the way: the indefatigable Lynette Smith OAM; Lyn Singleton and Steve Lewis; Bob and Jan Lawrence, who continue to lay wreaths at Hartland Point, Devon, in remembrance of Edie. Alison Middleditch, who took me on a tour of Belmont and surrounds – together we walked around Chipstead Woods and Box Hill, as Edie did. My father, Colin Kneeshaw; uncle Geoffrey Kneeshaw; cousin Leanne Kneeshaw; and especially Pat Pascoe, who has shared my interest and been good for a chat and a spot of speculation from the very beginning. Thanks to my children, Tom, Olivia and Patrick, and my husband, Paul, for their unwavering support of this project and without whom it could never have been achieved, although Paul chose to keep the peace by not reading a word.

Last but not least, thank you to Edie. I hope that she would not be concerned and would perhaps be 'a wee bit flattered' that I am sharing her words and that, somewhere, she knows she is not forgotten.

BIBLIOGRAPHY

PRIMARY SOURCES

Archival records

Australian War Memorial (AWM)
1DRL/0428, Australian Red Cross wounded and missing enquiry bureau files, 1914–18 war, 2110 Private Henry Herbert Bartrop, 3rd Battalion, 1915.
1DRL/0499, Millard, Reginald Jeffery (Colonel, b.1868 – d.1943), Typescript extracts from diary of Sir Reginald Jeffery Millard, 1914–16.
3DRL/3398(B), Davies, Evelyn (Sister, AANS, b.1884 – d.1966), 1915–21.
AWM4 10, Australian Imperial Force unit war diaries, 1914–18 war, Light Horse.
    2, 2nd Australian Light Horse Brigade, 1914–19.
    9, 4th Australian Light Horse Regiment, 1914–19.
    11, 6th Australian Light Horse Regiment, 1914–19.
AWM4 26/44, Australian Imperial Force unit war diaries, 1914–18 war, Medical, dental & nursing, 1st Australian Field Ambulance, 1914–19.
AWM27 373/12, Nursing services, Australia, Department of Defence, Roll of Australian nurses who served abroad with QAIMNS (Queen Alexandra's Imperial Military Nursing Service) (Nov 1921), 1921.
AWM41, Official history, 1914–18 war: records of A.G. Butler, historian of Australian Army Medical Services, Nurses narratives.
    992, Sister EW King, 1919–21.
    1035, Sister Scanlan, 1917–19.
    1054, Sister E Vickers Foote, 1917–19.
F 940.426092 B296d, AA Barwick, Diary of Sergeant A.A. Barwick, CdeG, 1st Battalion AIF, 1914–19.
PR05423, Edith Blake, Papers, 1915–18.
PR05855, Corfield, Agnes Beryl (Sister, b.1892 – d.1916), 1915–16.
PR82/135, Cook, Elsie Sheppard (Sister, AANS, AIF (1914–1916), attached Australian Red Cross Society (1916–1918) b.1890 – d.1972), 1914–18.

Imperial War Museum, United Kingdom
BRCS 25.5.4/26, British Red Cross Society, Programme for memorial service for deceased nurses St. Paul's Cathedral. Roll of honour for the nursing services. Memorial service for nurses, 10 April 1918.

National Archives of Australia (NAA)
B2455, First Australian Imperial Force personnel dossiers, 1914–20
    BARTROP H H, Henry Herbert Bartrop, 2110, POB Sydney.
    BROWN M C, Mildred Crocker Brown, nurse, POB Auburn, Cumberland, NSW.

Bibliography

COPEMAN F G, Frederick George Copeman, 2352, POB Narrabri, NSW.
DODD J C, Joseph Charles, 619, POB Battersea Park, England.
FLETCHER W M A, Wallis Mervyn Alfred Fletcher, major.
FRIZELL T J, Thomas James Frizell, major.
FURBER T M, Thomas Maynard Furber, major.
GRAHAM D E R, Donald Edwin Robinson Graham, 56, POB Jiggi, NSW.
MILLARD R J, Reginald Jeffery Millard, colonel, POB Newcastle, NSW.
PARKINS ALFRED JAMES, Alfred James Parkins, 773 3492, POB Sydney.
SWANNELL FREDERICK EDWARD, Frederick Edward Swannell, 3134 3380, POB Bungendore, NSW.
SOLLING ERIC MARTIN, Eric Martin Solling, lieutenant, POB Hexham.
SOLLING REGINALD, Reginald Solling, 7257, POB Stockton, NSW.
MT1487/1 BLAKE E, Edith Blake, RAMC, nurse, 16 October 1919 – 20 April 1920.

National Archives, United Kingdom (NAUK)
ADM 1/8511/19, Admiralty, and Ministry of Defence, Navy Department: correspondence and papers, Draft of despatches to Spanish ambassador re sinking of Hospital Ship Rewa. Hospital ships sunk by German submarines – Rewa, Glenart Castle, Llandovery Castle and Guildford Castle, 1918.
ADM 116, Admiralty, Record Office: cases
    1396, Alleged misuse of British hospital ships, vol. 2, 1916–18.
    1397, Alleged misuse of British hospital ships, vol. 3, 1917.
    1398, Alleged misuse of British hospital ships, vol. 4, 1916–17.
ADM 137, Admiralty, Historical Section: records used for Official history, First World War, 1860–1937
    3253, Inquiry into damage to HM Hospital Ship Glenart Castle by mine or torpedo: carrying of confidential documents in hospital ships, 1917.
    3424, HM Hospital Ship Glenart Castle: Court of Enquiry into sinking by enemy submarine, 26 Feb 1918, and issue of instructions and warnings to hospital ships following the sinking, 1918.
    4352, German naval officers: information photographs, press cuttings, 1908–12.
CO 323/785/68, Colonies, general: original correspondence, Circular despatch addressed to His Majesty's diplomatic representatives in allied and neutral countries respecting the torpedoing by German submarines of the British hospital ships 'Rewa', 'Glenart Castle', 'Guildford Castle' and 'Llandovery Castle', 1918.
FO 383/277, Foreign Office, Prisoners of War and Aliens Department: general correspondence from 1906, Germany: prisoners, including: reports of visits of inspection to the following internment camps and prison hospitals ... Belmont Hospital, 1917.
MT 23, Admiralty, Transport Department: correspondence and papers
    654, Admiralty, Transport Department: correspondence and papers, 1916.
    678/16, Statement on hospital ships carrying codes.
NATS 1/571, Ministry of National Service: records, Prisoners of war: repatriation, policy file, 1917–18.
WO 95/3989, War Office: First World War and Army of Occupation war diaries, Part I: France, Belgium and Germany, Lines of communication, Headquarters branches and services, Matron in chief, 1 January 1916 – 30 June 1917.

WO 95, War Office: First World War and Army of Occupation war diaries, Part I: France, Belgium and Germany, Lines of communication, Troops
    4144/5, Hospital Ship, Essequibo, February 1917 – December 1918.
    4145/2, Hospital Ship, Glenart Castle, October 1914 – February 1917.
WO 95/4739, War Office: First World War and Army of Occupation war diaries, Part IV: Egypt, Palestine and Syria, Lines of communication, Egypt and Palestine troops, 15 General Hospital (1915 Apr – 1918 Apr), 17 General Hospital (1915 Mar – 1920 Mar), 19 General Hospital (1915 Apr – 1919 Apr).
WO 162/341, Commander-in-Chief and War Office, Adjutant General's Department: papers, Report on the work of the Prisoners of War Information Bureau: includes examples of administrative papers, hospital and internment reports, 1 August 1914 – 31 December 1920.
WO 339/77725, War Office: Officers' services, First World War, long number papers (numerical), 2nd Lieutenant Charles Henry Blake. The Duke of Edinburgh's (Wiltshire Regiment), 1914–22.
WO 399, War Office: Directorate of Army Medical Services and Territorial Force: nursing service records, First World War
    494, Kate Beaufoy, 1914–20.
    582, Rebecca Beresford, 1914–20.
    683, Edith Blake, 1914–20.
    2459, Elizabeth Edgar, 1914–20.
    2584, Jane Evans, 1914–20.
    2619, Edith Fairchild, 1914–20.
    3760, Charlotte Henry, 1914–20.
    3725, Gertrude Henry, 1914–20.
    4543, Rose E Kendall, 1914–20.
    8131, Evelyn Swannell, 1914–20.
    11980, Harriet Henry, 1914–20.
    13088, Mary Mackinnon, 1914–20.

NSW State Archives
NRS 905 5/7348 15/27953 enclosing 15/27932, Colonial secretary, Main series of letters received, 1826–1982, letter from Office of the Director General of Public Health, Sydney to the Public Service Board dated 14 April 1915.
NRS 4405 3/5621-3/5625, Medical adviser to the government, Salary registers, 1895–1913, Coast Hospital, 1901-24.
RNCG-1216 A6082, Department of Education, Circulars relating to public servants who were on military leave during war, 1914–19.

State Library of NSW
MLMSS 2836 (K22194/Folder 2), Irene Victoria Read papers, pictorial material and relics, 1839–1951, Irene Victoria Read war letters, May–July 1915.

PRIVATE RECORDS, INTERVIEWS
Blake/Kneeshaw family
Blake, Alice, domestic science exercise book, Bracondale College, 1913.
Blake, Alice, letters to Arthur Blake, 15 and 26 April 1945.

Bibliography

Blake, Alice, letter to Charles Blake, 24 January 1917.
Blake, Frank, letter to Charles Blake, 24 January 1917.
Blake, Joyce, letter to Elizabeth Kneeshaw, 16 November 1980.
Blake, Joyce, letter to Robert Blake, 27 December 1990.
Blake, Robert, interview by Krista Vane-Tempest, Suffolk, 6–7 March 2018.
Gillson, A/g Lieutenant Colonel R M T, letter to Henry Blake, 18 December 1916.
K R O, Captain, letter to Henry Blake, 27 February 1918.
Thomas & John Brocklebank reference for Charles Blake, 9 August 1877.

Brown/Cull family
Brown, Mildred Crocker, diary, 1917–18.
Cull, Margaret, interview by Krista Vane-Tempest, Tamworth, 5 October 2018.

Fletcher/Bryan family
Bryan, Helen, interview by Krista Vane-Tempest, Forster, 28 April 2019.

Sinnott/Breen family
Breen, Ben, email to Krista Vane-Tempest, 8 April 2020.
Union-Castle Mail Steamship Company Limited, letter to Mrs Sinnott, Cahore, Gorey, County Wexford, 5 March 1918.
Sinnott, John, telegram to Sinnott family, 6 March 1918.

PUBLICATIONS AND LECTURES

Australasian Nurses' Journal, 1914–19.
British Journal of Nursing, 1918.
'Foundation of the Present Difficulties in VAD Service (1917)', reproduced at Scarlet Finders, accessed 5 August 2021, <www.scarletfinders.co.uk/186.html>.
Furnifull, Sarah Margaret, 'A World War I Nurse Remembers', *Australian Women's Weekly*, 31 October 1973, pp. 41, 43, 46.
Furse, Katharine, 'A Message from Katharine Furse, Commandant-in-Chief, British Red Cross Society Women's Voluntary Aid Detachments, to VADs Proceeding on Active Service', reproduced at Scarlet Finders, accessed 5 August 2021, <www.scarletfinders.co.uk/183.html>.
Higginbotham, Peter, 'South Metropolitan School District', The Workhouse accessed 5 August 2021, <www.workhouses.org.uk/SouthMetSD/>.
John Sands Ltd, *Sands Sydney, Suburban and Country Commercial Directory* (exact title varies) (Sydney: John Sands Ltd, 1858–59 to 1932–33), digitised at City of Sydney: Archives & History Resources, accessed 5 August 2021, <https://archives.cityofsydney.nsw.gov.au/nodes/view/495003>.
Lindsay, Kate, 'Headaches and Their Prevention', *Australasian Nurses' Journal*, 15 June 1914, pp. 189–192.
Loxton, HM, 'The Nursing of Malignant Diphtheria', *Australasian Nurses' Journal*, 15 January 1915, pp. 4–7.
Millard, RJ, 'The History of the Prince Henry (Coast) Hospital', *Australasian Nurses' Journal*, 15 March 1940, pp. 48–50.
Oseen, Helma, 'The Nursing of Tetanus', *Australasian Nurses' Journal*, 15 October 1914, pp. 346–347.

Ross, Ronald, 'A Lecture on the Treatment of Dysentery', Proceedings of the Royal Society of Medicine, London, 20 December 1915.
'Terms of Service with the Voluntary Aid Detachments of the British Red Cross Society and the Order of St. John', NSVW 14, reproduced at Scarlet Finders, accessed 5 August 2021, <www.scarletfinders.co.uk/182.html>.

DATABASES

'Burt, Bernard', in MH Massue, marquis de Ruvigny and Raineval (comp.), *De Ruvigny's Roll of Honour, 1914–18*, vol. 4, p. 23, reproduced at Ancestry, accessed 6 August 2021, <www.ancestry.com.au>(subscription required).
Commonwealth War Graves Commission, accessed 13 August 2021, <www.cwgc.org/find-records/find-war-dead>
Ireland, Sustainability Loan Fund, 1812–1868, Local associations, Galway, piece 094: Kilconickny note book, 1841–44, reproduced at Ancestry, accessed 6 August 2021, <www.ancestry.com.au> (subscription required).
New South Wales, Australia, assisted immigrant passenger lists, 1828–1896, reproduced at Ancestry, accessed 6 August 2021, <www.ancestry.com.au> (subscription required).
New South Wales, Australia, public service lists, 1858–1960, reproduced at Ancestry, accessed 6 August 2021, <www.ancestry.com.au> (subscription required).
New South Wales, Australia, unassisted immigrant passenger lists, 1826–1922, reproduced at Ancestry, accessed 6 August 2021, <www.ancestry.com.au> (subscription required).

NEWSPAPERS

Australia
Argus (Melbourne)
Border Morning Mail (Albury)
Brisbane Courier
Cumberland Argus and Fruitgrowers Advocate
Dubbo Liberal
Moora Herald and Midlands District Advocate
Northern Star (Lismore)
Register (Adelaide)
Sydney Mail
Sydney Morning Herald
Sydney Stock and Station Journal
Telegraph (Brisbane)
West Australian
World's News (Sydney)

United Kingdom
Belfast News-Letter
Birmingham Daily Post
Broughty Ferry Guide & Advertiser
Dundee Courier

Bibliography

Edinburgh Evening News
Graphic (London)
Hampshire Advertiser County Newspaper
Illustrated London News
Illustrated Police News (London)
Leeds Mercury
Liverpool Daily Post and Mercury
Middlesex County Times
Pall Mall Gazette (London)
People (London)
Scotsman (Midlothian)
Sheffield Daily Telegraph
Sussex Coast Mercury
Taunton Courier, and Western Advertiser
Western Mail (Glamorgan)
Western Morning News (Devon)

United States of America
New York Times

SECONDARY SOURCES

Books

Adie, Kate, *Corsets to Camouflage: Women and War* (London: Hodder & Stoughton, 2003).

Adie, Kate, *Fighting on the Home Front: The Legacy of Women in WWI* (London: Hodder & Stoughton, 2013; paperback edition 2014).

Barwick, Archie, *In Great Spirits: The WWI Diary of Archie Barwick* (Sydney: HarperCollins, 2013).

Bassett, Jan, *Guns and Brooches: Australian Army Nursing from the Boer War to the Gulf War* (Melbourne: Oxford University Press, 1992).

Bean, CEW, *Anzac to Amiens* (Canberra: Australian War Memorial, 1946; reprint 1993).

Bean, CEW, *The Official History of Australia in the War of 1914–1918*, vol. I, *The Story of Anzac: From the Outbreak of War to the End of the First Phase of the Gallipoli Campaign, May 4, 1915* (Sydney: Angus & Robertson, 1921).

Bean, CEW, *The Official History of Australia in the War of 1914–1918*, vol. II, *The Story of Anzac: From 4 May, 1915, to the Evacuation of the Gallipoli Peninsula* (Sydney: Angus & Robertson, 1924).

Beaumont, Joan, *Broken Nation: Australians in the Great War* (Sydney: Allen & Unwin, 2013).

Beaumont, Joan, Lachlan Grant & Aaron Pegram (eds), *Beyond Surrender: Australian Prisoners of War in the Twentieth Century* (Melbourne: Melbourne University Press, 2015).

Beckett, Ian FW, *The Home Front, 1914–1918: How Britain Survived the Great War* (Richmond, Surrey: National Archives, 2006).

Beeston, Joseph Lievesley, *Five Months at Anzac: A Narrative of Personal Experiences of the Officer Commanding the 4th Field Ambulance, Australian Imperial Force* (Sydney: Angus & Robertson, 1916).

Blythe, Ronald, *Akenfield: Portrait of an English Village* (London: Allen Lane, 1969).

Bou, Jean, *Light Horse: A History of Australia's Mounted Arm* (Sydney: Cambridge University Press, 2009).

Boughton, Clement R, *A Coast Chronicle: The History of the Prince Henry Hospital, 1881–1981; Centenary Issue* (2nd ed.), (Sydney: Board of the Prince Henry Hospital, 1963; reprint Waterloo, NSW: Knudsen Printing, 1981).

Bridgland, Tony, *Outrage at Sea: Naval Atrocities of the First World War* (Barnsley: Pen and Sword, 2002).

Butler, AG, *Official History of the Australian Army Medical Services in the War of 1914–1918*, vol. I, *Gallipoli, Palestine and New Guinea* (2nd ed.), (Melbourne: Australian War Memorial, 1943).

Butler, AG, *Official History of the Australian Army Medical Services in the War of 1914–1918*, vol. II, *The Western Front* (2nd ed.), (Canberra: Australian War Memorial, 1940).

Butler, AG, *Official History of the Australian Army Medical Services in the War of 1914–1918*, vol. III, *Special Problems and Services* (Canberra: Australian War Memorial, 1943).

Butler, Janet, *Kitty's War: The Remarkable Wartime Experiences of Kit McNaughton* (Brisbane: University of Queensland Press, 2013).

Cameron, David W, *The Battle for Lone Pine: Four Days of Hell at the Heart of Gallipoli* (Melbourne: Penguin Group (Australia), 2012; reprint 2015).

Chirnside, Mark, *The Olympic-Class Ships:* Olympic, Titanic & Britannic (Cheltenham: Tempus Publishing, 2004; reprint Cheltenham: History Press, 2011).

Cole, Christopher & EF Cheesman, *The Air Defence of Great Britain, 1914–1918* (London: Putnam, 1984).

Cordia, Maylean, *Nurses at Little Bay* (Little Bay, NSW: Prince Henry Trained Nurses' Association, 1990; reprint, revised 1995).

Feltman, Brian K, *The Stigma of Surrender: German Prisoners, British Captors, and Manhood in the Great War and Beyond* (Chapel Hill: University of North Carolina Press, 2015).

Fitzgerald, S, *Rising Damp: Sydney, 1870–90* (Melbourne: Oxford University Press, 1987).

Fredette, RH, *The Sky on Fire: The First Battle of Britain 1917–1918 and the Birth of the Royal Air Force* (Canada: Holt, Rinehart and Winston, 1966).

Friedman, Norman, *Seapower as Strategy: Navies and National Interests* (Annapolis, Maryland: Naval Institute Press, 2001).

Gammage, Bill, *The Broken Years: Australian Soldiers in the Great War* (Canberra: Australian National University Press, 1974; reprint Melbourne: Penguin Books Australia, 1981).

Gerard, James W, *My Four Years in Germany* (New York: George H Doran Company, 1917).

Goodman, Rupert, *Our War Nurses: The History of the Royal Australian Army Nursing Corps, 1902–1988* (Brisbane: Boolarong Publications, 1988).

Gray, Edwyn A, *The U-Boat War, 1914–1918* (London: Leo Cooper, 1972; reprint 1994).

Bibliography

Hallett, Christine E, *Containing Trauma: Nursing Work in the First World War* (Manchester: Manchester University Press, 2009).
Harris, Kirsty, *More Than Bombs and Bandages: Australian Army Nurses at Work in World War I* (Newport, NSW: Big Sky Publishing, 2011).
Harrison, Mark, *The Medical War: British Military Medicine in the First World War* (Oxford: Oxford University Press, 2010).
Hurd, Archibald, *History of the Great War: The Merchant Navy*, vol. I, *1914 to Spring 1915* (London: John Murray, 1921; Naval-History.net, accessed 6 August 2021, www.naval-history.net/WW1Book-MN1a-Merchant_Navy_in_WW1_Hurd.htm).
Hurd, Archibald, *History of the Great War: The Merchant Navy*, vol. II, *Summer 1915 to Early 1917* (London: John Murray, 1924).
Hurd, Archibald, *History of the Great War: The Merchant Navy*, vol. III, *Spring 1917 to November 1918* (London: John Murray, 1929).
Jellicoe, John Rushworth, *The Crisis of the Naval War* (London: Cassell and Company, 1920).
Macdonald, Lyn, *The Roses of No Man's Land* (London: Michael Joseph, 1980; reprint London: Penguin Books, 2013).
Moncrieff, Alexia, *Expertise, Authority and Control: The Australian Army Medical Corps in the First World War* (Melbourne: Cambridge University Press, 2020).
Moorehead, Alan, *Gallipoli* (Melbourne: Macmillan, 1956; reprint Melbourne: Macmillan, 1989).
Morris, E (ed.), *Australia's First Century, 1788–1888: Facsimiled from the Pages Devoted to Australia Appearing in Cassel's Picturesque Australasia MDCCCLXXXIX* (Hornsby: Child & Henry Publishing, 1980).
Nadin-Snelling, Erica, *Matron at War: The Story of Katy Beaufoy (1869–1918)* (Warwickshire: Brewin Books, 2014).
Payton, Philip, *Repat: A Concise History of Repatriation in Australia* (Canberra: Department of Veterans' Affairs, 2018; DVA, accessed 9 August 2021, <www.dva.gov.au/sites/default/files/files/publications/corporate/P03428.pdf>).
Pollock, John, *Kitchener: Comprising* The Road to Omdurman *and* The Saviour of the Nation (London: Constable, 2001).
Pugsley, Christopher, *Fighting for Empire: New Zealand and the Great War of 1914–1918* (Auckland: Bateman in association with Auckland War Memorial Museum, 2014).
Pugsley, Christopher & John Lockyer, *The Anzacs at Gallipoli: A Story for Anzac Day* (Auckland: Reed, 1999).
Rees, Peter, *The Other Anzacs* (Sydney: Allen & Unwin, 2008; reprinted as *Anzac Girls*, Sydney: Allen & Unwin, 2014).
Reid, Richard, *Gallipoli, 1915* (Canberra: Department of Veterans' Affairs & ABC Books, 2002).
Ring, Jim, *How the Navy Won the War: The Real Instrument of Victory, 1914–1918* (Barnsley: Seaforth Publishing, 2018).
Simkins, Peter, *Kitchener's Army: The Raising of the New Armies* (Manchester & New York: Manchester University Press, 1988).
Stanley, Peter, *Bad Characters: Sex, Crime, Mutiny, Murder and the Australian Imperial Force* (Sydney: Pier 9, 2010).
Sutton, Edward, *The Fitting Out and Administration of a Naval Hospital Ship* (Bristol: John Wright & Sons Ltd, 1918).

Tyquin, Michael, *Gallipoli: An Australian Medical Perspective* (Newport, NSW: Big Sky Publishing, 2012).
Tyquin, Michael, *Gallipoli: The Medical War; The Australian Army Medical Services in the Dardanelles Campaign of 1915* (Sydney: UNSW Press, 1993).

Articles, exhibitions, journals, pamphlets, websites

Abbott, Jacqueline, 'Cawood, Dorothy Gwendolen (1884–1962)', *Australian Dictionary of Biography*, vol. 7 (Melbourne: Melbourne University Press, 1979) online in 2006, accessed 12 August 2021, <www.adb.anu.edu.au/biography/cawood-dorothy-gwendolen-5537>.

Australian War Memorial, 'Conscription during the First World War, 1914–1918', AWM, last updated 6 March 2020, <www.awm.gov.au/articles/encyclopedia/conscription/ww1>.

AWM Website Admin, 'Dig Deeper: The First Convoy', Australian War Memorial, 31 October 2014, <www.awm.gov.au/articles/blog/dig-deeper-first-convoy>.

Bruton, Louise, 'The War at Sea', British Library, 29 January 2014, <www.bl.uk/world-war-one/articles/the-war-at-sea> .

Chamberlain, G, 'British Maternal Mortality in the 19th and early 20th Centuries', *Journal of the Royal Society of Medicine*, vol. 99, no. 11, November 2006, National Center for Biotechnology Information, accessed 6 August 2021, <www.ncbi.nim.nih.gov/pmc/articles/PMC1633559/>.

Cox, Francis, 'The First World War: Disease, the Only Victor', speech at Museum of London, 10 March 2014, transcript at Gresham College, 2014, <www.gresham.ac.uk/lectures-and-events/the-first-world-war-disease-the-only-victor>.

Fitzgerald, Shirley, 'Broadway', Dictionary of Sydney, 2009, <http://dictionaryofsydney.org/entry/broadway>.

Flood, J, 'The Case of Sydney, Australia', in Development Planning Unit, University College London & United Nations Human Settlements Programme, Understanding Slums: Case Studies for the Global Report on Human Settlements 2003, 2003, <www.ucl.ac.uk/dpu-projects/Global_Report/pdfs/Sydney.pdf>.

Ford, Steve & Katrina Bylykbashi, 'Quest to Record Names and Resting Places of WWI Nurses', *Nursing Times*, 25 September 2014, <www.nursingtimes.net/roles/nurse-managers/quest-to-record-names-and-resting-places-of-wwi-nurses-25-09-2014/>.

Friedman, Norman, 'World War I: A Maritime War?', in Andrew Forbes (ed.), *The War at Sea: 1914–18; Proceedings of the King-Hall Naval History Conference 2013* (Canberra: Sea Power Centre Australia, 2015; Navy, accessed 6 August 2021, <www.navy.gov.au/sites/default/files/documents/The_War_at_Sea_1914-18.pdf>), pp. 1–22.

Gilchrist, Catie, 'Socialist Opposition to World War I', Dictionary of Sydney, 2014, <https://dictionaryofsydney.org/entry/socialist_opposition_to_world_war_i>.

Grillini, Anna, 'Caporetto, Battle of ', 1914–1918 Online, International Encyclopedia of the First World War, last updated 28 April 2015, <https://encyclopedia.1914-1918-online.net/article/caporetto_battle_of>.

Hamilton, Reg, 'The History of the Australian Minimum Wage', Fair Work Commission, 2018, <www.fwc.gov.au/documents/documents/archives/exhibitions/minwage/exhibitionpaper-100yrsminwage.pdf>.

Bibliography

Helgason, Gudmundur, 'The U-Boats of World War One, 1914–1918', Uboat.net, accessed 6 August 2021, <https://uboat.net/wwi/boats/>.

History Press, 'Bread: A Slice of First World War History', History Press, accessed 6 August 2021, <www.thehistorypress.co.uk/articles/bread-a-slice-of-first-world-war-history/>.

International Committee of the Red Cross, 'The ICRC and the protection of prisoners of war: highlights from the ICRC Library's collections', 14 September 2020, accessed 14 August 2021, <https://blogs.icrc.org/cross-files/pows-library-collections/>.

James, Karl, 'I Hope You Are Not Too Ashamed of Me: Prisoners in the Siege of Tobruk, 1941', in *Beyond Surrender: Australian Prisoners of War in the Twentieth Century*, edited by Joan Beaumont, Lachlan Grant & Aaron Pegram (Melbourne: Melbourne University Press, 2015), pp. 96–115.

Jones, Heather, 'Prisoners of War', 1914–1918 Online, International Encyclopedia of the First World War, last updated 8 October 2014, <https://encyclopedia.1914-1918-online.net/article/prisoners_of_war>.

Kinsey, Gordon, *A History of Kesgrave Hall* (Ipswich: KDM International, 1995).

Law, Tim, 'Here She Comes!', People Helping People, accessed 6 August 2021, <www.peoplehelp.com.au/stories/arabia.html>.

Lundy, Darryl, 'Ellis Walford', The Peerage, last edited 23 May 2013, <www.thepeerage.com/p22237.htm#i222365>.

McCarthy, Perditta M, 'McCarthy, Dame Emma Maud (1859–1949)', *Australian Dictionary of Biography*, vol. 10 (Melbourne: Melbourne University Press, 1986), online in 2006, accessed 12 August 2021, <www.adb.anu.edu.au/biography/mccarthy-dame-emma-maud-7306>.

Meyer, Jessica, 'Don't Forget the Hospital Orderlies of World War I, On or Off the Screen', *Conversation*, 15 May 2014, <https://theconversation.com/dont-forget-the-hospital-orderlies-of-world-war-i-on-or-off-the-screen-26669>.

Moore, Wendy, 'Oh! What a Lovely Diet', *Guardian*, 14 January 2001, <www.theguardian.com/theobserver/2001/jan/14/life1.lifemagazine5>.

National Archives of Australia & Australia, Department of Veteran's Affairs, *Shell-Shocked: Australia after Armistice*, exhibition, Canberra, 8 November 2008 – 27 April 2009.

National Museum of Australia, 'Age and Invalid Pensions', NMA, last updated 17 June 2020, <www.nma.gov.au/defining-moments/resources/age-and-invalid-pensions>.

Negus Cleary, Michelle, 'Flies, Filth and Bully Beef: Life at Gallipoli in 1915', *Conversation*, 10 April 2015, <https://theconversation.com/flies-filth-and-bully-beef-life-at-gallipoli-in-1915-39321>.

New Zealand, Ministry for Culture and Heritage, *The Great War Exhibition*, Massey University, Wellington, 2014–18.

Parsons, FG, 'Anthropological Observations on German Prisoners of War', *Journal of the Royal Anthropological Institute of Great Britain and Ireland*, vol. 49, January–June 1919, pp. 20–35.

Paxman, Jeremy, 'The Strange Death of Lord Kitchener', *Financial Times*, 7 November 2014, <www.ft.com/content/f3760af0-6545-11e4-91b1-00144feabdc0>.

Peck, J, 'The Story of the Book', *Pettistree People*, no. 63, December 2013, p. 11, <http://pettistreesuffolk.org.uk/pettistreepeople/issue_63.pdf>.

Pegram, Aaron, 'Bold Bids for Freedom: Escape and Australian Prisoners in Germany, 1916–18', in Joan Beaumont, Lachlan Grant & Aaron Pegram (eds), *Beyond Surrender: Australian Prisoners of War in the Twentieth Century* (Melbourne: Melbourne University Press, 2015), pp. 18–39.

QARANC, 'QAIMNS World War I Queen Alexandra's Imperial Military Nursing Service QAIMNS Nurses', QARANC, accessed 6 August 2021, <www.qaranc.co.uk/qaimns.php>.

Rafaat, Samir, 'Aussies in Maadi (Meadi) Camp, Egypt, 1914–19', *Egyptian Mail*, 20 April 1996, transcribed at Digger History, accessed 6 August 2021, <www.diggerhistory.info/pages-conflicts-periods/ww1/maadi.htm>.

Siers, Robyn, 'Friends, Sisters and Pioneers', *Wartime*, no. 58, April 2012, <www.awm.gov.au/wartime/58/friends-sisters-and-pioneers>.

Snow, Dan, 'Viewpoint: 10 Big Myths about World War One Debunked', BBC News, 25 February 2014, <www.bbc.com/news/magazine-25776836>.

Stilwell, Martin, 'Farming in World War 1: Surrey's Contribution', Surrey in the Great War: A County Remembers, 5 December 2017, <www.surreyinthegreatwar.org.uk/story/farming-in-world-war-1-surreys-contribution/>.

Stowers, Richard, 'Could the Attack on Chunuk Bair Have Succeeded?', WW100, last updated 13 November 2015, <www.ww100.govt.nz/could-the-attack-on-chunuk-bair-have-succeeded>.

Thiel, Jens & Christian Westerhoff, 'Forced Labour', 1914–1918 Online, International Encyclopedia of the First World War, last updated 8 October 2014, <https://encyclopedia.1914-1918-online.net/article/forced_labour>.

Woolfenden, Tony, *A Church for Belmont: St John's, Its History and a Guide* (Belmont: St John's Church, 2015).

NOTES

Prologue
1. HM Hospital Ship Glenart Castle: Court of Enquiry into sinking by enemy submarine, 26 Feb 1918, and issue of instructions and warnings to hospital ships following the sinking, 1918, National Archives, United Kingdom (hereafter NAUK), ADM 137/3424.
2. See chapter 42, endnote 45.

1 Getting started
1. Edith Blake, letter to Charles, Catherine, Grace and Alice Blake, 26 April 1916, Australian War Memorial (hereafter AWM), PR05423. Hereafter, dates of Edith Blake's letters to her family and diary entries (the latter preceded by 'Diary') are given in the text.
2. 'Educational. Bracondale, Albert St, Petersham', *Sydney Stock and Station Journal*, 26 January 1909, p. 3.
3. Alice Blake, domestic science exercise book, Bracondale College, 1913, Blake/ Kneeshaw family records.
4. Clement R Boughton, *A Coast Chronicle: The History of the Prince Henry Hospital, 1881–1981; Centenary Issue*, 2nd edn (Waterloo, NSW: Knudsen Printing, 1981), pp. 1–6.
5. Boughton, p. v.
6. Boughton, pp. 34–35.
7. Maylean Cordia, *Nurses at Little Bay*, rev. edn (Little Bay, NSW: Prince Henry Trained Nurses' Association, 1995), p. 36.
8. Cordia, p. 145.
9. Cordia, pp. 94–95.
10. Day shifts usually alternated between 6 am – 6 pm and 6 am – 2 pm then 6–8 pm: Cordia, pp. 19, 91, 99.

2 Edie at the Coast
1. Maylean Cordia, *Nurses at Little Bay*, rev. edn (Little Bay, NSW: Prince Henry Trained Nurses' Association, 1995), p. 56.
2. Clement R Boughton, *A Coast Chronicle: The History of the Prince Henry Hospital, 1881–1981; Centenary Issue*, 2nd edn (Waterloo, NSW: Knudsen Printing, 1981), pp. 22–23; Cordia, pp. 14–15, 83.
3. Margaret Cull, interview by Krista Vane-Tempest, Tamworth, 5 October 2018.
4. Cordia, pp. 94, 95.
5. Kirsty Harris, *More Than Bombs and Bandages: Australian Army Nurses at Work in World War I* (Newport, NSW: Big Sky Publishing, 2011), p. 23.
6. Cordia, p. 91.
7. Cordia, p. 91.
8. Cordia, p. 216.

9   Boughton, p. 15.
10 HM Loxton, 'The Nursing of Malignant Diphtheria', *Australasian Nurses' Journal*, 15 January 1915, p. 6.
11 Cordia, p. 161.
12 Cordia, p. 64.
13 *Australasian Nurses' Journal*, 15 February 1915, p. 58.
14 Dr Baret, who succeeded Dr Millard as medical superintendent in 1933, instituted a protocol that these patients could not be admitted until examined by a senior nurse: Cordia, p. 141.
15 Cordia, p. 75.
16 Cordia, pp. 124–25.
17 Catherine Deely of Toolooban, Galway, received funds from the Kilconickny Loan in the 1840s, one of the sustainability loan funds provided for the 'industrious poor' – most likely because her shoemaker husband, Thomas, had passed away: Ireland, Sustainability Loan Fund, 1812–68, Kilconickny note book, 1841–44, reproduced at Ancestry, accessed 6 August 2021, <www.ancestry.com.au> (subscription required).
18 Harris, p. 24.
19 Cordia, p. 85.
20 Sarah Margaret Furnifull, 'A World War I Nurse Remembers', *Australian Women's Weekly*, 31 October 1973, p. 41; Office of the Director General of Public Health, Sydney, reference for Edith Blake, 6 April 1915, AWM, PR05423.
21 Furnifull, p. 41.
22 Boughton, p. 94.

3 Australia goes to war
1   'Our Very Best', *Sydney Morning Herald*, 3 August 1914, p. 10.
2   'Farewell to the Governor-General', *Sydney Morning Herald*, 18 April 1914, p. 20.
3   Joan Beaumont, *Broken Nation: Australians in the Great War* (Sydney: Allen & Unwin, 2013), pp. 22–24.
4   'Doctors for the Front. Great Response to Call. Leading Men Volunteer. Allotment to Posts', *Argus* (Melbourne), 3 October 1914, p. 14.
5   'The Army Nursing Service', *Australasian Nurses' Journal*, 15 August 1914, p. 266.
6   The AANS Reserves consisted of 'efficients' and 'non-efficients'. Efficients had to qualify in first aid and attend lectures each year on the organisation of military hospitals, hygiene and military surgery, and could be called up in time of war: Kirsty Harris, *More Than Bombs and Bandages: Australian Army Nurses at Work in World War I* (Newport, NSW: Big Sky Publishing, 2011), p. 39; Robyn Siers, 'Friends, Sisters and Pioneers', *Wartime*, no. 58, April 2012, <www.awm.gov.au/wartime/58/friends-sisters-and-pioneers>.
7   ML 355.81/A, Standing Orders for the Australian Army Medical Services, 1914, p. 28, cited in Harris, p. 41. By 1918 the span was twenty to forty-five years of age: AG Butler, *Official History of the Australian Army Medical Services in the War of 1914–1918*, vol. III, *Special Problems and Services* (Canberra: Australian War Memorial, 1943), p. 545.
8   That is, a hospital of eighty or more beds where lectures must be attended.
9   A Watson, Coast Hospital reference for Edith Blake, 12 August 1914, AWM, PR05423.

10 Alice Blake, letter to Arthur Blake, 26 April 1945, Blake/Kneeshaw family records.
11 Alice Blake, letter to Arthur Blake, 15 April 1945, Blake/Kneeshaw family records.
12 Gordon Kinsey, *A History of Kesgrave Hall* (Ipswich: KDM International, 1995).
13 Alice Blake, letter to Arthur Blake, 26 April 1945 .
14 During his four-year apprenticeship, Charles Blake sailed to Hong Kong on the clipper *Maiden Queen* from February 1873 to January 1874; made three voyages to Calcutta on the *Baroda* between 1874 and 1876; then joined the *Burdwan*'s nine-month journey to Singapore, returning in August 1877: Thomas & John Brocklebank reference for Charles Blake, 9 August 1877, Blake/Kneeshaw family records.
15 New South Wales unassisted immigrant passenger lists, 1826–1922, reproduced at Ancestry, accessed 6 August 2021, <www.ancestry.com.au> (subscription required).
16 His Majesty's Australian Transport *Kyarra* was employed as a hospital ship until March 1915 then became a troop transport.
17 'The Australian Army Hospitals', *Australasian Nurses' Journal*, 15 August 1914, pp. 398–400.
18 'Australian Army Hospitals'.
19 'Hospital Steamer Kyarra. Contraband on Board', *Brisbane Courier*, 5 January 1915, p. 7.

4. Why the British?

1 QARANC, 'QAIMNS World War I Queen Alexandra's Imperial Military Nursing Service QAIMNS Nurses', QARANC, accessed 6 August 2021, <www.qaranc.co.uk/qaimns.php>. However, at the declaration of war QAIMNS had fewer than 300 Regulars, 200 Reserves and 600 civilian nurses available: Kate Adie, *Fighting on the Home Front: The Legacy of Women in WWI* (London: Hodder & Stoughton, 2014), p. 105.
2 AG Butler, *Official History of the Australian Army Medical Services in the War of 1914–1918*, vol. III, *Special Problems and Services* (Canberra: Australian War Memorial, 1943), p. 535.
3 General Fetherston recommended to the minister after his tour of inspection of Egypt in 1915–16 that Australian nurses should wear badges, as 'Australian nurses suffered considerable disability through absence of badges of rank indicating their position as officers', but '[m]any nurses expressed their disapproval of the step': Butler, vol. III, p. 548.
4 AG Butler, *Official History of the Australian Army Medical Services in the War of 1914–1918*, vol. I, *Gallipoli, Palestine and New Guinea*, 2nd edn (Melbourne: Australian War Memorial, 1943), p. 405.
5 'Ready for Service', *Australasian Nurses' Journal*, 15 September 1914, p. 290.
6 'A Cable from the High Commissioner', *Australasian Nurses' Journal*, 15 March 1915, p. 69.
7 According to AG Butler, 'Members of the Australian nursing profession, eager to serve – especially abroad – began to realise that the chance of doing so with the AIF was limited. But another avenue opened up ... This was service with the British forces' (vol. III, p. 539).
8 Sister Scanlan, narrative, AWM, AWM41/1035.
9 Sister E Vickers Foote, narrative, 1917–19, AWM, AWM41/1054.

10 AG Butler refers to '130' Australians serving with the QAIMNSR (vol. III, p. 539), but 128 are listed in the Australian Department of Defence's Roll of Australian nurses who served abroad with QAIMNS (Queen Alexandra's Imperial Military Nursing Service) (Nov 1921), 1921, AWM, AWM27 373/12.
11 Office of the Director General of Public Health, Sydney to the Public Service Board, 14 April 1915, NRS 905 5/7348 15/27953 enclosing 15/27932.
12 The hospital's salary ledger recorded that Edie had joined the Expeditionary Forces (rather than the QAIMNSR) and was being paid '£60pa': NRS 4405 3/5621-3/5625, Medical adviser to the government, Salary registers, 1895–1913, Coast Hospital, 1901–24.
13 'War Gratuity Payment to Certain Members of the QAIMNS', *Moora Herald and Midlands District Advocate*, 14 October 1921, p. 4.
14 Butler, vol. III, pp. 540, 575–77.

5. Leaving Australia
1 *Australasian Nurses' Journal*, 15 April 1915, p. 136.
2 A Watson, reference for Edith Blake, 4 April 1915, AWM, PR05423.
3 Office of the Director General of Public Health, Sydney, reference for Edith Blake, 6 April 1915, AWM, PR05423.
4 'Social and Personal', *Telegraph* (Brisbane), 24 July 1915, p. 8.
5 'A.T.N.A. Belgian Relief Fund', *Australasian Nurses' Journal*, 15 March 1915, p. 70.
6 Although 'Eveline' is used on her birth and public service records, she evidently adopted the spelling 'Evelyn', which is used in letters in her war service records, death notice and plaque.

6 Into the blue
1 'The Emden's Loss, Told in the Trenches', *Sydney Morning Herald*, 27 November 1914, p. 7.
2 QAIMNS matron-in-chief Maud McCarthy recorded for 1915 that five nurses married but stayed, while fifteen nurses and one VAD resigned to marry: Jan Bassett, *Guns and Brooches: Australian Army Nursing from the Boer War to the Gulf War* (Melbourne: Oxford University Press, 1992), p. 40.
3 Janet Butler, *Kitty's War: The Remarkable Wartime Experiences of Kit McNaughton* (Brisbane: University of Queensland Press, 2013), p. 22.
4 The Ottomans had actually suffered 8000 casualties in the first week's fighting at Anzac. The Australians suffered more: some 8500, including 2300 dead: CEW Bean, *The Official History of Australia in the War of 1914–1918*, vol. I, *The Story of Anzac: From the Outbreak of War to the End of the First Phase of the Gallipoli Campaign, May 4, 1915* (Sydney: Angus & Robertson, 1921), p. xxii.

7 The landings
1 CEW Bean, *The Official History of Australia in the War of 1914–1918*, vol. I, *The Story of Anzac: From the Outbreak of War to the End of the First Phase of the Gallipoli Campaign, May 4, 1915* (Sydney: Angus & Robertson, 1921), chapter IX.
2 'Anzac' was originally an acronym for the Australian and New Zealand Army Corps, first used as a telegraphic code. By August 1915 it was being used to describe the place, and later the men.
3 Bill Gammage, *The Broken Years: Australian Soldiers in the Great War* (Melbourne:

Penguin Books Australia, 1981), p. 53. Primary sources vary as to the exact time, but by 4.30 am is most likely.
4   Eric Martin Solling, National Archives of Australia (hereafter NAA), B2455.
5   Perhaps Eric's death inspired his brother Reginald to enlist on 19 May 1915. He served as a gunner in France, but survived the war: Reginald Solling, NAA, B2455.
6   Agnes 'Beryl' Corfield , letter to friend Lizzie, 6 July 1915, AWM, PR05855.
7   Bean, p. xii.
8   Bean, p. 461.
9   Kirsty Harris, *More Than Bombs and Bandages: Australian Army Nurses at Work in World War I* (Newport, NSW: Big Sky Publishing, 2011), pp. 78–80.
10 Irene Read, letter to Mrs Langer Owen, 30 May 1915, State Library of NSW, MLMSS 2836 (K22194/Folder 2).
11 AG Butler, *Official History of the Australian Army Medical Services in the War of 1914–1918*, vol. I, *Gallipoli, Palestine and New Guinea*, 2nd edn (Melbourne: Australian War Memorial, 1943), p. 165.
12 Butler, p. 115.
13 Butler, p. 193.
14 Including infectious, venereal diseases and convalescent hospitals, 1AGH was ultimately responsible for some 10 600 beds: Michael Tyquin, *Gallipoli: The Medical War; The Australian Army Medical Services in the Dardanelles Campaign of 1915* (Sydney: UNSW Press, 1993), pp. 101–102.
15 Sister EW King, narrative, 1919–21, AWM, AWM41/992.
16 King.
17 Butler, p. 196.
18 Australia, Department of Defence, Roll of Australian nurses who served abroad with QAIMNS (Queen Alexandra's Imperial Military Nursing Service) (Nov 1921), 1921, AWM, AWM27 373/12.

8   On duty once more
1   Rupert Goodman, *Our War Nurses: The History of the Royal Australian Army Nursing Corps, 1902–1988* (Brisbane: Boolarong Publications, 1988), p. 45.
2   This is the only letter Edie left undated. Her diary indicates it was written on 5 May 1915: AWM, PR05423.
3   Bill Gammage, *The Broken Years: Australian Soldiers in the Great War* (Melbourne: Penguin Books Australia, 1981), p. 61.
4   Sister EW King, narrative, 1919–21, AWM, AWM41/992.
5   King.
6   Evelyn 'Tev' Davies, letter to mother, 15 July 1915, AWM, 3DRL/3398(B).
7   Thomas Maynard Furber, NAA, B2455.
8   Donald Edwin Robinson Graham, NAA, B2455; 2nd Australian Light Horse Brigade, war diaries, 1914–19, AWM, AWM4 10/2.
9   Jean Bou, *Light Horse: A History of Australia's Mounted Arm* (Sydney: Cambridge University Press, 2009), pp. x–xi, chapter 6.

9   Pyramids by moonlight
1   AG Butler, *Official History of the Australian Army Medical Services in the War of 1914–1918*, vol. I, *Gallipoli, Palestine and New Guinea*, 2nd edn (Melbourne: Australian War Memorial, 1943), pp. 198–99.

2   Likely they were accommodated in the mansion built for Prince Ibrahim Halim. The Khedivate of Egypt was an autonomous state ruled by the khedives after Napoleon Bonaparte's forces were expelled at the turn of the nineteenth century. The state paid tribute to the Ottoman Empire, maintaining that status even after the British occupied Egypt following the 1882 Anglo-Egyptian War. After the Ottoman Empire declared war on the side of the Central Powers the British deposed the ruling khedive and established a formal protectorate, the Sultanate of Egypt.
3   AA Barwick, diary, pp. 12–13, AWM063662, F 940.426092 B296d.
4   Regimental order no. 22, 4th Australian Light Horse Regiment, war diary, 29 April 1915, p. 51, AWM, AWM4 10/9/6.
5   Jan Bassett, *Guns and Brooches: Australian Army Nursing from the Boer War to the Gulf War* (Melbourne: Oxford University Press, 1992), pp. 80–81.
6   Agnes 'Beryl' Corfield, letter to friend Lizzie, 6 July 1915, AWM, PR05855.

10   In the land of uncertainty
1   'Devoted Red Cross Winner. Chat with Sister Graham', *Register* (Adelaide), 26 February 1917, p. 8.

11   Culture shock
1   'Letter from the Front. "The Bob a Day Tourists"', *Dubbo Liberal*, 22 June 1915, p. 2.
2   Richard Reid, *Gallipoli, 1915* (Canberra: Department of Veterans' Affairs & ABC Books, 2002), p. 3.
3   Notice from AIF Staff Pay Office, 4th Australian Light Horse Regiment (4LHR), war diary, March 1915, p. 52, AWM, AWM4 10/9/5.
4   4LHR, war diaries, 1914–19, AWM, AWM4 10/9; 6th Australian Light Horse Regiment (6LHR), war diaries, 1914–19, AWM, AWM4 10/11.
5   4LHR, February 1915, p. 47, AWM4 10/9/4.
6   4LHR, January 1915, p. 54, AWM4 10/9/3.
7   4LHR, November–December 1914, p. 93, AWM4 10/9/2.
8   6LHR, April 1915, p. 14, AWM4 10/11/5.
9   6LHR, March 1915, p. 16, AWM4 10/11/4.
10 6LHR, March 1915, p. 25.
11 4LHR, January 1915, p. 9, AWM4 10/9/3.
12 4LHR, January 1915, p. 47.
13 Peter Stanley, *Bad Characters: Sex, Crime, Mutiny, Murder and the Australian Imperial Force* (Sydney: Pier 9, 2010), p. 33.
14 Stanley, p. 29.
15 Samir Rafaat, 'Aussies in Maadi (Meadi) Camp, Egypt, 1914–19', *Egyptian Mail*, 20 April 1996, transcribed at Digger History, accessed 6 August 2021, <www.diggerhistory.info/pages-conflicts-periods/ww1/maadi.htm>.
16 This may not have been an isolated incident. The AIF instructed, 'All vehicles driven by soldiers or natives must be driven at a walking pace at all times, whether in the Streets or outside the town. In cases of real urgency they may proceed at a slow jog trot [with written permission]': Routine order no. 118, 6LHR, 3 March 1915, p. 8.

12 Arrival in Alexandria

1. AG Butler, *Official History of the Australian Army Medical Services in the War of 1914–1918*, vol. I, *Gallipoli, Palestine and New Guinea*, 2nd edn (Melbourne: Australian War Memorial, 1943), pp. 186–95.
2. 15 General Hospital, war diaries, April 1915 – April 1918, NAUK, WO 95/4739.
3. 17 General Hospital, war diary, 12 April 1915, NAUK, WO 95/4739.
4. 17 General Hospital, 29 April 1915.
5. 17 General Hospital, 15 May 1915.
6. Sister E Vickers Foote, narrative, 1917–19, AWM, AWM41/1054.
7. Elsie Sheppard Cook, diary, 26–27 June 1915, AWM, PR82/135.
8. Agnes 'Beryl' Corfield, letter to friend Lizzie, 6 July 1915, AWM, PR05855.
9. AG Butler, *Official History of the Australian Army Medical Services in the War of 1914–1918*, vol. III, *Special Problems and Services* (Canberra: Australian War Memorial, 1943), p. 535.
10. Jessica Meyer, 'Don't Forget the Hospital Orderlies of World War I, On or Off the Screen', *Conversation*, 15 May 2014, <https://theconversation.com/dont-forget-the-hospital-orderlies-of-world-war-i-on-or-off-the-screen-26669>.
11. Butler, vol. III, p. 554.
12. Butler, vol. III, p. 554.

13 Flies, faeces and food

1. Most support for the poor or disabled was provided by families and religious charitable organisations. The NSW government introduced an old-age pension in 1900, and an invalid pension in 1908. The Commonwealth parliament passed the *Invalid and Old-Age Pensions Act* in 1908 (noting that at Federation only around 4 per cent of the population could expect to live to sixty-five to claim the old-age pension): National Museum of Australia, 'Age and Invalid Pensions', NMA, last updated 17 June 2020, <www.nma.gov.au/defining-moments/resources/age-and-invalid-pensions>, citing Australian Bureau of Statistics, 'Australian Historical Population Statistics, 2014', ABS, 2014, <www.abs.gov.au/AUSSTATS/abs@.nsf/Lookup/3105.0.65.001Main+Features12014>.
2. Agnes 'Beryl' Corfield, letter to friend Lizzie, 28 August 1915, AWM, PR05855.
3. Michael Tyquin, *Gallipoli: The Medical War; The Australian Army Medical Services in the Dardanelles Campaign of 1915* (Sydney: UNSW Press, 1993), p. 63.
4. Helma Oseen, 'The Nursing of Tetanus', *Australasian Nurses' Journal*, 15 October 1914, pp. 346–47.
5. Mark Harrison, *The Medical War: British Military Medicine in the First World War* (Oxford: Oxford University Press, 2010), p. 101.
6. Reginald Jeffery Millard, diary, 30 July 1915, AWM, 1DRL/0499.
7. Joyce Blake, letter to Elizabeth Kneeshaw, 16 November 1980, Blake/Kneeshaw family records.
8. Bill Gammage, *The Broken Years: Australian Soldiers in the Great War* (Melbourne: Penguin Books Australia, 1981), pp. 64, 76–77; Tyquin, pp. 126–29.
9. Christopher Pugsley & John Lockyer, *The Anzacs at Gallipoli: A Story for Anzac Day* (Auckland: Reed, 1999), p. 224.
10. AG Butler, *Official History of the Australian Army Medical Services in the War of 1914–1918*, vol. I, *Gallipoli, Palestine and New Guinea*, 2nd edn (Melbourne: Australian War Memorial, 1943), p. 242.

Notes to pages 89-96

11   Alan Moorehead, *Gallipoli* (Melbourne: Macmillan, 1989), p. 249.
12   Anzac was fortunately apparently free of typhus and trench fever: CEW Bean, *The Official History of Australia in the War of 1914–1918*, vol. II, *The Story of Anzac: From 4 May, 1915, to the Evacuation of the Gallipoli Peninsula* (Sydney: Angus & Robertson, 1924), p. 377. Almost all troops on the Western Front were affected at some time by trench fever. It was realised only late in the war that the debilitating condition was caused by a bacterium carried by lice: Francis Cox, 'The First World War: Disease, the Only Victor', speech at Museum of London, 10 March 2014, transcript at Gresham College, 2014, <www.gresham.ac.uk/lectures-and-events/the-first-world-war-disease-the-only-victor>, p. 5.
13   Butler, p. 232.
14   Gammage, p. 65.
15   Butler, p. 244.
16   Cox, p. 4.
17   Tyquin, p. 119.
18   Tyquin, p. 118.
19   Clement R Boughton, *A Coast Chronicle: The History of the Prince Henry Hospital, 1881–1981; Centenary Issue*, 2nd edn (Waterloo, NSW: Knudsen Printing, 1981), p. 20.
20   Maylean Cordia, *Nurses at Little Bay*, rev. edn (Little Bay, NSW: Prince Henry Trained Nurses' Association, 1995), pp. 82–83.
21   For example, the New Zealand Field Ambulance unit diary for 25 April – 31 July 1915 recorded only 25 per cent fit for combat (the casualties were: 28 per cent sick, 41 per cent wounded, 31 per cent dead): New Zealand, Ministry for Culture and Heritage, *The Great War Exhibition*, Massey University, Wellington, 2014–18.

14   Not one whole man
1   Alan Moorehead, *Gallipoli* (Melbourne: Macmillan, 1989), p. 206.
2   AG Butler, *Official History of the Australian Army Medical Services in the War of 1914–1918*, vol. I, *Gallipoli, Palestine and New Guinea*, 2nd edn (Melbourne: Australian War Memorial, 1943), p. 282.
3   Butler, p. 282.
4   Moorehead, p. 209.
5   CEW Bean, *Anzac to Amiens* (Canberra: Australian War Memorial, 1993), p. 148.
6   Butler, p. 293.
7   Moorehead, p. 239.
8   Major WH Cunningham, letter to Lieutenant Colonel R Hughes, 23 February 1916, quoted in Christopher Pugsley, *Fighting for Empire: New Zealand and the Great War of 1914–1918* (Auckland: Bateman in association with Auckland War Memorial Museum, 2014).
9   CEW Bean, *The Official History of Australia in the War of 1914–1918*, vol. II, *The Story of Anzac: From 4 May, 1915, to the Evacuation of the Gallipoli Peninsula* (Sydney: Angus & Robertson, 1924), p. 679; Richard Stowers, 'Could the Attack on Chunuk Bair Have Succeeded?', WW100, last updated 13 November 2015, <www.ww100.govt.nz/could-the-attack-on-chunuk-bair-have-succeeded>.
10   Bean, *Official History*, p. 711.
11   Bean, *Official History*, p. 713; Richard Reid, *Gallipoli, 1915* (Canberra: Department of Veterans' Affairs & ABC Books, 2002), p. 8.

12 Michael Tyquin, *Gallipoli: The Medical War; The Australian Army Medical Services in the Dardanelles Campaign of 1915* (Sydney: UNSW Press, 1993), p. 37.
13 Tyquin, pp. 38–39.
14 Tyquin, p. 42.
15 Tyquin, pp. 61–69.
16 Butler, p. 41.
17 Reid, p. 67.
18 Butler, p. 252.
19 Rupert Goodman, *Our War Nurses: The History of the Royal Australian Army Nursing Corps, 1902–1988* (Brisbane: Boolarong Publications, 1988), pp. 41–42.
20 17 General Hospital, war diaries, March 1915 – March 1920, NAUK, WO 95/4739.
21 Butler, p. 400.
22 War Office, memorandum to Meditarranean Expeditionary Force, 5 October 1915, quoted in Tyquin, p. 43.
23 Bean, *Anzac to Amiens*, p. 165.

15 The fortunes of war
1 AG Butler, *Official History of the Australian Army Medical Services in the War of 1914–1918*, vol. I, *Gallipoli, Palestine and New Guinea*, 2nd edn (Melbourne: Australian War Memorial, 1943), p. 400.
2 17BGH admitted nearly 400 patients on 25 August 1915 alone: 17 General Hospital, war diaries, March 1915 – March 1920, NAUK, WO 95/4739.
3 Joseph Charles Dodd, NAA, B2455.
4 Henry Herbert Bartrop, NAA, B2455.
5 2110 Private Henry Herbert Bartrop, 3rd Battalion, 1915, AWM, 1DRL/0428.
6 Bartrop, NAA, B2455, pp. 24, 26.

16 Nothing doing on the peninsula
1 Prior to the August battles 3.5 per cent of men reported sick. Three weeks later the proportion had risen to 8.9 per cent, then it fell slightly as colder weather killed the flies: Bill Gammage, *The Broken Years: Australian Soldiers in the Great War* (Melbourne: Penguin Books Australia, 1981), p. 76.
2 Michael Tyquin, *Gallipoli: The Medical War; The Australian Army Medical Services in the Dardanelles Campaign of 1915* (Sydney: UNSW Press, 1993), p. 228.
3 Men in Class A were 'fit to rejoin their units', and those in B were 'convalescent, fit for service on lines of communication only': AG Butler, *Official History of the Australian Army Medical Services in the War of 1914–1918*, vol. I, *Gallipoli, Palestine and New Guinea*, 2nd edn (Melbourne: Australian War Memorial, 1943), p. 408.
4 Alan Moorehead, *Gallipoli* (Melbourne: Macmillan, 1989), p. 249.
5 Gammage, p. 76.
6 17 General Hospital, war diary, September–December 1915, NAUK, WO 95/4739.
7 Lyn Macdonald, *The Roses of No Man's Land* (London: Penguin Books, 2013) pp. 118, 123.
8 Ronald Ross, 'A Lecture on the Treatment of Dysentery', *Proceedings of the Royal Society of Medicine*, London, 20 December 1915, transcript, pp. 78–80.

9 Michelle Negus Cleary, 'Flies, Filth and Bully Beef: Life at Gallipoli in 1915', *Conversation*, 10 April 2015, <https://theconversation.com/flies-filth-and-bully-beef-life-at-gallipoli-in-1915-39321>.
10 In early September 1915 the French offered a substantial force of four additional army divisions, but General Hamilton's celebrations were short-lived, as the news soon followed that the French troops would not be available until mid-November. Worse news was to come: Bulgaria mobilised in late September and poised to join the German and Austrian forces in attacking Serbia. Any assault on Bulgaria had to be launched through Greece, and Greece demanded assistance if she was to enter the war. Therefore, instead of receiving more men at Gallipoli, one division each of French and British troops was removed to Salonika, but those units were ultimately in no position to help when Serbia was attacked in early October 1915, and was then lost. King Constantine was unimpressed and returned Greece to neutrality.
11 Moorehead, p. 264.
12 Moorehead, pp. 270–71.
13 Butler, p. 440.
14 Gammage, p. 77. Moorehead cites 10 000 casualties (pp. 271–72); Macdonald cites over 16 000 frostbite cases (p. 126).

17 Such a Christmas we have had

1 The volunteers received a small sum to defray costs. After one month's probation, those contracted received £20 per annum for six months, with increments to a maximum £30 per annum, plus allowances for uniform, and for travelling, board, lodging and washing if they went overseas: 'Terms of Service with the Voluntary Aid Detachments of the British Red Cross Society and the Order of St. John', NSVW 14, reproduced at Scarlet Finders, accessed 5 August 2021, <www.scarletfinders.co.uk/182.html>.
2 Kate Adie, *Fighting on the Home Front: The Legacy of Women in WWI* (London: Hodder & Stoughton, 2014), pp. 107–108. In turn, VAD complaints in 1917 included trained nurses' jealousy of the untrained women: 'Foundation of the Present Difficulties in VAD Service (1917)', reproduced at Scarlet Finders, accessed 5 August 2021, <www.scarletfinders.co.uk/186.html>.
3 Perhaps over 70 000 throughout the war: Adie, p. 106.
4 Katharine Furse, 'A Message from Katharine Furse, Commandant-in-Chief, British Red Cross Society Women's Voluntary Aid Detachments, to VADs Proceeding on Active Service', form, VAD, reproduced at Scarlet Finders, accessed 5 August 2021, <www.scarletfinders.co.uk/183.html>.
5 Frederick George Copeman, NAA, B2455.
6 'Waits' were official English waitnight carol singers.

18 Don't think that I've lost my heart

1 Concert program sent home with Edith Blake's letter dated 31 December 1915: AWM, PR05423.
2 17 General Hospital, war diary, 26 December 1915, NAUK, WO 95/4739.
3 17 General Hospital, 22 January and 20 September 1916.
4 Alfred James Parkins, NAA, B2455.

Notes to pages 129–165

5 Parkins was not satisfied sitting at home: eighteen months later he joined up again (distinguishing mark: bullet wound to left forearm) and spent the rest of the war in Palestine with the 6th Australian Light Horse Regiment: Parkins.
6 Mildred Crocker Brown, diary, 23 May 1917, Brown/Cull family records.

19 Waiting for the next move
1 Letter to the editor, *Argus* (Melbourne), 18 September 1915, p. 18.
2 Hughes replaced Andrew Fisher as prime minister of Australia in 1915. Hughes relished the demands of wartime leadership with which Fisher had struggled.
3 Of all admissions to AGHs, 11.2 per cent were Australians, but on the Western Front the proportion was only 6.5 per cent: Rupert Goodman, *Our War Nurses: The History of the Royal Australian Army Nursing Corps, 1902–1988* (Brisbane: Boolarong Publications, 1988), p. 60.
4 'Rioting. Soldiers Refuse to Drill. One Man Killed', *Sydney Morning Herald*, 15 February 1916, p. 9.
5 CEW Bean, *Anzac to Amiens* (Canberra: Australian War Memorial, 1993), pp. 194–95.

20 It is an education
1 Seven of 128 Australian nurses allocated to the QAIMNS: Australia, Department of Defence, Roll of Australian nurses who served abroad with QAIMNS (Queen Alexandra's Imperial Military Nursing Service) (Nov 1921), 1921, AWM, AWM27 373/12.
2 Katy Beaufoy, diary, 14 April 1916, quoted in Erica Nadin-Snelling, *Matron at War: The Story of Katy Beaufoy (1869–1918)* (Warwickshire: Brewin Books, 2014), p. 60.

21 Sunburn, sand – and slack
1 17BGH admitted 435 patients on 13 May 1916 and 520 on 9 July 1916: 17. General Hospital, war diaries, March 1915 – March 1920, NAUK, WO 95/4739.

22 The nicest ship I have been on
1 Personnel on ships were instructed that correspondence referring to names or movements of ships, dates of sailing, ports of call or destination, would be stopped. See, for example, Regimental order no. 73, 4th Light Horse Regiment, war diary, 29 October 1914, p. 123, AWM, AWM4 10/9/1.
2 Edie had given Queen a green cloth-bound copy of *The Myths of Greece and Rome* for her sixteenth birthday.
3 Edward Sutton, *The Fitting Out and Administration of a Naval Hospital Ship* (Bristol: John Wright & Sons Ltd, 1918), preface.
4 Sutton, pp. 25–26.
5 Charles Blake was 58, turning 59 in December 1916.

23 Passing through all dangers
1 'R.M.S. Arabia. Sunk by Torpedo. Attack in Mediterranean', *Argus* (Melbourne), 9 November 1916, p. 6.
2 Tim Law, 'Here She Comes!', People Helping People, accessed 6 August 2021, <www.peoplehelp.com.au/stories/arabia.html>.

Notes to pages 165–195

3   'Torpedoed! A Woman in Peril', *West Australian*, 13 July 1935, p. 5.
4   'Torpedoed!'
5   'Torpedoed!'
6   'R.M.S. Arabia. Sunk by Torpedo. Attack in Mediterranean', *Argus* (Melbourne), 9 November 1916, p. 6.
7   HMHS *Britannic* was intended to have all eight sets motorised but was pressed into war service before this work could be completed. The final three sets were manually operated, as RMS *Titanic*'s had been: Mark Chirnside, *The Olympic-Class Ships:* Olympic, Titanic & Britannic (Cheltenham: History Press, 2011), pp. 220, 224.

24 The war at sea

1   Eberhard Weichold, *The War at Sea in the Mediterranean* (Washington, DC: US Navy, 1947), quoted in Norman Friedman, 'World War I: A Maritime War?', in Andrew Forbes (ed.), *The War at Sea: 1914–18; Proceedings of the King-Hall Naval History Conference, 2013* (Navy, accessed 6 August 2021, <www.navy.gov.au/sites/default/files/documents/The_War_at_Sea_1914-18.pdf>), p. 3.
2   John Rushworth Jellicoe, *The Crisis of the Naval War* (London: Cassell and Company, 1920), p. 1.
3   Edwyn A Gray, *The U-Boat War, 1914–1918* (London: Leo Cooper, 1994), p. 53.
4   Jim Ring, *How the Navy Won the War: The Real Instrument of Victory, 1914–1918* (Barnsley: Seaforth Publishing, 2018), p. xvi.
5   John Pollock, *Kitchener: Comprising* The Road to Omdurman *and* The Saviour of the Nation (London: Constable, 2001), p. 192.
6   Pollock, chapter 25; Jeremy Paxman, 'The Strange Death of Lord Kitchener', *Financial Times*, 7 November 2014, <www.ft.com/content/f3760af0-6545-11e4-91b1-00144feabdc0>.
7   Jellicoe, p. 4.
8   Gray, p. 171.

26 Back to the old place

1   Mildred Crocker Brown, diary, 9 February 1917, Brown/Cull family records.
2   J Peck, 'The Story of the Book', *Pettistree People*, no. 63, December 2013, p. 11, <http://pettistreesuffolk.org.uk/pettistreepeople/issue_63.pdf>, citing *Suffolk Roots* (Suffolk Family History Society), vol. 34, no. 1; Robert Blake, interview by Krista Vane-Tempest, Suffolk, 6–7 March 2018.
3   The bell rang at 8 am, 10 am and 5 pm: Joyce Blake, letter to Robert Blake, 27 December 1990, Blake/Kneeshaw family records.
4   Ronald Blythe, *Akenfield: Portrait of an English Village* (London: Allen Lane, 1969), pp. 126–27.
5   Blythe, p. 113.
6   R Blake, 2018.

27 'A pleasant voyage'

1   Hospital Ship, Essequibo, war diary, 3 March 1917, NAUK, WO 95/4144/5.
2   Edwyn A Gray, *The U-Boat War, 1914–1918* (London: Leo Cooper, 1994), p. 20.
3   Gray, p. 171.
4   The restricted maritime area was between Flamborough Head-Terschelling to

the east, and Ushant-Land's End to the west: Draft of despatches to Spanish ambassador re sinking of Hospital Ship Rewa. Hospital ships sunk by German submarines – Rewa, Glenart Castle, Llandovery Castle and Guildford Castle, 1918, NAUK, ADM 1/8511/19. The German action was not unprecedented: in August 1916 the Russians announced that they would not recognise Ottoman hospital ships in the Black Sea: Memorandum, 28 August 1916, NAUK, ADM 116/1396.
5   Draft of despatches to Spanish ambassador.
6   Gray, p. 183.
7   A F Bowdler, Captain RAMC HS Essequibo, countersigned by John D Gimlette, Major RAMC HS Essequibo, letter to the Officer Commanding Troops, HS Essequibo, 15 March 1917, NAUK, WO 399/8131.
8   Matron in chief, war diaries, 1 January 1916 – 30 June 1917, NAUK, WO 95/3989.
9   Perditta M McCarthy, 'McCarthy, Dame Emma Maud (1859–1949)', *Australian Dictionary of Biography*, vol. 10 (Melbourne: Melbourne University Press, 1986), online in 2006, accessed 12 August 2021, <www.adb.anu.edu.au/biography/mccarthy-dame-emma-maud-7306>.

28 Somewhere on the Atlantic Ocean
1   Hospital Ship, Essequibo, war diary, 31 March 1917, NAUK, WO 95/4144/5.
2   Hospital Ship, Essequibo, 2 April 1917.
3   Statement on hospital ships carrying codes, 1916, NAUK, MT 23/678/16.
4   Admiralty, memorandum, 19 April 1917; and Brief for information of the War Cabinet, 17 May 1917, NAUK, ADM 116/1396.
5   Admiralty, memorandum, 2 February 1917, NAUK, ADM 116/1396.
6   Memorandum, November 1916, NAUK, ADM 116/1396.
7   Memorandum, 2 February 1917, NAUK, ADM 116/1396.
8   British ships sunk by U-boats that attacked without warning: 21 per cent in 1915; 29 per cent in 1916; 64 per cent in the first four months of 1917: John Rushworth Jellicoe, *The Crisis of the Naval War* (London: Cassell and Company, 1920), p. 38.
9   Louise Bruton, 'The War at Sea', British Library, 29 January 2014, <www.bl.uk/world-war-one/articles/the-war-at-sea>, citing Julian Thompson, *The Imperial War Museum Book of the War at Sea, 1914–1918* (London: Sidgwick & Jackson, 2005), p. 326.
10 Archibald Hurd, *History of the Great War: The Merchant Navy*, vol. III, *Spring 1917 to November 1918* (London: John Murray, 1929), appendix C.
11 Jellicoe, p. vii.
12 Memorandum, 2 June 1917, NAUK, ADM 116/1397.
13 Memorandum, 23 April 1917, NAUK, ADM 116/1397.
14 Memoranda, 13 April 1917 and 4 May 1917, NAUK, ADM 116/1397.
15 Memorandum, 24 May 1917, NAUK, ADM 116/1397.
16 Malaria ran rampant in Macedonia from 1916 to 1918, affecting all armies. Estimates suggest the British lost over 2 million man days to malaria: Francis Cox, 'The First World War: Disease, the Only Victor', speech at Museum of London, 10 March 2014, transcript at Gresham College, 2014, <www.gresham.ac.uk/lectures-and-events/the-first-world-war-disease-the-only-victor>, p. 5.

29 I'm not going to nurse any Germans

1. Advertisements, 1913, in Tony Woolfenden, *A Church for Belmont: St John's, Its History and A Guide* (Belmont: St John's Church, 2015).
2. 'The South Metropolitan Industrial Schools at Sutton, Surrey', *Illustrated London News*, Saturday 18 March 1854, p 10.
3. 'The Fulham Workhouse and Infirmary', *Middlesex County Times*, 7 April 1917, p. 1.
4. Germany: prisoners, including: reports of visits of inspection to the following internment camps and prison hospitals ... Belmont Hospital, 1917, NAUK, FO 383/277.
5. The *Ballarat* was an Australian troopship torpedoed in the English Channel on 25 April 1917; no lives were lost.

30 Our feelings are very mixed here

1. Heather Jones, 'Prisoners of War', 1914–1918 Online, International Encyclopedia of the First World War, last updated 8 October 2014, <https://encyclopedia.1914-1918-online.net/article/prisoners_of_war>.
2. FG Parsons, 'Anthropological Observations on German Prisoners of War', *Journal of the Royal Anthropological Institute of Great Britain and Ireland*, vol. 49, January–June 1919, pp. 20–35.
3. More mines were planted, but several did not detonate that day.
4. 'Haig's Brilliant Victory', *People* (London), 10 June 1917, p. 7.
5. CEW Bean, *The Official History of Australia in the War of 1914–1918*, vol. II, *The Story of Anzac: From 4 May, 1915, to the Evacuation of the Gallipoli Peninsula* (Sydney: Angus & Robertson, 1924), p. 162.
6. Brian K Feltman, *The Stigma of Surrender: German Prisoners, British Captors, and Manhood in the Great War and Beyond* (Chapel Hill: University of North Carolina Press, 2015), pp. 2, 15; Karl James, 'I Hope You Are Not Too Ashamed of Me: Prisoners in the Siege of Tobruk, 1941', in Joan Beaumont, Lachlan Grant & Aaron Pegram (eds), *Beyond Surrender: Australian Prisoners of War in the Twentieth Century* (Melbourne: Melbourne University Press, 2015), pp. 101–102.

31 These men have to work

1. Heather Jones, 'Prisoners of War', 1914–1918 Online, International Encyclopedia of the First World War, last updated 8 October 2014, <https://encyclopedia.1914-1918-online.net/article/prisoners_of_war>.
2. Brian K Feltman, *The Stigma of Surrender: German Prisoners, British Captors, and Manhood in the Great War and Beyond* (Chapel Hill: University of North Carolina Press, 2015), p. 2.
3. That is, the Convention for the Amelioration of the Condition of the Wounded and Sick in Armies in the Field, Geneva, 6 July 1906, and the Convention on the Laws and Customs of War on Land, The Hague, 18 October 1907. The Convention relative to the Treatment of Prisoners of War, Geneva, passed 27 July 1929 followed the same principles as the earlier treaties concerning treatment of prisoners, but introduced compliance provisions and mechanisms because of violations by the belligerents during the First World War, when the International Committee of the Red Cross 'advocated for [prisoners of war] rights through diplomatic channels and negotiated with the belligerents to be allowed to visit

[POW] camps. From 1915 to 1918, its delegates visited 534 POW camps, mainly in Europe but also in North Africa and Asia': <https://blogs.icrc.org/cross-files/pows-library-collections/>. These conventions were precursors to, and far less comprehensive than, the requirements of the 1949 Third Geneva Convention relative to the Treatment of Prisoners of War.
4   Report on the work of the Prisoners of War Information Bureau: includes examples of administrative papers, hospital and internment reports, 1 August 1914 – 31 December 1920, NAUK, WO162/341.
5   Jens Thiel & Christian Westerhoff, 'Forced Labour', 1914–1918 Online, International Encyclopedia of the First World War, last updated 8 October 2014, <https://encyclopedia.1914-1918-online.net/article/forced_labour>.
6   4th Light Horse Regiment, war diary, January 1915, p. 31, AWM, AWM4 10/9/3.
7   Jones.
8   POW camp, Wakrey, Northants, report, 10 July 1917, NAUK, Germany: prisoners, including: reports of visits of inspection to the following internment camps and prison hospitals … Belmont Hospital, 1917, NAUK, FO 383/277.
9   Officers' camp, Colsterdale, Masham, Yorkshire, report, 26 June 1917, NAUK, FO383/277.
10 Dan Snow, 'Viewpoint: 10 Big Myths about World War One Debunked', BBC News, 25 February 2014, <www.bbc.com/news/magazine-25776836>.
11 Charles Blake, Statement of circumstances of capture, 17 January 1919, NAUK, WO339/77725.
12 R M T Gillson, A/g Lieutenant Colonel, letter to Henry Blake, 18 December 1916, Blake/Kneeshaw family records.
13 Prisoners of war: repatriation, policy file, 1917–18, NAUK, NATS 1/571.
14 'K R O', Captain, letter to Henry Blake, 27 February 1918, Blake/Kneeshaw family records.
15 'K R O', Captain.

32 The food question is a serious one now
1   Heather Jones, 'Prisoners of War', 1914–1918 Online, International Encyclopedia of the First World War, last updated 8 October 2014, <https://encyclopedia.1914-1918-online.net/article/prisoners_of_war>.
2   For example, 'Starving Anzacs. Grim Story of Two Escaped Prisoners', *Edinburgh Evening News*, 1 June 1917, p. 5. The men captured at Bullecourt received harsher treatment in reprisal for the British and French using German prisoners for captive labour: Aaron Pegram, 'Bold Bids for Freedom: Escape and Australian Prisoners in Germany, 1916–18', in Joan Beaumont, Lachlan Grant & Aaron Pegram (eds), *Beyond Surrender: Australian Prisoners of War in the Twentieth Century* (Melbourne: Melbourne University Press, 2015), pp. 26–28.
3   POW hospital, Belmont, Surrey, report, 26 July 1917, NAUK, Germany: prisoners, including: reports of visits of inspection to the following internment camps and prison hospitals … Belmont Hospital, 1917, NAUK, FO 383/277.
4   POW hospital, Belmont, Surrey, report, 4 October 1917, NAUK, FO383/277.
5   POW hospital, Belmont, Surrey, report, 4 October 1917, NAUK, FO383/277.
6   Martin Stilwell, 'Farming in World War 1: Surrey's Contribution', Surrey in the Great War: A County Remembers, 5 December 2017, <www.surreyinthegreatwar.org.uk/story/farming-in-world-war-1-surreys-contribution/>.

7   History Press, 'Bread: A Slice of First World War History', History Press, accessed 6 August 2021, <www.thehistorypress.co.uk/articles/bread-a-slice-of-first-world-war-history/>.
8   History Press.
9   Ian FW Beckett, *The Home Front, 1914–1918: How Britain Survived the Great War* (Richmond, Surrey: National Archives, 2006), pp. 380–82.
10 History Press.
11 History Press.
12 Wendy Moore, 'Oh! What a Lovely Diet', *Guardian*, 14 January 2001, <www.theguardian.com/theobserver/2001/jan/14/life1.lifemagazine5>.
13 History Press.

33 Murder in my heart
1   Christopher Cole & EF Cheesman, *The Air Defence of Great Britain, 1914–1918* (London: Putnam, 1984), p. 31.
2   'The Zeppelin Menace', *Broughty Ferry Guide & Advertiser*, 11 June 1915, p. 6.
3   Cole & Cheesman, pp. 243–46.
4   Officially, fifty-seven were killed and 193 wounded: Cole & Cheesman, p. 260.
5   RH Fredette, *The Sky on Fire: The First Battle of Britain 1917–1918 and the Birth of the Royal Air Force* (Canada: Holt, Rinehart and Winston, 1966), pp. 75–81.
6   'Anti-German Riots in London', *Leeds Mercury*, 9 July 1917, p. 4.
7   'London Air Raid. Discussion in Parliament', *Liverpool Daily Post and Mercury*, 10 July 1917, p. 5.
8   Fredette, pp. 82–84.
9   Only ten balloon barrages were installed: Cole & Cheesman, p. 307.
10 Cole & Cheesman, p. 307.

34 'Baby killers'
1   Christopher Cole & EF Cheesman, *The Air Defence of Great Britain, 1914–1918* (London: Putnam, 1984), pp. 288–300.
2   Most died in an attack on Chatham Naval Barracks on 3 September 1917: Cole & Cheesman, pp. 301–307.

35 It is delightful walking here
1   Rebecca Beresford, NAUK, WO 399/582.
2   Probably the teahouse at Mugswell, a 10-mile round trip for the ramblers.

36 Family footsteps
1   The Carrel-Dakin Method instilled an antiseptic solution into a wound via perforated rubber tubes to prevent infection and necrosis, averting many amputations.
2   Alice Blake, letter to Charles Blake, 24 January 1917, Blake/Kneeshaw family records.
3   Frank Blake, letter to Charles Blake, 24 January 1917, Blake/Kneeshaw family records.

37 For weal or woe
1. Australian War Memorial, 'Conscription during the First World War, 1914–1918', AWM, last updated 6 March 2020, <www.awm.gov.au/articles/encyclopedia/conscription/ww1>.
2. 'I.W.W. Treason Charges', *Sydney Morning Herald*, 11 October 1916, p. 11.
3. Edith Fairchild, NAUK, WO 399/2619.

38 HMHS *Glenart Castle*
1. 'Burt, Bernard', in MH Massue, marquis de Ruvigny and Raineval (comp.), *De Ruvigny's Roll of Honour, 1914–18*, vol. 4, p. 23, reproduced at Ancestry, accessed 6 August 2021, <www.ancestry.com.au> (subscription required).
2. 'The Lost Vessel. An Early Adventure of the War', *Liverpool Daily Post and Mercury*, 28 February 1918, p. 5.
3. The number was 525 according to Hospital Ship, Glenart Castle, war diaries, October 1914 – February 1917, NAUK, WO 95/4145/2; and Inquiry into damage to HM Hospital Ship Glenart Castle by mine or torpedo: carrying of confidential documents in hospital ships, 1917, folio 216, NAUK, ADM 137/3253, but it was 532 according to Inquiry into damage, folio 278.
4. Inquiry into damage, folios 217, 236, 238, 253.
5. Inquiry into damage, folios 255, 256.
6. Inquiry into damage, folios 254, 255.
7. Inquiry into damage, folio 255.
8. Inquiry into damage, folios 229, 242.
9. Inquiry into damage, folio 258.
10. Inquiry into damage, folios 228, 240, 277, 280, 285.
11. Hospital Ship, Glenart Castle, 17 November 1917.

39 A very boisterous cradle
1. Hospital Ship, Glenart Castle, war diary, 20 November 1917, NAUK, WO 95/4145/2.
2. Hospital Ship, Glenart Castle, 29 November – 4 December 1917.
3. Hospital Ship, Glenart Castle, 11 December 1917.
4. Draft of despatches to Spanish ambassador re sinking of Hospital Ship Rewa. Hospital ships sunk by German submarines – Rewa, Glenart Castle, Llandovery Castle and Guildford Castle, 1918, NAUK, ADM 1/8511/19. The declaration of 15 October 1917 confirmed the declarations of 29 January and 29 March 1917.
5. Hospital Ship, Glenart Castle, 11 December 1917.
6. Hospital Ship, Glenart Castle, 11 December 1917.
7. James W Gerard, *My Four Years in Germany* (New York: George H Doran Company, 1917), foreword.
8. Erica Nadin-Snelling, *Matron at War: The Story of Katy Beaufoy (1869–1918)* (Warwickshire: Brewin Books, 2014); Kate Beaufoy, NAUK, WO 399/494.
9. Hospital Ship, Glenart Castle, 24 December 1917.
10. Edward Sutton, *The Fitting Out and Administration of a Naval Hospital Ship* (Bristol: John Wright & Sons Ltd, 1918), p. 42.
11. Hospital Ship, Glenart Castle, 7 January 1918.
12. Hospital Ship, Glenart Castle, 27 December 1917.
13. Hospital Ship, Glenart Castle, 30 December 1917, 25 January 1918.

14 Hospital Ship, Glenart Castle, 28 January 1918.
15 Hospital Ship, Glenart Castle, 1 February 1918.
16 Hospital Ship, Glenart Castle, 3 February 1918. Numerous recent shipwrecks could have been responsible for the wreckage.
17 Hospital Ship, Glenart Castle, 3–7 February 1918.

40 Taking leave
1 Mildred Crocker Brown, diary, 6 January 1918, Brown/Cull family records.
2 Brown, 16 February 1918.
3 Jacqueline Abbott, 'Cawood, Dorothy Gwendolen (1884–1962)', *Australian Dictionary of Biography*, vol. 7 (Melbourne: Melbourne University Press, 1979), online in 2006, accessed 12 August 2021, <www.adb.anu.edu.au/biography/cawood-dorothy-gwendolen-5537>.
4 Brown, 29 November 1917.
5 Brown, 20 February 1918.
6 Brown, 20 February 1918.
7 Brown, 23 February 1918.
8 'Signed on at Newport', *Western Mail* (Glamorgan), 28 February 1918, p. 3.
9 'Southampton Notes and News. A Part Dependent', *Hampshire Advertiser County Newspaper*, 25 May 1918, p. 6.
10 DDMS, Embarkation, Southampton, Standing orders and instructions for officers commanding troops in hospital ships, 1916, NAUK, MT 23/654.
11 Rebecca Beresford, NAUK, WO 399/582.
12 Elizabeth Edgar, NAUK, WO 399/2459.
13 Mary Mackinnon, NAUK, WO 399/13088.
14 Charlotte Henry, NAUK, WO 399/3760; Gertrude Henry, NAUK, WO 399/3725; Harriet Henry, NAUK, WO 399/11980.
15 Rose E Kendall, NAUK, WO 399/4543.
16 Jane Evans, NAUK, WO 399/2584.
17 HM Hospital Ship Glenart Castle: Court of Enquiry into sinking by enemy submarine, 26 Feb 1918, and issue of instructions and warnings to hospital ships following the sinking, 1918, NAUK, ADM 137/3424.
18 Archibald Hurd, *History of the Great War: The Merchant Navy*, vol. III, *Spring 1917 to November 1918* (London: John Murray, 1929), pp. 106–34.
19 Draft of despatches to Spanish ambassador re sinking of Hospital Ship Rewa. Hospital ships sunk by German submarines – Rewa, Glenart Castle, Llandovery Castle and Guildford Castle, 1918, NAUK, ADM 1/8511/19.
20 For example, 'Hospital Ship Sunk in Bristol Channel. Displayed All Red Cross Markings', *Dundee Courier*, 10 January 1918, p. 2.

41 What the fishermen saw
1 John Hill, 2nd hand, *Swansea Castle*, statement, NAUK, ADM 137/3424.
2 Archibald Hurd, *History of the Great War: The Merchant Navy*, vol. I, *1914 to Spring 1915* (<Naval-History.net>, accessed 6 August 2021, <www.naval-history.net/WW1Book-MN1a-Merchant_Navy_in_WW1_Hurd.htm>), chapter VI.
3 Hurd, chapter VI.
4 Thomas Matthews, bosun's mate, *Glenart Castle*, statement, NAUK, ADM 137/3424. In his statement, Matthews refers to 'Jockhon' being the 'look-out man'.

The only similar surnames were 'Joachim', 'Johnson' and 'Jacobsen'. Seaman Harold Joachim seems most likely.
5   Agnes 'Beryl' Corfield, letter to friend Lizzie, 29 August 1915, AWM, PR05855, describing calls between the watch and bridge.
6   In his statement to the court of enquiry, NAUK, ADM 137/3424, Matthews refers to 'Second Officer'. The name of Second Mate Ralph Woollett has been used because he held this positions.
7   Lt Charles Beaven, CO HM Trawler *Okino*, statement, 1 March 1918, NAUK, ADM 1/8511/19.
8   William H Fletcher, skipper, *Dynevor Castle*, statement, NAUK, ADM 137/3424.
9   'Jacob Sheler', quartermaster, *Glenart Castle*, statement, NAUK, ADM 137/3424. Spellings of his surname vary, but most subsequent reports use 'Schiller'.
10 Sheler.
11 Sheler.
12 Kiesewetter took command of UC-56 in April 1917: Tony Bridgland, *Outrage at Sea: Naval Atrocities of the First World War* (Barnsley: Pen and Sword, 2002), chapter 11; German naval officers: information photographs, press cuttings, 1908–12, NAUK, ADM 137/4352.
13 Bridgland, Chapter 11.
14 Hill.
15 Hill.
16 Joseph Rust, statement, NAUK, ADM 137/3424.
17 Hill.
18 Rust.
19 Hill.
20 See Chapter 42, endnote 45.

42 The sinking
1   Thomas Matthews, bosun's mate, *Glenart Castle*, statement, NAUK, ADM 137/3424.
2   'Story of the Outrage. Interviews with Survivors', *Belfast News-Letter*, 28 February 1918, p. 5.
3   The operator could have been the senior man Jabez George Bull, who was the wireless operator on duty when the *Glenart Castle* was mined on 1 March 1917, or junior wireless operator Michael Sinnott, who, his family believe, trained with Bull at the Marconi marine station in County Kerry: Ben Breen, email to Krista Vane-Tempest, 8 April 2020.
4   Alfred Bale, greaser, *Glenart Castle*, statement, NAUK, ADM 137/3424.
5   Bale.
6   Thomas Casey, fireman, *Glenart Castle*, statement, NAUK, ADM 137/3424.
7   Casey.
8   Jacob Sheler, statement; and Thomas Matthews, statement, NAUK, ADM 137/3424.
9   C Beveridge, lance corporal, RAMC, *Glenart Castle*, statement, NAUK, ADM 137/3424.
10 Beveridge.
11 In statements to the court of enquiry, NAUK, ADM 137/3424, Alfred Bale and George Frederick Scarlett refer to the 'Chief Officer'. The name of Chief Mate Samuel Hutchings has been used because he held this position.

12 Sheler.
13 Sheler; Matthews.
14 Casey.
15 Sheler; Matthews.
16 Bale.
17 George Frederick Scarlett, 4th officer, *Glenart Castle*, statement, NAUK, ADM 137/3424.
18 Scarlett.
19 Beveridge.
20 Scarlett.
21 Bale.
22 Bale.
23 Bale.
24 Beveridge.
25 Beveridge.
26 Sheler.
27 'The Brutal Hun. Sinks Another Hospital Ship in the Bristol Channel', *Illustrated Police News*, 7 March 1918, p. 2.
28 'Rescues from the Glenart Castle. Medals for French Seamen', *Scotsman* (Midlothian), 9 August 1918, named the French crew who were awarded the 'Silver Medal for Gallantry by the King': Joseph Marie Stephant, master; Louie Marie Dermain, mate; Julien Kersocho and Joseph Marie Raude, sailors; and Emile Joseph Calloch, apprentice.
29 'Fate of Small Boats. Little Hope of More Survivors', *Liverpool Daily Post and Mercury*, 1 March 1918, p. 5.
30 Bale; Archibald Hurd, *History of the Great War: The Merchant Navy*, vol. III, *Spring 1917 to November 1918* (London: John Murray, 1929), pp. 297–339.
31 United Kingdom, House of Commons, *Debates*, vol. 104, 13 March 1918, c. 316 (F. Flannery), transcript at UK Parliament, Hansard, accessed 9 August 2021, <https://hansard.parliament.uk/commons/1918-03-13/debates/603e77f9-e9b8-4caf-a057-4325f5e19d99/GallantryOfAmericanSailors>. Men from USS *Parker* who risked their lives to rescue the stranded men were Halsey Powell, USN, commander; JC Cole, quartermaster; RE Hosses, boatswain's mate; David Goldman, machinist's mate; Jerry Quinn, coxswain; FW Beeghley, yeoman; WW Matthews, ship's cook; and J Newman and TF Troue, seamen.
32 'American Gallantry. Bluejackets Who Jumped Overboard to Save Life', *Pall Mall Gazette* (London), 13 March 1918, p. 2.
33 Commander Halsey Powell, USN, Commanding Officer USS *Parker*, Form SA ID sent to Senior Officer, Milford Haven, 26 February 1918, NAUK, ADM 137/3424; Commonwealth War Graves Commission <www.cwgc.org/find-records/find-war-dead/casualty-details/670426/HARRY%20LUND/>.
34 Matthews.
35 Alfred Olden, fireman, *Glenart Castle*, statement, NAUK, ADM 137/3424.
36 Sheler.
37 Casey.
38 Joseph Rust, statement, NAUK, ADM 137/3424.
39 Sheler.
40 William H Fletcher, statement, NAUK, ADM 137/3424; 'Boots and Stockings Found in Damaged Boat', *Birmingham Daily Post*, 28 February 1918, p. 5.

41 Union-Castle Mail Steamship Company Limited, letter to Mrs Sinnott, 5 March 1918, Sinnott/Breen family records.
42 Breen.
43 John Sinnott, telegram to Sinnott family, 6 March 1918, Sinnott/Breen family records.
44 'Were Survivors Fired Upon?', *Scotsman* (Midlothian), 11 March 1918, p. 3.
45 Although official despatches later quoted HMHS *Glenart Castle* as having 186 on board, the Press Association established that 182 were aboard: for example, 'Vessel Goes Down in Seven Minutes. Matron and Nine Nurses Missing', *Birmingham Daily Post*, 28 February 1918, p. 5: 'The Exchange Telegraph Company gives the total as 206, but the Press Association makes the number 182, as follows: 5 doctors, 1 matron, 7 sisters, 2 chaplains, 42 RAMC, 4 officers, 5 engineers, 115 crew & master Captain Burt'. 182 accords with 153 dead and 29 survivors. The names of 153 dead have been cross-referenced against cemetery records. The number of 29 survivors is taken from lists in contemporary newspaper reports and the court of inquiry. Only three survivors picked up by the USS *Parker* cannot be named. Discrepancies in the number of survivors may arise as the number of 'nine' persons brought in by the USS *Parker* is confused by the death on board of Jesse White and the subsequent death of Samuel 'Harry' Lund in Pembroke Hospital, so 'nine' on board became 'nine' survivors, incorrectly inflating the total survivors to thirty-one. Further, some newspapers counted thirty-eight survivors (twenty-two landed in Swansea, nine in Milford and seven in Pembroke: for example, 'Hospital Ship Sunk – Another Red Cross Outrage', *Taunton Courier, and Western Advertiser*, 6 March 1918, p. 3). The confusion appears to come from a double count of those picked up by the USS *Parker*, such that the 'nine' landed in Milford (including White and Lund) was added to 'seven' survivors in Pembroke, as the ports of Milford and Pembroke lie opposite each other and both were involved in the rescue.
46 'Fate of Nine Nurses', *Sheffield Daily Telegraph*, 28 February 1918, p. 5.
47 Matthews.

43 The news they had dreaded
1 Edith Blake, NAUK, WO 399/683. The War Office issued a certificate of death on 11 July 1918.
2 Mildred Crocker Brown, diary, 27 February 1918, Brown/Cull family records.
3 Matron Fairchild to AW Blake, 19 March 1918, AWM, PR05423.
4 British Red Cross Society, Programme for memorial service for deceased nurses St. Paul's Cathedral. Roll of honour for the nursing services, Memorial service for nurses, 10 April 1918, Imperial War Museum, BRCS 25.5.4/26.
5 Of some 350 nurses and VADs listed in the memorial service roll of honour (Imperial War Museum, BRCS 25.5.4/26): fifty drowned when hospital ships sank; fifteen were killed in air raids, accidents, and so on; one, Edith Cavell, was executed; and around 280 died of disease and illness: nearly 65 per cent of the nurses and nearly 95 per cent of the 183 VADs.
6 Brown, 10 April 1918.
7 Edith Blake, NAA, MT1487/1.
8 In her Last Will and Testament, Edie left everything she had to her mother: NAA, MT1487/1.

Notes to pages 306–312

9   'The Latest Act of Hun Fiendishness', *Graphic* (London), 9 March 1918, p. 13.
10 *British Journal of Nursing*, 16 March 1918, p. 185.
11 Draft of despatches to Spanish ambassador re sinking of Hospital Ship Rewa. Hospital ships sunk by German submarines – Rewa, Glenart Castle, Llandovery Castle and Guildford Castle, 1918, NAUK, ADM 1/8511/19.
12 One torpedo missed after HMHS *Essequibo* took evasive action; another may have hit but failed to explode: Archibald Hurd, *History of the Great War: The Merchant Navy*, Vol III, Spring 1917 to November 1918 (London: John Murray, 1929), Chapter XI, The Sinking of Hospital Ships, pp. 297-339, 'Attack on "Guildford Castle"'.
13 'The Truth about the Lusitania!', *World's News* (Sydney), 20 December 1919, p. 12.
14 'U-Boat Assassin', *Western Morning News*, 13 August 1919, p. 4.
15 'Naval "Black List"', *Pall Mall Gazette* (London), 7 February 1920, p. 2.
16 Tony Bridgland, *Outrage at Sea: Naval Atrocities of the First World War* (Barnsley: Pen and Sword, 2002), chapter 11; 'Admiralty Stirred by German's Release', *New York Times*, 2 December 1919.
17 British memorandum, 5 February 1920, NAUK, ADM 1/8511/19.
18 German memorandum, 16 July 1920, NAUK, ADM 1/8511/19.
19 Gudmundur Helgason, 'The U-Boats of World War One, 1914–1918', <Uboat.net>, accessed 6 August 2021, <https://uboat.net/wwi/boats/>.
20 'The Truth about the Lusitania!'

44 After the war
1   The number of Australians enlisted for service was 416 809, representing 38.7 per cent of the total male population aged eighteen to forty-four: National Archives of Australia & Australia, Department of Veteran's Affairs, *Shell-Shocked: Australia after Armistice*, exhibition, Canberra, 8 November 2008 – 27 April 2009.
2   Australia's casualties numbered 215 585, representing 64.98 per cent of the 331 781 who served overseas (n.b. some suffered multiple injuries): National Archives of Australia & Australia, Department of Veteran's Affairs.
3   Francis Cox, 'The First World War: Disease, the Only Victor', speech at Museum of London, 10 March 2014, transcript at Gresham College, 2014, <www.gresham.ac.uk/lectures-and-events/the-first-world-war-disease-the-only-victor>, pp. 3, 6.
4   Steve Ford & Katrina Bylykbashi, 'Quest to Record Names and Resting Places of WWI Nurses', *Nursing Times*, 25 September 2014, <www.nursingtimes.net/roles/nurse-managers/quest-to-record-names-and-resting-places-of-wwi-nurses-25-09-2014/>.
5   Philip Payton, *Repat: A Concise History of Repatriation in Australia* (Department of Veterans' Affairs, accessed 9 August 2021, <www.dva.gov.au/sites/default/files/files/publications/corporate/P03428.pdf>).
6   Payton, p. 27.
7   Evelyn Swannell, NAUK, WO 399/8131.
8 ' Personal Pars', *Cumberland Argus and Fruitgrowers Advocate*, 23 November 1918, p. 6.
9   'About People', *Border Morning Mail* (Albury), 8 February 1944, p. 2.
10 Dorothy Cawood was one of four nurses to be awarded the Military Medal after No. 2 Australian Casualty Clearing Station was bombed near Armentières in July 1917. Edie proudly wrote home, 'Bravo Cawood!' (1 September 1917). When she

arrived home in Parramatta in July 1919 Sister Cawood was met by the mayor and an informal guard of honour of returned soldiers and a large welcome home committee that lined the streets: 'Sister Cawood Home. Returned Soldier "Boys" Join In', *Cumberland Argus and Fruitgrowers Advocate*, 5 July 1919, p. 6.
11 Thomas James Frizell, NAA, B2455; 1st Australian Field Ambulance, war diary, October 1917, AWM, AWM4 26/44/31.
12 Wallis Mervyn Alfred Fletcher, NAA, B2455.
13 Clement R Boughton, *A Coast Chronicle: The History of the Prince Henry Hospital, 1881–1981; Centenary Issue*, 2nd edn (Waterloo, NSW: Knudsen Printing, 1981), pp. 33, 35.
14 Maylean Cordia, *Nurses at Little Bay*, rev. edn (Little Bay, NSW: Prince Henry Trained Nurses' Association, 1995), p. 94.
15 Cordia, p. 102.
16 Cordia, p. 80.
17 Cordia, p. 82.
18 RJ Millard, 'The History of the Prince Henry (Coast) Hospital', *Australasian Nurses' Journal*, 15 March 1940, p. 49.

www.ingramcontent.com/pod-product-compliance
Lightning Source LLC
Chambersburg PA
CBHW031721230426
43669CB00007B/204